1988

HERE IS YOUR
COMPLIMENTARY

Examination
Copy

Sandford-Yeager:
PRINCIPLES OF EFFECTIVE
SPEAKING, Sixth Edition

$4.75

We believe you will find the book well
suited to the needs of your course and will
want to consider it for adoption.

THE RONALD PRESS COMPANY
15 East 26th St., New York 10, N.Y.

WILLIAM PHILLIPS SANDFORD, Ph.D., The Ohio State University, is Professor of Speech at St. Louis University. He previously taught at the University of Minnesota, The Ohio State University, and the University of Illinois prior to twelve years of private practice in business speech. Professor Sandford is co-author of four principal works with Professor Yeager and author of several others, and has conducted training courses and acted as counsel on speaking and selling for more than one hundred firms and associations in twenty-five states.

WILLARD HAYES YEAGER, LL.D., Morris Harvey College, is Professor and Chairman, Department of Speech, at The Ohio State University. He previously taught at the University of Illinois and at George Washington University. Professor Yeager is author or co-author of ten other books and is a past president of the Speech Association of America and of the Speech Association of the Eastern States.

Principles of
Effective Speaking

WILLIAM PHILLIPS SANDFORD
ST. LOUIS UNIVERSITY

WILLARD HAYES YEAGER
THE OHIO STATE UNIVERSITY

Sixth Edition

THE RONALD PRESS COMPANY · NEW YORK

Library of Congress Catalog Card Number: 63-9242

PRINTED IN THE UNITED STATES OF AMERICA

Preface

Principles of Effective Speaking, now offered in its Sixth Edition, has, since 1928, served many generations of college students. Changing conditions and new points of emphasis through the years have brought about modifications, but its original dedication to the purpose of "practical instruction in all phases of speaking" has not changed.

For years, we have stressed the applicability of classical rhetoric, not only to public speaking, but to conversational speech in everyday business and community life. This edition emphasizes, even more than its predecessors, what is now popularly termed "oral communication" as a day-to-day activity.

To be understood is a primary purpose of all speech; and in this edition the *rationale* of good idea-structure and relevancy in detail is stressed to that end. *To be interesting and persuasive* in all communication is essential; so the psychology of the hearer and of the speaker in their relation to each other is presented. Public speaking is treated from the viewpoint of the design of informative, persuasive and entertaining talks. Speech masterpieces and good student speeches furnish illustrative material, as in all of our previous editions.

Certain specialized chapters, such as those on debate, discussion, business speech, and parliamentary procedure, have been eliminated, simply because excellent textbooks in these areas, published in the last decade, make them unnecessary. Over all, we have shortened the book somewhat, and have concentrated upon material which, we believe, can furnish the background for a *thorough, basic training* in oral communication. We have gone beyond the simple structural analysis of presentations to include functional techniques

iii

of vividness, activation, and style, believing these important at the college level.

To those of our professional colleagues who have honored us by the use of earlier editions, and to the tens of thousands of students who have worked with them and with us, we repeat the expression of hope with which we prefaced the edition of 1928, "that this book may serve usefully in the cause of speech education."

WILLIAM PHILLIPS SANDFORD
WILLARD HAYES YEAGER

St. Louis, Missouri
Columbus, Ohio
January, 1963

Contents

Part One

THE BASICS OF ORAL COMMUNICATION

Part Two

BUILDING PROFICIENCY IN PUBLIC SPEAKING

CONTENTS

Part Three

SPEECHES FOR ANALYSIS AND APPRECIATION

Part Four

ASSIGNMENTS FOR SPEAKING PRACTICE

Part One

THE BASICS OF ORAL COMMUNICATION

1

Oral Communication in
Your Life

You are judged by what you say, and how you say it.
V. A. KETCHAM

W<small>HY</small> study oral communication? The reason, tersely stated by a distinguished teacher, is given above. In talking with an individual, in a group discussion, or to an audience, *what you say and how you say it* determine the impression you make. People will understand what you are attempting to explain; they will agree that your views are right; they will be interested, entertained, or persuaded—all of these—if you talk clearly and well.

We communicate with others primarily through speech—conveying ideas, words, feelings, opinions. More than 90 per cent of all communication is oral. It behooves us, therefore, to achieve a high level in this vital skill.

Its scope. Oral communication includes our everyday talk with family and friends. It includes our questions and answers in the classroom. It is involved in our dealings with our employers, customers, and fellow-workers. It is important in the discussions and debates of public life. It takes place in the meetings of organizations to which we belong. It is used in such communication media as the telephone, radio, and television.

In short, there is no level of activity, from the most casual to the most important, in which what we say and how we say it do not affect our success. Everyone—from the research scientist and the engineer to the lawyer, clergyman, and teacher—needs to develop effective oral communication. It is a necessary part of one's education and helps to make effectual the knowledge gained in high school and college courses and through experience.

Knowledge may come first in importance, but knowledge plus the ability to communicate it to others is knowledge in action. It has been said, with more than casual meaning, that "if you can't express your knowledge about a subject so that others can understand it, you don't really have full knowledge."

Proof of its importance. We have stated that oral communication is important to everyone. You may be skeptical. "After all," you may reason, "the authors are teachers of this subject and overstate the case."

Let's look at some facts. One is the tremendous growth during the last few decades of courses in speech, and large departments of speech, in virtually every college in the land. There is a similar development on the high school level. Another fact is the growing demand for courses in speech in the adult education movement. Still another is the emphasis on effective oral communication in company training courses. Training in industry is given to supervisors and group discussion leaders, to salesmen, to personnel men, to public relations men, to junior executives, to foremen. Finally, commercial enterprises have arisen whose activities range from speechwriting to "crash" courses in speech. These, most certainly, are "signs of the times."

The testimony is convincing. Let us quote a few statements by people who are not professional teachers of speech to the effect that oral communication is a vital subject. To quote them all would require this entire book.

Benjamin F. Lamme, distinguished inventor and engineer of the Westinghouse Company, in response to a student's question, "What courses would you take if you were to return to college?":

If I were to return to college, I would take all the courses in effective speaking I could get. The engineer of today is a businessman. He must persuade boards of directors that his plans should be put into effect. He must add this skill to his technical accomplishments if he is to succeed.

Murray W. Cochrane, personnel director of the west coast plant of one of the large automobile concerns:

We can train men in the specifics of company policy. I am in favor of a broad liberal education. As to absolute requirements, I would insist upon just two: philosophy, to teach the student how to think, and speech, to teach him how to express his ideas.

Clarence Randall, former chairman of the board of the Inland Steel Corporation and chairman of the board of the Fund for Adult Education in 1956:

At every point to which he (the business executive) turns in his work, he senses the necessity for the adequate communication of ideas. Each hour of the day, from the humblest foreman to the chief executive of the company, the person bearing responsibility must engage in telling others what to do and how to do it. Knowledge and wisdom are wasted if unexpressed; genius is completely unharnessed if the lips are inarticulate. The businessman today must be able to write and speak the English language with clarity and felicity, or stand aside and let his chair be occupied by some one who can.

S. C. Allyn, president of the National Cash Register Company, in an article entitled "Speech and Leadership in Business" in the April 1948 issue of the *Quarterly Journal of Speech:*

Ability to speak well is no longer a professional art to be mastered only by lawyers, preachers, teachers, and entertainers. The man preparing for leadership in business needs this ability too, because leadership expresses itself primarily through speech.

Owen D. Young, industrialist and diplomat, in a commencement address:

Have you developed skill in communication with others? If you can't answer that question satisfactorily, you will find it difficult to succeed.

To conclude these statements, we quote one which covers a broader field and emphasizes the central importance of good speech in all aspects of life. It is by H. A. Overstreet in his book *The Mature Mind:*

Speech is that through which we most constantly influence one another. From the words of a mother to her babe to the words of one diplomat to another, speech is a maker of psychological universes. . . . Again, it is that through which we clarify our ideas and beliefs.

Few . . . in adulthood, are so able to say what they want to say—with confidence, precision, beauty, and a sensitive awareness of what is fitting in the situation—that the communicative experience holds more of success than of failure. *In no area of our maturing, in fact, is arrested development more common than in the area of communication.*

Thus does the distinguished philosopher-psychologist state the reasons for training in oral communication. Through our speech—what is said and how it is said—we influence others and clarify our own thinking. *Few use speech well.* Still fewer reach maximum efficiency, the "sensitive awareness of what is fitting in the situation." Yet optimum skill in dealing with others is a priceless asset in every human contact.

THE SOCIAL IMPORTANCE OF
ORAL COMMUNICATION

We have discussed thus far the importance of oral communication to the individual. Its *social* significance is even greater.

Group action and group representation are facts of modern life. On the economic front practically every business, profession, or occupation has its local, state, and national association. In St. Louis, for example, more than ninety business associations are listed in the directory and many more labor organizations. Nationally there are more than 1,500 associations, covering every type of business. And the great farm organizations, such as the American Farm Bureau Federation with its component state Farm Bureaus, the National Grange, and others are spokesmen for agriculture. The AFL-CIO, and others, with many millions of members, function at local, state, and national levels.

In the economic sphere lie great responsibilities and opportunities for the person trained in oral communication. Internally, all organizations such as those mentioned above must maintain contact with members, obtain their participation in policy determination, and in general keep the membership active and informed. In part, this is done through written communication in the form of organization news sheets, magazines, and bulletins. But perhaps most of it is achieved through meetings, conferences, and conventions. Here the ability to talk with individuals, to take part in committee meetings and conferences, and to make effective speeches to audiences large and small is indispensable. Grassroots, person-to-person contact with members and leaders is a cardinal point in the conduct of organizations.

Externally, a labor union, farm organization, or professional or business association seeks to influence public opinion on behalf of its members and policies. Legislation is often sought or opposed. Here again, the skills of the effective conversationalist and speaker come into play.

It is no wonder that organized groups seek officers and staff employees "who can stand on their two feet and express their ideas" and who can take part in management-labor negotiations, intergroup meetings, and radio and television discussions.

The person trained in oral communication of all kinds was never more in demand than today.

Social and political groups. Everything that has been said about the role of the speaker-conversationalist in the economic field applies in other fields of group activity.

The promotion of better understanding among members of various religious denominations, among racial or national origin groups, among the different sections of our country, and indeed between our country and Latin America, Europe, and Asia—all of these and many more offer opportunities for dedicated people who can speak clearly, tactfully, and persuasively—in short, for sincere and effective oral communicators.

In government and politics the successful leader has always had to meet the test of persuasive communication through the spoken word. This involves not only speech making—although with radio and television the importance of this form of communication has reached an all-time high—but, even more, it demands skill in conversational speech, in the conferences of party leaders, with the press, and with volunteer and paid campaign workers.

The promotion of reforms that have a nonpartisan basis, as well as the adjustment of governmental problems, through interviews, conferences, and speeches is another field of public life demanding effective speech.

Legislative and administrative officers in many states periodically must reapportion Congressional districts, to adjust to population shifts revealed in the census. There is endless discussion and debate in such a situation. A movement to consolidate suburbs and the central city in a vast metropolitan area under one government has its sponsors and opponents, and, therefore, we have conferences, television-radio broadcasts, speeches. Congressional business is transacted in committee meetings and hearings, and the same is true of state legislative procedure. The President confers with leaders of the House and Senate and with advisers on domestic and foreign policy. Conferences and speeches permeate our entire governmental structure.

One has but to look around him to see many more civic, social, or governmental uses for effective communication and to note the key responsibility of conferrers and speakers in them.

Consolidated and independent charitable campaigns; the

efforts of institutions such as colleges, hospitals, and the like to raise funds for development or expansion; the advocacy of bond issues, community movements, reforms—all use the paid or volunteer efforts of hundreds of people. Everywhere, the person who can inform, persuade, and interest others is in demand.

The new concept of speech. A century ago, and, indeed, during most of the twenty-five centuries in which oral communication has been studied as a useful art, the "image" of the end product was that of the statesman speaking on great issues in Congress or Parliament, the priest or minister presenting his sermon, or the attorney pleading before judge or jury. Effective speech remains one of the elements in the success of such professional men, but today it is recognized that the use of speech in everyday relationships, in the world of business and industry, and in socio-governmental affairs at all levels is equally important. "What to say and how to say it" is being studied today by more people than at any previous time in history. This skill is fully recognized as an essential aim of education. For the individual and for the group, it is vital.

SETTING GOALS FOR ACHIEVEMENT

If good oral communication rewards the individual and society, it follows that the attainment of maximum skill is a worthwhile goal. How may this be achieved? What are the sources of effectiveness? What are the most helpful mental attitudes? What are the specific goals, the attainment of which leads to the highest efficiency?

"Nature, art, and practice." All of us have some inborn talent for self-expression. This, of course, varies with the individual. Yet the greatest talent if unused and undeveloped *is only a potential asset.* "Good speakers are made, not born" is a saying that has proved true throughout history. A Demosthenes practicing to improve a reportedly poor voice and to overcome a speech defect; a Henry Clay rehearsing youthful speeches in the farmyard; and a Daniel Webster assuring fellow-Senators, "I have been preparing this speech all of my life"—these are just a few examples which show how men with high talents have worked to improve. The evolution of Lincoln from a backwoods campaigner to the President whose inaugural speeches and Gettysburg Address are classics of style is another. And such instances are the rule—not the exception.

Any normal person can learn to speak with considerable effectiveness. This is our firm belief after four decades of teaching and practicing. Up to the limits of individual intelligence, desire, and knowledge one can develop into an effective speaker, even an outstanding one.

The methods are established. One reason why training, rather than native talent, is a determining factor is this: the principles and methods of learning are well established. *Effective speech was not invented yesterday.* It has been a subject of intensive study for 2,500 years. Men of every century have written about it. Among the great names are Aristotle, Cicero, Quintilian, Saint Augustine, Francis Bacon, John Quincy Adams, Henry Ward Beecher, and William Jennings Bryan. Except Quintilian, the great Roman teacher, none of these was a specialist in speech theory, but each thought it worth his time and effort to contribute to its development. Hundreds of men, professional teachers of speech and others, have added their ideas. The result, with the researches and reinterpretations of this century, is a body of theory, or principles, in which the student can have full confidence. *Learn and apply the principles,* and you become more effective.

A brief outline of this established theory will give you an idea of its inclusiveness.

THE FIVE FOUNDATIONS

Early in the history of speech training, the great rhetoricians defined the theory of public address and analyzed, from a broad viewpoint, the factors that make a speaker effective. Beginning with a definition that included "all the available means of persuasion" open to the speaker and observing that his function is to inform, move, and please his hearers, they arrived at these five foundations of effectiveness: *invention, arrangement, style, memory,* and *delivery.*

Invention

Invention is the thinking process that necessarily precedes all effective oral communication, whether in purposive conversation or in public address. The speaker must select from all available ideas and facts those best qualified to achieve his purpose. *What he says* is more important than how he says it. He does not "invent" facts in the modern sense; he surveys the possible means of conveying information, of persuading, or of entertaining his hearers. The invention comes in his exercise of good judgment in deciding what to say. There are three sources from which he may draw: logic, emotional appeal, and the appeal of his own personality.

LOGIC. Logic—in the sense of good reasoning and factual data—is, let us emphasize, vital to long-range effectiveness. It cannot be denied that flamboyant appeals to feeling and unfounded assertions at times seem to be successful; but the sober second thought that comes to most people usually cancels out the effect of such tactics. Witness the overstated claims in some television commercials and other advertising. Used without a foundation of solid proof, pressure tactics often backfire.

Not only is there a moral obligation to tell the truth, but for practical reasons one must have a foundation of common sense and fact in what he says. A student should start at once to improve his reasoning processes and learn to respect evidence. His thinking should have an underpinning of logic, formal or informal. He should strive to avoid hasty conclusions and irrelevancies. Sound logic is necessary to effectiveness.

EMOTION. It is true that "a man convinced against his will retains the same opinion still." This means simply that, along with common-sense logic, the speaker must consider the wants and desires of people. He must show that his subject is of vital interest to them. He must make his speech or other presentation specific, striking, and colorful enough to hold their attention. He must get people to listen attentively and motivate them to believe or act.

Anyone interested in moving others acquires very early the habit of asking: "What are the interests of my hearers? What do they *want?* How can they profit by understanding what I am trying to make clear, or by doing what I am asking them to do?

PERSONAL EFFECTIVENESS. It is a man or woman who speaks or converses, and to other men or women. Quite plainly, then, it can be seen that the speaker's personal qualities help or hinder him. This is true not only of such things as appearance, speech, manner, and attitude at the time of contact; it is also true in respect to the opinions that the audience has of the speaker. Before an audience, therefore, one will try to be at his best in all respects. More deeply, he will try to increase the confidence that people have in him by what he does and says. He will guard his reputation and guide his actions by acceptable work habits and moral standards. He will cultivate greater consideration of others. These are foundations for personal persuasiveness.

Invention, then, consists of logical, emotional, and personal appeal by the wisely considered use of which the speaker decides what to say and how to say it. It is the most vital part in the process of effective oral communication.

Arrangement

Arrangement, or disposition as it was formerly called, has to do with the ordering or composition—the putting together —of the facts and ideas the speaker has selected by the thinking process of invention described above. It includes the parts of the speech. It also includes the consideration of the most effective order for the presentation of ideas.

Style

Style has to do with the form in which ideas are presented. It concerns the choice of words, the use of various types of sentences and phrases, and the use of figures of speech and of thought. Sometimes considered mere ornamentation, good style can be highly functional in affording more effective expression. In this concept, it is an aid in presenting what has been invented and arranged.

Memory

Memory can be trained to enable a speaker to recall the ideas and facts he wishes to present, not by rote word-for-word recall but by remembering the framework of the speech. It also has to do with remembering sources of material and specific facts.

Delivery

Lastly, a well-designed speech or other type of oral communication depends upon the effectiveness with which it is spoken. What has been invented, arranged, styled, and learned has to be delivered. The speaker's communicative power, his animation, and his sincerity must be at a high point, and he must be expressive enough to attain maximum effectiveness.

THE GOALS OF EFFECTIVENESS

Not only are these five elements the foundation of effectiveness, but they must be considered as major goals of the student who is seeking to attain such effectiveness. In short, the major goals are to become more proficient in the design of a speech through use of the threefold means of logical, emotional, and personal persuasiveness; and to learn better arrangement, effective methods of recall, better language, and more effective delivery.

Clarity

An important general goal is to attain greater clarity. Always the aim of communication is to be understood by the hearer, to be "able to get a message across." This is related to the five major goals we have just reviewed. Clear thinking in the selection of ideas and facts, and in their arrangement, wording, and delivery, is the way to that *instant understandability* that one must possess.

Adaptation to the Hearer

Oral communication is not something merely uttered; *it is something said to a hearer or hearers.* Its success depends upon its reception by the hearer and his reaction to it. Hearers are not all alike; they vary in intelligence, knowledge, experience, and interests. They also vary in their attitude at the moment toward the speaker and his subject. So the effective oral communicator develops a high degree of hearer-consciousness. He adapts what he says to the listeners. If he talks "over their heads" or fails to consider their interests and attitudes, he is almost surely going to be unsuccessful. Not only in what is said, but in the manner of speaking, hearer-consciousness is vital. The good talker possesses a strong sense of communication. He talks *directly* to people, looks at individuals, observes their reactions, and tries in every possible way to set up and maintain direct contact with them. The converser who seems to be talking to himself, the speaker who looks down at the floor or out of the window—these people are "soloists," not communicators.

Hearer-consciousness is reflected in invention, especially in consideration of emotional appeal; in style, in the adaptation of language to the persons addressed; in delivery, through highly communicative presentation. Only when what is said is received by the hearer is there any communication. Remember, a radio or television program isn't successful just because it is put on the air. It succeeds only when receiving sets are kept tuned in. The same thing is true of speaker-audience or converser-hearer situations.

SUMMARY. The positive goals that one should seek can be stated very briefly: improved thinking in designing a speech (invention), with proficiency in logical, emotional, and personal persuasiveness; good arrangement, good style, effective memory, and good oral delivery; clarity, and adaptation to the hearer. These are attainable aims, and the ones on which your attention should be focused.

Practice is necessary. It goes without saying that practice —repeated, methodical practice—is necessary. One does not become a good speaker or conferrer by reading about speaking, discussion, or conference technique. He *does* learn by practice. This is especially true *if the practice is guided, not random.* This is where theory, or principle, comes in. The ideal training is that which provides frequent speaking and which directs the attention of the student to the practical application of sound methods. Random, or unguided, practice, although of some value, might result in confirming bad habits or in little if any change in over-all effectiveness.

Your instructor and the ideas provided in this book have a function like that of a football coach. By designing plays the coach sets up methods that the team then tries to follow. You would not think much of a coach who said simply, "Go out and practice . . . you'll learn by experience." Patterns, both offensive and defensive, are needed. With them, the football practice becomes an exercise *in applying methods.* That is precisely what a well-planned course in oral communication should be.

Your attitude is important. Your personal attitude toward a course in effective oral communication will largely determine whether you profit by it. Affirmative attitudes can make success almost certain; negative or defeatist ones can make it a total loss. Whether the course is elective or required, it offers an opportunity for you; yours is the decision whether to accept that opportunity.

What are some of the positive attitudes that can aid in a course in oral communication?

First, the viewpoint that *learning to speak effectively is worth the effort.* There is no more useful art, no more important way of influencing others, no more vital means of supporting good causes and worthy ideals. No other discipline can do more for the individual in the cultivation of desirable personality traits or contribute more toward harmonious understanding between groups, races, and nations. College students have had enough experience with communication, both successful and unsuccessful, to appreciate that a study that enables them to say clearly and interestingly what they believe, want, or know is indeed worthy of their attention. If one's education has consisted mainly in acquiring knowledge and ideas, it surely seems desirable to learn how better to express those ideas to others.

Second, the realization that *oral communication with others is a natural, practical thing,* not a "performance" or an "exhibition." We all talk. We have done so since about age two. We use thousands of words daily to convey our ideas to others. There is nothing artificial about this act of speech. This is true of conversation, group discussion, and public speaking. It is not a question, then, of learning something entirely new and strange; rather, it is a matter of improving in what we already have learned to do.

Third, the confidence that *our experiences, our knowledge, and our views are worth-while,* and that—properly expressed —they will be interesting to other people. No one of college age is without something to talk about. Not only what has been learned by direct experience and everyday contacts, but material learned in subject-matter courses and from current events as reported in the press and over radio and television is available. There can be no such thing as a lack of important and interesting subject matter.

Fourth, and perhaps most important, *that it is possible to improve.* This applies to those with or without previous formal training in speech. As we have pointed out, this subject is not a mysterious or experimental one; it has been studied, taught, and practiced for centuries. Its principles are well known. A beginner, if only he tries, can learn and apply them —and find a surprising change in his effectiveness before a term is more than half over. One who has had previous training can refine and correct what he now does; and he, too, if willing, can show marked progress.

Fifth, *an attitude of cooperation and mutual encouragement.* This includes *being good listeners,* not only to what is said by the instructor, but even more importantly, to the talks by other members of the class. Inattention, or bored preoccupation with one's own thoughts, can be most discouraging to a classmate who is trying to interest you. Whether silent or speaking, you should be a constant participant in what is going on in the class. In that way you learn more, and you help others to learn. Also, after a certain stage of development has been reached, you may be asked to comment constructively on the talks given by others. By this sort of cooperative attention, you meet a social obligation, that of being an actively participating member of a group.

Minimize the negative. Contrast the attitudes described above with those of some people who find themselves in a course in speech: "I don't need it." "There's nothing to Speech." "It's a pipe course." "I'm (determined to be) scared." "What you say isn't important; it's what you know." And so forth and so on!

How can you be sure you don't need good training in Speech, even if you once won an oratorical contest? Did that highly stylized discourse make you effective for all time to come? Is there nothing to Speech; is it a pipe course? Try it and see. The five-point outline of its requirements given above may give you pause. The really great speakers, political and business leaders, have found there is a great deal to it. And what you know is only half of the job; the ability to communicate it is the other.

Confidence grows with competence. You don't expect to be at home in the water on your first visit to a swimming pool or a poised, confident bowler the first time you roll a ball toward that elusive 1–3 pocket. You have a degree of nervousness or uncertainty whenever you attempt to learn a new game or a new skill. It is rightly called "beginners' embarrassment." Yet, as you learn to swim or bowl and develop some of the skills that produce results, the initial nervousness disappears. As competence develops, confidence comes.

This is true of speaking to a group. There is nothing to fear. It is you, talking to other human beings. As you learn to speak well, and with guided practice and growing competence, the over-rated bugaboo of stage fright disappears. Your nervous energy comes under control. Rather than worrying about initial nervousness, concentrate on good preparation and on attaining the positive goals we have outlined. Make every talk your best possible effort to communicate. Confidence will grow. Let us say frankly that if you apply what is set forth, especially in Chapter 5, on how to be effective in the way you talk, there will remain no basis for timidity.

Affirmative attitudes, including a willingness to learn, are essential. Goals then may be set, practice begun, and the direct path to success mapped out.

SUMMARY AND PREVIEW

Positive goals, and positive attitudes, should be keynotes in your study of oral communication. Better thinking prior to the speech, with consideration of the basic elements of logic, emotional appeal, and personal effectiveness, is the starting point. Arrangement, style, memory, and delivery—each has its function in making what you say effective. Clarity and hearer-consciousness join with these as goals—and all of them are attainable through practice.

In the last analysis, nearly everything depends upon your own attitude and motivation: whether you have the desire and the drive to attain effectiveness in one of the most important arts known to man. It is, in the main, up to you.

The next four chapters in Part One present specifically the basics of communicative skill: clarity attained through good thinking and good speech structure, and through intelligent handling of details; interestingness, through established psychological principles applied to the speaker-audience relationship; the speaker's personal persuasiveness; and the principles of effective presentation, or delivery. These apply, let us reemphasize, to all forms of oral communication, from the conversation to the public address.

Part Two deals specifically with the *planning of speeches*, including invention, arrangement, and style. In Chapters 7, 8, 9, and 10 additional techniques are presented which can raise your proficiency above that of the average speaker. These are applicable also in purposive conversational speech.

Part Three presents speech masterpieces of the past and present. You can learn much from these examples of effective public speaking.

In Part Four, a condensed chart of the principles of speech composition and suggestions for carrying out classroom speaking assignments which may be made are given.

We hope that this textbook will assist you as you work for more effective speech. Its principles are tested; *they do work when applied.* We may add that many thousands of students have used the five previous editions. We trust that in its new form the text may help you, as it has helped others.

2

How to Get Your Ideas
Understood: Good Structure

*It cannot be repeated too often that the capacity to write
and speak the English language clearly is indispensable
today for advancement in business.*

CLARENCE RANDALL

MR. RANDALL, in the Harvard lecture referred to in Chapter 1, made the statement quoted above. If there is one dominant idea in the expressions of business and professional leaders about speech, it is that being *clear* comes first.

The trustees of an important educational foundation gave the University of Chicago $500,000 to establish a professorship with the purpose of teaching students to express themselves clearly. Their letter of transmittal said in part:

"The trustees . . . are deeply concerned at the failure of many of our schools and colleges to teach students to use the English language effectively. . . . In particular, they hope that students will learn to express themselves with clarity and precision in good, straight-forward English."

This emphasis upon the compelling need of clarity is not new. In the eighteenth century, Hugh Blair, in his *Lectures on Rhetoric and Belles Lettres,* said "Perspicuity is the fundamental quality of style: a quality so essential that for the want of it nothing can be done." Without clarity there can be no satisfactory communication.

The speaker or converser must say what he means, and say it so that the hearer understands—instantly! And that, in today's slang, is a neat trick if you can do it!

WHAT DOES CLARITY DEMAND?

The over-all plan. Clarity makes many demands upon the oral communicator. He must know specifically what he *wants* to say; thus, his thinking must be precise and definite. He must be able so *to organize* his thoughts that ideas follow each other in logical order and that each detail is exact and relevant. He must know how to summarize each idea and to indicate clearly one transition to the next. The old-fashioned virtues of unity, staying with a central aim; coherence, a logical sequence of ideas; and emphasis are involved.

A carefully planned, simply organized presentation is the basis for that instant understanding that the converser or speaker seeks.

Words and sentences. This well-organized pattern of thought must find expression in *words* and *sentences*. The speaker's words must be accurate, appropriate, and, at times, vivid. The sentences conveying meaning must be direct, easy to follow, and varied in their structure. They, and the phrases of which they consist, must be such that a hearer can follow with ease.

Clarity, attained through good planning and arrangement of ideas, is the topic of this chapter.

CLARITY THROUGH GOOD STRUCTURE

What is purposive structure? The word "purposive" perhaps best defines good idea-structure. One communicates in order to produce a direct effect. He marshalls ideas and facts in order to do this. To illustrate: you wish to give a new employee instructions on the routine of his job; or you wish to explain the filing system in your office to this new staff member. Your purpose is *to give information.* You wish to get comprehension, that is, understanding, from your employee in relation to one or the other of these subjects. You succeed if this information is understood. There is no collateral or indirect purpose: entertainment is not sought; cultural advancement is not sought; persuasion is not sought. You are trying to convey certain facts—and these only. This is a direct purpose, an aim. All of your efforts are focused on its attainment.

Or perhaps a younger person, say a child, asks why so much is written today about the Civil War. In your conversation you seek to give him information to show the importance of that conflict. You stress how deep were the issues that caused it; how serious was its effect upon national life; how some of the sectional cleavages have persisted for a century. Your aim here, too, is informative, not argumentative. You are trying to make clear and to impress upon your hearer the vast importance of the Civil War. You are communicating facts.

Rather than aiming to give information, you may be seeking *to persuade.* Although your conversation will *contain information,* the facts are used to support your arguments. An example might be a discussion with a high school senior in which you urge him to go to college or, perhaps, to convince him that one particular college would be best for him to attend. Here, again, there is one over-riding aim. Your purpose is *to persuade,* either to agreement or to immediate, overt action. You succeed if this agreement or action is obtained.

Again, you may have returned recently from a trip to England and are to speak to your Kiwanis Club on "Cricket as I Saw It." Perhaps your only purpose is to entertain, to amuse. You will compare cricket to baseball and contrast the decorous, English "Well played" to the raucous cheers of American baseball fans. You will pick out humorous aspects of the game and relate incidents that amused you. Again you have one over-riding purpose: to entertain.

Summary on purposiveness. Oral communication is purposive and with very definite kinds of objectives. The *General Purposes* are classified as informative, persuasive, or entertaining.

Oral communication stresses not only a definite and single purpose, but is characterized by the *immediacy* of its aim: to get the new employee oriented in his job; to persuade Congress that we should spend more money on space exploration; to amuse the audience by a discussion of the student's trials in physical education.

Business letters, printed instructions, and advertisements, and some other written communications have the characteristics of singleness and immediacy of purpose, and their structure resembles that of speeches and interviews.

Occasionally, it is true, a speaker may explain or persuade with some hidden or collateral purposes, such as to enhance personal prestige or to win good will for his company or organization; but these do not affect the structure of the speech. They are *incidental* results which may follow, when the primary aim of information, persuasion, or entertainment is achieved.

To conclude: every attempt at oral communication has a single aim, and it is achieved successfully when that one purpose is attained.

The specific purpose. We have pointed out that the *kinds* of purposes in oral communication are three: to inform, to persuade, and to entertain. These lead to the classification of speeches as informative, persuasive, or entertaining.

But informative about what? and to whom? Persuasive about what? and to whom? Obviously, clearness would not be served by a speaker who said "I want to be informative about taxation," or "I want to persuade an audience about the bond issue." To inform whom? and about what kind or phase of taxation: personal property, real estate, income taxation; its productivity, assessment, or what?

Thus, clear thinking and clarity in presentation demand more than just a general purpose, as to inform, and a general subject, as taxation. We must determine *our exact aim,* in terms of precisely what we want to give information about and precisely *to whom.* This exact aim is called the *Specific Purpose.* It may be contrasted with the General Purpose, which in this case is to inform. So, too, in persuasive or entertaining speeches.

The Specific Purpose may be defined as a concise statement of the *exact* aim of the speaker or converser, specifying the precise result desired in relation to subject and hearer. For example:

1. To explain to an audience of liberal arts students how a jet plane is propelled.
2. To make clear the scope of authority of the Student Council. (Freshmen make up the audience.)
3. To explain to this new employee the duties of a payroll clerk.

These examples, all for talks of explanation or instruction, show the distinction between General and Specific Purposes. All have the *General* Purpose of giving information, but the *what* and *to whom* are definitely stated.

When the General Purpose is *to persuade,* the Specific Purpose states exactly *who is to be persuaded and precisely to what belief or action* in respect to the speaker's subject. For example:

1. To persuade John Brown to become a candidate for a Woodrow Wilson fellowship.
2. To persuade the Kiwanis Club members that the United Nations has been a force for world peace.
3. To persuade the television audience to contribute to Radio Free Europe.

In entertaining talks the Specific Purpose likewise "comes down to specifics." It should show what phase or characteristic of the subject is to be made entertaining.

Value of the specific purpose. No one can hope to talk clearly, or even to think clearly, without knowing his goal.

It is to determine that exact goal, with respect to subject, purpose, and audience, that a Specific Purpose must be selected.

A properly chosen and worded Specific Purpose enables the oral communicator to have unity in his presentation; he selects ideas and details, not at random, but with a view to their value in attaining the goal. It promotes coherence, or orderly progression. It permits him to limit the scope of his talk, in view of the knowledge or attitude of his hearers, to that which can reasonably be attempted. A non-technical group, for example, could not be led to understand all phases of jet plane operation, but could grasp the basic principle of its propulsion.

For the speaker himself, the Specific Purpose furnishes a guide. He will not, for example, be tempted in a speech explaining how a jet plane is propelled to wander over into persuasion by commenting on the superiority of one make or model over another. He will not talk about risks, or the need of longer runways, or the inadequacy of some airports, because in the very beginning he has limited himself to one task: to explain how a jet plane works. All of this means time-saving, clear, orderly presentation.

Choose the specific purpose carefully. The mental discipline involved in deciding definitely just what your Specific Purpose will be, and limiting yourself accordingly, will promote clearness. Three considerations should govern its choice:

First of all, make your Specific Purpose *specific*. A vague or generally stated purpose is no purpose at all. Exactly what do you want to explain, and to whom? Precisely what belief or action do you want to get, and from whom?

Second, *limit the scope* of your Specific Purpose to that which you can hope to achieve in the time allotted you. You may want to cut down a speech trying to prove that the United Nations is a general success to a specific argument that it was right in its stand during the Congo troubles.

Third, plan your Specific Purpose *with regard to the edu-*

129,143

*cational level, experience, and knowledge of the general sub-
ject that the audience now possesses; or with regard to its
known attitude toward your subject.* Obviously, an explanation of how grain is marketed delivered to an audience of
students in a city college would be vastly different from a
report given to the directors of a grain marketing corporation. Similarly, in a persuasive talk on urban renewal projects,
it would make a difference whether the audience was composed of property owners initially against the project or of
tenants who seek better rental housing.

Distinguish fact from opinion. In summarizing this discussion of General and Specific Purposes, let us emphasize the
necessity of distinguishing clearly between the presentation
of fact (the informative speech) and of opinions (the persuasive speech). In explaining how the automatic transmission
of an automobile works, you are dealing with matters of *fact.*
Opinion, for instance, whether manually operated gearshift-
ing is more efficient than the automatic, is not your concern.
Your sole object is to get understanding, that is, comprehension on the part of the hearer. If you are commemorating the
anniversary of John Glenn's orbital flight, you are again dealing with matters of fact. The audience in such a situation
would agree in advance that the flight was important and
worth commemorating; otherwise, it would not be in attendance. So you do not deal with controversial matters, but present facts which stress some of the significances of the event.

In persuasion, on the other hand, your objective is to form
or change opinion. You argue that a certain course of action
in regard to negotiations with Russia is better than some
other one, or you urge a person to abandon his aversion to life
insurance and to apply for a policy. True, you present *facts*
to support your arguments, but you are dealing with matters
on which there may be two or more opinions and are seeking
to get your opinions accepted. Your hearer or audience may
have, at the outset, a neutral or opposed opinion, and it is
your job to get that opinion changed to one favorable to
yours.

Failure to recognize this clear-cut distinction between the objectives of informative speech and those of persuasion is in itself a bar to clearness. It reflects itself, among other ways, in the use of vague terms, as "I will *explain* to him why he should save money regularly" when, actually, the intended meaning is "I will try to *persuade* him to start saving money."

Summary on purposes. The *General* Purposes are informative, persuasive, or entertaining. These terms denote the *kind* of effect one wishes to have upon his hearers. It should be clear that when the General Purpose is informative, one is conveying facts as such, and is not trying to establish or to change the hearers' opinions. Likewise, it should be clear that when the General Purpose is persuasive, one's aim *is* to influence or change opinions. In entertainment there is usually no serious attempt to influence opinions.

The *Specific* Purpose states the exact aim of the speaker, in terms of subject and desired effect upon the hearer. It should be definite, limited in scope to that which can be accomplished in the allotted time, and adjusted to the known educational level and attitude of the hearer.

With the General and Specific Purposes properly chosen and stated, the speaker, interviewer, or converser is ready to proceed further with systematic planning.

The principal ideas. The next step in attaining over-all clarity is to choose Principal Ideas. These are statements that, when properly developed, will enable the speaker to achieve his goal, as set forth in the Specific Purpose.

One frequent cause of unintelligibility is that of poor idea-selection. Important and unimportant points, some of them even not relating to the Specific Purpose, are presented one after the other. The result is a jumble of confusion. The speaker's task is to determine what Principal Ideas will best assist in achieving the aim of his talk. Others should be discarded. Then it is possible to concentrate on a few vital points, and to develop them fully enough so that the desired understanding or persuasion is achieved.

The relation between Specific Purpose and Principal Ideas is illustrated in this chart:

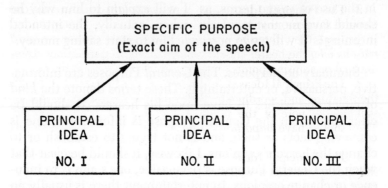

The arrows indicate that each Principal Idea contributes directly to the attainment of the Specific Purpose. In an informative talk each idea defines, describes, or furnishes a step forward in the process of explanation. In persuasion each idea should be a reason why the belief or action asked in the Specific Purpose should be agreed to. In this sense, a good alternative term for Principal Ideas would be Supporting Ideas. They are *principal* in the sense that they are important and relatively few; they are *supporting* in their function toward the Specific Purpose.

Around Principal Ideas, by developing them with *Speech Details* such as examples, comparisons, statistics, and testimony, the entire speech or interview-plan is built.

Choosing and wording principal ideas. Because the Principal Ideas are the pivotal points of a presentation, great care in choosing and wording them is necessary. Their limitation in number and a clear order of presentation are also important.

The following list of requirements deserves careful study and compliance. Its use will greatly assist in arriving at the most effective Principal Ideas for a given talk:

1. The Principal Ideas must clearly and logically support the Specific Purpose. They must relate directly to it as supporting points. This point has been developed above.

2. The Principal Ideas must conform in their nature to the General Purpose, that is, informative, persuasive, or entertaining. In general, they *describe* or *define* in the informative type; give *reasons why* the hearer should believe or act in persuasion; stress unusual or amusing points about the subject in entertainment.

3. The Principal Ideas should be interesting: appealing through their nature and wording to the wants or desires of people or striking the note of the familiar, the unusual, or the specific. They should have *importance,* and be worded so as to create interest.

4. The Principal Ideas should be thought-provoking both to the speaker, in that a well-chosen idea suggests its own development, and to the hearer, in that they cause him to listen with interest and to follow the speaker's reasoning with attention. *Generative* and *challenging* are words that also express this desirable feature.

5. The Principal Ideas should be chosen from one consistent, stable point of view. If, for instance, your Specific Purpose is to convince the hearers that the council-manager form of government is advantageous, the ideas should all present specific *advantages,* and you should not digress in the middle of the talk to tell how the council-manager form of government originated.

6. The Principal Ideas should be few in number. Too many points mean confusion.

7. The Principal Ideas should be stated in the form of complete sentences, rather than in catch phrases or single words. This is necessary in order that their meaning be clear both to the speaker and hearer. Catch phrases, such as "necessity" or "Why this is good" are obviously vague. They lack, therefore, communicative strength.

Examples of purpose-idea structure. The core of a well-designed speech, or well-planned interview, is simple but precise. It consists of the Specific Purpose, supported or developed by Principal Ideas. These Principal Ideas, in turn, are developed by Speech Details.

It is impossible to over-emphasize the importance of *understanding* and *using* this type of structure. Without it, clearness is almost unattainable. Moreover, this plan is compact, time-saving, and thus effective.

To illustrate the relationship and functions of purpose and ideas, as well as the application of the rules for each, the following "skeleton outlines" are offered.

GENERAL PURPOSE—Informative (explanation)

SPECIFIC PURPOSE:

To explain the city manager-council form of municipal government to students

PRINCIPAL IDEAS:

1. The elective council, headed by the mayor, makes policy through passage of ordinances.
2. The council employs and supervises the work of the professionally trained city manager.
3. The manager, as the executive responsible to the council, directs the actual operation of all city departments.

Here the Specific Purpose is definite, is sufficiently limited in scope, and is adapted to a student audience. The Principal Ideas conform to the seven rules given above: each supports the Specific Purpose, is definitive in nature, thus conforming to the informative type, can be made interesting, is thought-provoking, is chosen from a consistent viewpoint, and is stated as a declarative sentence; and there are only three Principal Ideas.

GENERAL PURPOSE—Persuasive, seeking Belief

SPECIFIC PURPOSE:

To convince the audience of the efficiency of the council-manager form of city government

PRINCIPAL IDEAS:

1. It provides skilled and centralized authority over all operations.
2. It sharply reduces the possibility of political influence on departmental operations.
3. It permits operating economies and improved procedures.

When supported by Speech Details, such as testimony, examples, statistics, and comparisons, the Principal Ideas here given would tend to convince the hearers of the efficiency of the council-manager form of government. Each idea is a reason why this form of government is efficient, or can be. Centralized authority, reduced political influence, and operating improvements—each contribute toward the notion of efficiency.

What we have been attempting to explain and illustrate may be termed the *basic speech plan*. Twenty-three centuries ago, Aristotle, in his *Rhetoric*, said, "The essential parts of a speech are two: statement and proof." In other words, Specific Purpose and Principal Ideas, developed by appropriate details. This basic speech plan is the foundation of clearness.

Beginning and ending. It will be noted that we have not included a treatment of the introduction and conclusion as parts of the basic speech plan.

In spite of the survival of the idea that the "introduction, body, and conclusion" are the essential parts of speeches and other presentations, it must be pointed out that the purposes and ideas of the speech are the *real* essentials.

Effective beginnings and endings are, of course, helpful, but can be planned only *after* the core of the speech has been decided upon. And, especially under modern time limits, the introduction is often confined to a brief statement of purpose or subject, with perhaps a short indication of its importance to the audience; and the conclusion usually sums up the main points and, perhaps, makes a brief plea for action. The more elaborate openings and endings of former days have fallen into virtual disuse. The tendency now is to get to the main points of the talk rapidly and to conclude briefly.

The vital parts of a speech, let us repeat, are the purpose and the developed ideas that help achieve it. These ought to have our first and most thorough attention.

Further suggestions on clarity. Although not intended to be used in every talk, the following suggestions may aid clarity in the speech as a whole.

1. You may announce, not only your subject, but your Specific Purpose in opening your talk.

2. In your opening you may also tell in advance what your Principal Ideas are to be.

3. You may use a *topical sentence* in starting each Principal Idea, that is, you may state it concisely before presenting the details.

4. You may sum up, in a brief sentence, a Principal Idea before going on to the next one.

5. You may combine summary and topical sentences in making a transition from one Principal Idea to another; for example, "Not only is the tax on food unfair, but it is bad for the nation's health."

6. In presenting successive ideas, you may use "first, second, third" as an aid to clarity.

7. You *should* usually summarize your points in your conclusion. This may be done formally, as "I have tried to show you that the tax on food is unfair and a detriment to the nation's health," or informally, as "Surely a tax that discriminates against the poor and denies adequate nutrition to our people is undesirable."

8. Often you may end with a restatement of your Specific Purpose, so that the hearers will have no doubt what they are supposed to understand, believe, or do: "So vote for the repeal of the food tax when you go to the polls next Tuesday."

Clear thinking is the keynote. If you want to be clear to others, your own thinking must be clear. Through the *basic speech plan* you employ clear thinking as to purpose and supporting ideas. The process of choosing and wording these promotes definiteness and concentration. It helps you to simplify and to be specific. This increases your ability to be understood by others.

An incidental advantage of the basic speech plan is that it furnishes an *important aid to memory*. Instead of trying to recall a manuscript or an elaborate outline, all that is necessary is to have a mental picture of the purpose and ideas that constitute the framework of your talk. Details can be remembered in association with each Principal Idea. Thus, a basis for note-free, extemporaneous speaking is laid. You learn to "think on your feet." Your talk then is not only clearer, but it has a far more communicative, "I–to–you" quality. It becomes genuine communication, and not an artificial "performance."

"Extemporaneous," the term used above for speaking from prepared ideas, is the method employed by the most effective and communicative talkers. The extemporaneous speaker learns to concentrate on *ideas* and to express them and their details in whatever words seem appropriate at the moment of utterance. This skill, as it develops, promotes fluency and confidence.

Ability thus to use the basic speech plan leads to another important skill, that of speaking *impromptu,* that is, without previous preparation. Called on unexpectedly, a trained speaker instantly decides upon his purpose and formulates one or two or more ideas that will support it. The untrained speaker often is confused and perhaps fails altogether to give a purposive or coherent talk. Many of the situations of business and personal life, in conversation, demand ability to express one's ideas instantly and clearly.

Listening skill is also increased by the clear outline of thought which we have presented in this chapter. Those hearing a speech or engaged in conversation discern ideas more readily if the speaker follows the basic plan. If a speaker's or converser's outline is clear, the well-disposed listener can not only recognize ideas more efficiently, but can evaluate them as they are developed. It is one of the responsibilities of the speaker to be clear, in order that the speech may encourage the hearer to listen with good attention. A further advantage of learning and mastering the basic design for speeches and interviews is that this plan carries over into such fields as business letter writing and other written communication. The purpose-idea-detail structure can make you more effective. Your letters, bulletins, notices, reports, and instructions will be clearer.

Clarity depends upon good structure. Summarizing what we have said thus far: clarity—instant intelligibility—is vital to effectiveness. Clarity depends on clear thinking and clear speech structure. Good speech structure begins with the determination of the General Purpose: informative, persuasive, or entertaining. There follow the choice and wording of the Specific Purpose—the *exact* aim of the speaker with subject and audience—and the selection of Principal (supporting) Ideas. These, when properly developed through Speech Details, lead to the accomplishment of the Specific Purpose. We have just set forth some important advantages that this simple, basic speech plan offers to the communicator. They are well worth your consideration.

3

Clarity in the Details of a Presentation

Exemplum docet. (The example teaches.)
QUINTILIAN

ALL that has been said in Chapter 2 points to the connection between clear thinking and clarity of *ideas.* Thus, we studied good speech structure. Clear structure of ideas means clarity in the speech or interview as a whole. Likewise, clear structure in the *development* of ideas is necessary to insure instant understanding on the part of the hearer. This involves oral "paragraphs," the Speech Details, sentences, and words.

The oral "paragraph." We have seen that the structural unit of a speech is a Principal Idea, one of those statements of fact or opinion that supports the Specific Purpose. In a short speech, it is simply developed by appropriate details, and perhaps summarized. Thus, in his War Address of December 8, 1941, President Franklin D. Roosevelt briefly developed the Principal Idea that the Pearl Harbor attack by Japan was the result of preconcerted plan:

It will be recorded that the distance of Hawaii from Japan makes it obvious that the attack was deliberately planned many days or even weeks ago. During the intervening time, the Japanese government has deliberately sought to deceive the United

States by false statements and expressions of hope for peace in the Pacific.

The attack yesterday on the Hawaiian Islands has caused severe damage to American military and naval forces. Many American lives have been lost. In addition, American ships have been reported torpedoed on the high seas between San Francisco and Honolulu.

Yesterday the Japanese Government also launched an attack against Malaya.

Last night Japanese forces attacked Hong Kong.

Last night Japanese forces attacked Guam.

Last night Japanese forces attacked the Philippine Islands.

Last night the Japanese attacked Wake Island.

Last night the Japanese attacked Midway Island.

Japan has, therefore, undertaken a surprise offensive extending throughout the Pacific area. The facts of yesterday speak for themselves.

This excerpt constitutes one unit of thought. *Like a written paragraph,* it has a topical sentence, stating the gist of the thought, followed by supporting details and finally by a summary sentence. It is not rigidly worded, since the first few lines approach the topic from the viewpoint of "deliberate deceit" and the summary uses the term "a surprise offensive"; yet the structure of the idea is immediately apparent.

Subordinate ideas are "paragraphs." In a speech of greater length and more detail, the Principal Ideas are often divided into what may be termed Subordinate Ideas, each of which supports the thought of the Principal Idea of which it is a part. Thus President John F. Kennedy, in his speech announcing the planned resumption of nuclear testing in the atmosphere, March 2, 1962, had among others, one Principal Idea dealing with the reaction of other nations to his announcement. It might be outlined as follows, showing its subdivision into three Subordinate Ideas:

I. Principal Idea: Different countries will react differently to this announcement.

A. There will be those in other countries who will urge us to refrain from testing at all.

B. Free peoples generally will support our resumption of these tests.
C. Russia's reaction will be unfavorable.

Each of the Subordinate Ideas here could be considered an oral paragraph. For example, consider this "paragraph" involving part B of the Principal Idea.

But those free peoples who value their freedom and security, and look to our relative strength to protect them from danger—those who know of our good faith in seeking an end to testing and an end to the arms race—will, I am confident, want the United States to do whatever it must do to deter the threat of aggression.

If they felt we could be swayed by threats or intimidation—if they thought we could permit a repetition of last summer's deception—then surely they would lose faith in our will and our wisdom as well as our weaponry.

I have no doubt that most of our friends around the world have shared my own hope that we would never find it necessary to test again—and my own belief that, in the long run, the only real security in this age of nuclear perils rests not in armament but in disarmament.

But I am equally certain that they would insist on our testing once that is deemed necessary to protect free world security. They know that we are not deciding to test for political or psychological reasons—and they also know that we cannot avoid such tests for political or psychological reasons.

Good oral paragraph structure is thus an aid to instant understanding. Every Principal or Subordinate Idea can be kept clear if the speaker will observe these three simple rules: *state the idea, develop it, and restate it.* This does not mean that every oral "paragraph" must be mechanical or rigid. For example, Adlai Stevenson, in his speech dedicating the Lovejoy Memorial at Alton, Illinois, November 9, 1952, developed one idea in this manner:

Elijah Lovejoy, however, served a greater cause than that of the abolition of Negro slavery. And it was his devotion to this cause, I dare say, which we will long remember after the struggle over the abolition of slavery has all but been forgotten.

This greater cause, if you please, was the right—and the duty— of the individual to speak out for the truth. I make the reference to "duty" advisedly because that was the way Lovejoy thought of it. To his fellow citizens of Alton in meeting assembled to protest the turmoil provoked by his outspokenness, he said something like this:

"I am impelled in the cause I have taken because I fear God. As I shall answer to my God in the great day, I dare not abandon my sentiments nor cease in all proper ways to propagate them. I can die at my post but I cannot desert it."

The summation need not, it will be observed from the examples we have given, be in the identical words of the topical statement: it may use synonyms effectively.

Sometimes a summary sentence is combined with the next topical sentence, in what is usually termed a summary-transition statement; for example:

"The Republican platform not only repudiates the League of Nations, but praises, without discrimination all of the Republican senators who participated in its defeat."—Homer S. Cummings, keynote speech in 1920 Democratic convention.

"Such are the authentic proofs of the validity and vitality of democracy. Here, no less, hides the mystery of democracy."— Woodrow Wilson, accepting for the nation the gift of the Lincoln birthplace farm.

"Our nation is tempted to depart from its 'standard of morality' and adopt a policy of 'criminal aggression.' But will it yield?"—William Jennings Bryan, *America's Mission*.

These distinguished speakers used summary-transitions, repeating the essence of one idea before passing on to the next. In general, the scanning of any speech in the collections of outstanding addresses will show that the topical sentence-development-summation plan is followed in a large majority of cases.

The ordering of details. Within the framework of the oral paragraph, details—such as examples, comparisons, statistics, or testimony—should all logically relate to the topic sentence. The paragraphs we have quoted from Roosevelt, Kennedy, and Stevenson illustrate in different ways this principle. They likewise illustrate an orderly and natural sequence of detail to detail. The thought proceeds in a straight line which promotes clearness. And in none of them is there a detail that does not relate to the idea then being developed.

Clarity is aided, especially in the Roosevelt speech, by the use of reiteration within the idea: the use of repetitive "Last night" beginnings; the repeated use of the phrase "Japanese forces attacked." Reiteration used in this manner, as well as in summaries, adds emphasis and increases clarity.

The speech details. There are five kinds of Speech Details, through the use of which ideas may be developed. They are:

COMPARISON. This likens an idea to something of the same nature (literal comparison) or to something in which the resemblance is imagined (figurative comparison). For example, literal comparison is involved in the following statement, "Chess and checkers are played on the same kind of board." Figurative comparison is illustrated by comparison with something of a different kind, as "Chess resembles medieval warfare, with its pawns, knights, king, and queen." *Simile,* in which specific words indicating comparison are used, such as *like, resembles,* etc., and *metaphor,* in which the comparison is made without such words, are the figures of speech involved.

"Like an armed warrior, like a plumed knight, James G. Blaine marched down the halls of Congress."—Ingersoll, nominating Blaine for the presidency.

"She [America] was indeed the fountain of our wealth, the nerve of our strength, the nursery and basis of our naval power." —William Pitt.

"'A house divided against itself cannot stand.' I believe this government cannot endure permanently half slave and half free."— Lincoln.

Whether for clarity or vividness, or both, the use of comparison is an important means of developing an idea. Lincoln's "house divided" comparison illustrated clearly the point that he wished to make. *Contrast,* showing dissimilarities between things of the same kind or between different things that have some imaginary resemblance is, in principle, like comparison: it illustrates the speaker's point by reference to that which is known or imagined.

"The stroke used on an electric typewriter is far lighter than that employed when using a manual machine. In the electric, a light touch causes the motor to actuate the keys; in the manual, you furnish the energy."

"And this wonderful power, it was not a thunderstorm: he flanked you with his wit, he surprised you out of yourself; you were conquered before you knew it."—Wendell Phillips, *Eulogy of O'Connell.*

Compare, or *contrast,* that which you are trying to make clear to that which the audience understands and you achieve greater understanding. Thus comparison and its helpmate, contrast, aid in making clear one's meaning. When used in persuasion, comparison and contrast, by referring to those ideas or feelings that have previously been believed or felt by the audience, aid in moving people to belief or action.

EXAMPLES. Even more important weapons of the speaker than comparison, are actual cases, incidents, or happenings that tend to support an idea. Roosevelt in his War Message, of which part is quoted above, used actual cases which tended to establish his point that Japan had undertaken a surprise offensive: Hawaii, Malaya, Hong Kong, Guam, the Philippines, Wake Island, Midway Island.

In the historic debate of 1920 over our proposed membership in the League of Nations, Homer S. Cummings, Attorney General under Wilson, made a prophetic speech before the Democratic convention centering on the issue of the League. He made use of many examples throughout. One passage will illustrate his method:

A League of Nations already exists. It is not a project, it is a fact. We must either enter it or remain out of it.

What nations have actually signed and ratified the treaty?

Brazil, Bolivia, Great Britain, Canada, Australia, South Africa, New Zealand, India, Czecho-Slovakia, Guatemala, Liberia, Panama, Peru Uruguay, Siam, Greece, Poland, Japan, Italy, France and Belgium.

What neutral states, invited to join the League, have actually done so?

Norway, Venezuela, the Netherlands, Denmark, Colombia, Chile, Argentina, Paraguay, Persia, Salvador, Spain, Sweden and Switzerland.

Even China will become a member when she ratifies the Austrian treaty.

Germany has signed and is preparing to take the place that awaits her in the League of Nations.

What nations stand outside? Revolutionary Mexico, Bolshevist Russia, Unspeakable Turkey, and—the United States of America.

It is not yet too late. Let us stand with the forces of civilization.

Mr. Cummings, one of the most able speakers of our century, was especially apt in cumulating brief examples to sustain a point. Naturally, some examples may be given in greater detail, according to a speaker's purpose and the nature of his subject.

The example is probably the most effective means of developing persuasive ideas; however, it has a great use in speeches of the informative type, whether for simple explanation or for the impressive-informative sort of talk. For example, in explaining what the League of Women Voters does, the following paragraph makes use of examples:

One function of the League of Women Voters is to take definite stands upon issues of the day, local, state and national, after thorough study. For instance, its proposed agenda for 1962 suggested that the League consider the United Nations, its support and evaluation of means of strengthening it, as one item on its agenda. Another proposed item was foreign economic policy. "Continuing responsibilities," those programs on which an official stand had previously been taken, included these: conservation of water resources, the loyalty-security problem, self-government and representation in Congress for the District of Columbia, support of the "item veto," the right of the President to veto individual items in appropriation bills, opposition to constitutional limitations on tax rates, and opposition to constitutional changes that would limit the existing powers of the President and Congress over foreign relations. These were the national issues on which the League centered its efforts.

These examples helped make clear what the League does in supporting or opposing national proposals.

In a well-planned informative-impressive talk, a St. Louis University student listed Civil War battles and other events that happened in St. Louis and the leadership that came from St. Louis during the conflict, to make impressive his Specific Purpose, which was to show the large part the city played in the war. These examples thus aided impressiveness.

Examples involve incidents, happenings, events, or persons that are known to the audience, thus employing the principle of the *familiar;* they involve also the *specific,* the quality of definiteness and exactness, sometimes called concreteness. Thus they are usually interesting and forceful. Because they are specific and may be known, they help the hearer to understand and thus promote clarity.

Someone has said, "The most valuable words in a speaker's vocabulary are 'for example,' or 'for instance.'" Insofar as these phrases encourage and promote the citation of examples, the statement has a great deal of truth in it.

STATISTICS. Many subjects *require* statistical treatment, because of the great number of facts involved; others can profit from the use of some figures. When one speaks, as did a police official in a radio program, on the increase in crime in a city area, the use of grand totals, percentages of increase, and increases within each class of crime is almost unavoidable. If a speaker combines several examples with statistics tending to show that his examples are typical of the whole body of fact, he reenforces his persuasive effect.

Although primarily, perhaps, useful in the logical process of persuasion, statistics can also be used with good effect in some informative talks. The dimensions of a factory and of its departments might aid in explaining how automobiles are made. Too, the number of steps in each part of the process of manufacture might be given. In a speech of the impressive-informative type, a nursing student made vivid the complexity of the human nervous system by giving the total number of nerves in the body.

Statistics should be accurate, derived from a reliable source and representative of the truth. Usually their use should be sparing, and exclusive dependence upon them is generally to be avoided. They should be considered as reenforcing material rather than as a sole means of explanation or proof. Their power to convince lies in the fact that they are specific.

TESTIMONY. The statements of others, like statistics, tend to reenforce comparisons and examples, rather than to constitute complete proof or explanation by themselves.

The verdict of a person who is an authority on the subject matter and is known to be such by the hearers or the judgment of a man held in high respect by the audience tends to help convince the hearers that the speaker is right in the opinions he is presenting. The same is true of quotations from high courts or great documents, such as the United States Constitution. Biblical quotations and literary references, proverbs and axioms, act as testimony.

In cases at law, of course, the testimony of *witnesses* is important. If a person was in a position to observe—and was physically and mentally capable of accurate observation—and had no motive to testify against the truth, what he tells helps to establish the facts in the case. In less formal situations, the observations made by a capable and disinterested person may also help to establish matters of fact.

In informative speeches giving explanations or instructions, the testimony of others may be used when someone has stated a principle with great clarity. In the informative-impressive talk, vivid quotations from others stressing some quality or characteristic of the topic may be of great assistance.

Some of the several uses of testimony are illustrated in the following quotations:

Bishop Fulton J. Sheen has this to say about the need of clear thinking to a speaker: "Clarity is derived from understanding a subject. A professor in a class in cosmology once asked me the definition of time. I said; 'I know what it is, but I can't tell you.' He said, 'If you knew what it is, you could tell me.' "—From a lecture on speaking.

"I will vouch John Randolph of Roanoke, the Virginia slave-holder, who hated an Irishman almost as much as he hated a Yankee. Hearing O'Connell, he exclaimed, 'This is the man, these are the lips, the most eloquent that speak English in my day.'"—Phillips, *Eulogy of O'Connell*.

"In the language of the late chief justice: 'It is not required that the abettor shall be actually on the spot when the murder is committed, or even in sight of the more immediate perpetrator of the act. If he be at a distance, cooperating in the act . . . this, in the eye of the law, is being present, aiding and abetting, so as to make him a principal in the murder.'"—Webster, *White Murder Case*.

Thus testimony may add clarity and vividness both to informative speeches and to persuasive ones. Its limitations: the notion that "You can get an expert on either side of a subject," "Testimonials aren't proof," etc., should not cause one to ignore it as a means of backing up or reenforcing his other means of explanation or proof.

REITERATION. We have already spoken of the value of *repeating*, in identical or other words, the statement of a Principal Idea to summarize the point. Such reiteration is necessary, as a rule, to keep the meaning clear to the audience. Reiteration may also be employed in summarizing a speech as a whole. Finally, immediately after stating an idea, it may be repeated, either in the same, or in different words:

"You cannot conciliate America by your present measures. You cannot subdue her by your present, or by any measures. What, then, can you do? You cannot conquer, you cannot gain; but you can address; you can lull the fears and anxieties of the moment into an ignorance of the danger that should produce them."— William Pitt, *The Attempt to Subjugate America*.

"The eighth commandment reads, 'Thou shalt not steal.' It does not read, 'Thou shalt not steal from the rich man.' It does not read, 'Thou shalt not steal from the poor man.' It reads simply and plainly, 'Thou shalt not steal.'"—Theodore Roosevelt, *Man With a Muckrake*.

Oral communication, whether in a speech or in conversation, employs more reiteration than is needed in written composition. The reason, very simply, is that one cannot usually ask a speaker to repeat a statement. The understanding on the hearer's part must be immediate. Thus reiteration, as we have outlined its uses here, is important to clarity.

Summary on speech details. Comparison, examples, statistics, testimony, and reiteration have been defined and illustrated here. They contribute to clarity when they are directly in support of the ideas of the speaker and when stated concisely. That no one type of Speech Detail should be relied upon exclusively has been emphasized. People react differently to each one. Comparison appeals to the more imaginative; examples to the logically minded; statistics and testimony reenforce other proof and vary in their appeal; and reiteration keeps meaning before the hearer. The effective oral communicator uses all five kinds.

Visual aids, such as charts, exhibits, models, demonstrations, and auditory aids employing recorded sound help in the presentation of the Speech Details. These, and other aids to effectiveness in presenting details, will be treated in Chapter 7. The following chart illustrates the Basic Speech Plan, including Specific Purpose, Principal Ideas, and the five kinds of Speech Details:

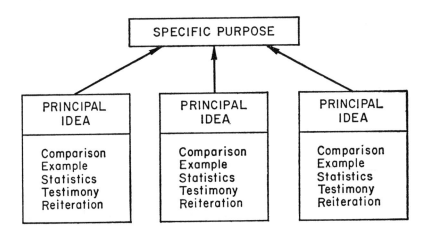

CLARITY THROUGH SENTENCES
AND WORDS

Specific Purpose, Principal Ideas, and Speech Details are expressed in *sentences* and *words*. Assuming that the idea-structure is clear, and that details are well related to the ideas they develop, an over-all clarity of thought is achieved. This over-all clarity, based on clear thinking, paves the way for clear, readily understandable sentences and words.

Clarity in sentences. The speaker or converser has many types of sentences at his command, but the direct, straightforward declarative form comes first. Subject, verb, and object, stated clearly, can indicate meaning tersely and directly:

"I do not expect the house to fall; but I do expect that it will cease to be divided."—Lincoln.

"There has been a change of government. It began two years ago, when the House of Representatives became Democratic by a decisive majority. It has now been completed. The offices of President and Vice-President have been put into the hands of the Democrats."—Wilson, *First Inaugural.*

The *interrogative sentence,* as a variant from the declarative, points up and emphasizes a point. It may be a *rhetorical* question which implies its own answer or simply a question to be answered by the speaker. Wilson, after the statements just quoted, used a question to introduce the theme of his speech. He said:

"What does the change mean? That is the question that I am going to try to answer. . . ."

The rhetorical question suggests its own answer. In the supposed speech of Patrick Henry before the House of Burgesses in 1775, this one occurs:

"Is this the part of wise men, engaged in a great and arduous struggle for liberty?"

The *imperative sentence,* "commanding" the hearer to

give his attention to a point, when used with discretion, serves the purposes of clarity and emphasis:

"Compare the two. This I offer to give is plain and simple. The other, full of perplexed and intricate mazes."—Burke, *Conciliation Speech*.

"New York gave us Grover Cleveland, teaching in Albany that public office is a public trust; Theodore Roosevelt, preaching the doctrine of the square deal for all; Virginia and New Jersey gave to us that pioneer of fellowship between nations, our great leader, Woodrow Wilson.

"Let us measure our present Governor by those standards."—Franklin D. Roosevelt, nominating Alfred E. Smith for the Presidency.

It is with these three kinds of sentences that the speaker mainly deals. The many variations in sentence structure, such as parallel construction, periodicity, inverted order, and the many stylistic possibilities such as antithesis, like beginnings, like endings, and rhythm, may be left for later study. All, and many more, are illustrated in the speeches in Part Three. For the present, we may offer a few suggestions having to do with clarity:

1. The short sentence is usually clearer than a long, involved one.
2. If a long sentence, however, is composed of short and readily-understood phrases, it is usually clear.
3. The active voice, rather than the passive, is conducive to clarity.
4. A variety of sentence-types breaks monotony and thus aids in audience-attention.
5. A variety in the length of sentences is desirable.
6. The exclamation, popular in the speeches of the 18th and early 19th centuries, is not used so frequently by present-day speakers.
7. Clarity is assisted when parenthetical phrases, qualifying phrases and the like are avoided. These complicate a sentence without adding much to its understandability. Therefore "come to the point" in your statements.

"Talk yourself clear," was the frequent suggestion of a great teacher, Thomas C. Trueblood, founder of the Department of Speech at the University of Michigan. Although his advice applies to the over-all structure of a speech as well, it is particularly useful in clarifying one's sentences. For those who were unable to "come to the point," he suggested writing out a paragraph and then blue-pencilling all phrases that were not necessary to convey meaning. Then for "big words" he suggested simpler ones. This aided many of his students to achieve a simple directness and brevity. The suggestion is a good one.

Clarity in words. It is a common saying that the speaker "should not talk over the heads of his audience," that is, use words that they do not understand. Yet this is negative advice. Obviously, one tries for the simple word when talking to an audience of very young children, or to one composed of illiterates. But too often the warning not to go "over their heads" is interpreted as meaning that no word longer than four or five letters should be used. The level of one's speaking vocabulary should be adjusted to the audience, the occasion, and the subject, always with the first aim of being understood. There is no reason to address everything to the lowest level of audience intelligence, nor for the speaker to descend to vulgarity, excessive slang, or ungrammatical English. He will command respect far better by clear-cut and correct expressions.

Words are the symbols of meaning; when used in phrases and sentences, they convey meaning. Granted that the simpler word of two possible choices is usually preferable, *accuracy* in meaning is important.

The word used should convey the meaning that the speaker wishes to convey. If the mental picture produced by a word is sharp and clear, meaning has been communicated. Take the word "dog." This produces any number of mental images, from the toy lapdog to the Great Dane. But if the word "chow" were used, a medium-sized, red, compactly built dog would be visualized. Add to this an appropriate adjective, such as "snarling," and you get a specific impression.

Accuracy in language rests upon the choice of words that are as specific as possible. Consider the word *house:* perhaps it first occurs to you to express a meaning. But there are many more specific words, more descriptive ones. One of the following might be better to use for the sake of exact meaning: mansion, split-level, ranch house, cabin, bungalow, home, residence, shack, etc. The individual name, rather than a general statement, is good: Stonewall Jackson rather than a Confederate general, Corregidor rather than a fort in the Philippines, Man of War rather than a champion racehorse.

Semantics stresses the fact that words may mean one thing to one individual, another to someone else. It is important to use words with the shade of meaning that the hearer will accept. The phrase, "peaceful coexistence," has different meanings for Americans and for Russians, for example.

Careful consideration of words and the meanings they seek to communicate is therefore necessary. This is not the place for consideration of semantics; but one should be conscious of the impact of various terms on different individuals. Accuracy, if striven for, and definiteness of language, can help keep meaning clear. "Who, when, where, why, what, and how" is a good guide.

To meet the demands of clarity and exactness, the student speaker should strive to increase the range and flexibility of his vocabulary. A standard dictionary will prove useful in this connection. There are also books of synonyms and antonyms, such as Roget's *Thesaurus.* Vocabulary can be improved by listening to the speech of educated people, and of finding the meaning of unfamiliar words by reference to dictionaries.

APPROPRIATENESS OF LANGUAGE. After accuracy and clearness, a major consideration about the use of words is that they shall be appropriate to the speaker, the audience and occasion, and the subject. A young speaker using ornate and high-flown language suitable for a Daniel Webster would only create amusement. An academic gathering, a political rally, church services, and labor meetings would obviously call for different kinds of language. And in regard to subject matter, a routine explanation in a business office, a political debate, and a eulogy of a great man—each demand entirely different levels of vocabulary.

The story of Lincoln's painstaking efforts to be clear and precise in his use of words, to the point of saying exactly what he wished to say and in a way that permitted no misunderstanding, holds much of value for lesser speakers. His "House Divided" speech, briefly quoted before in this chapter, and his *Cooper Union Address,* in which he carefully defined the exact issue he wished to discuss, will repay reading from this viewpoint alone.

SUMMARY ON CLARITY

Without utmost clarity there can be no effective communication of ideas. In these two chapters, we have pointed out that clarity is best achieved by use of *the basic speech plan,* with a well-defined Specific Purpose, well-chosen Principal Ideas, and effective introduction and conclusion. The *development* of each part of a speech depends upon clear "paragraph" structure, with topical sentences, details, and summary sentences keeping the outline of thought before the hearer. General simplicity in the sentences, and accuracy in language, have been stressed. Following is a complete chart of speech structure:

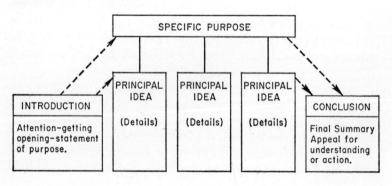

Thus clearness, the ability instantly to be understood, depends upon many factors. The principal one, and one that underlies all others, however, is clear and definite thinking.

Let us emphasize, in closing, that not only the public speech, but every form of oral communication: conversation, interview, conference, discussion, has clarity as an aim. What we have said about over-all speech structure applies with equal force to the structure of a purposive interview or other form of conversational speech. The first job of the oral communicator is *to be understood.*

4

How to Interest People
in What You Say

What we attend to controls our behavior. What we can get other people to attend to controls their behavior.

H. A. OVERSTREET

Let us take inventory at this point. In the two chapters just completed, we have learned that a necessary aim of the speaker, at any level of communication, is *to be understood.* We have found that this means a clear-cut structure of ideas, so that the speaker's thought may be followed easily by the hearer. We have found, also, that the details of a presentation must relate clearly to the ideas, and in themselves be clear and relevant.

Yet clarity and logic alone do not solve the problem of the speaker or converser. A speech or an interview must get the *interested attention of the hearer.* The speech must get itself listened to. How to make what is already clear and logical more appealing and interesting is the theme of this chapter.

THE APPEAL TO WANTS

"Find out what the prospect, or the audience, wants. Then show him that your proposal will satisfy those wants." This pointed statement by the late James A. Worsham, expert in salesmanship, sounds the keynote of persuasion. Overstreet, in *Influencing Human Behavior,* stresses the necessity of considering the wants that motivate people, in the statement, "No appeal to reason that is not at the same time an appeal to wants is ever successful."

If you want people to be interested in your talk, choose a subject that is concerned with their vital interests. Show them how it relates to their health, their income, their desire for recognition, the welfare of their family, their city, their country. In informative talks, motivate them to listen by establishing a connection with their desires for these things. In persuasion, show them that if they will do what you suggest, they will benefit in one of these areas. The task of interesting people is basically that simple.

The wants of an individual may include dozens, even hundreds of specific items. "I want a better car; I want a raise; I want a tailored suit; I want a vacation; I want to be a better golfer," etc. Listen in on any conversation and you will be aware of how often the words "I want" are used. Bring these wants to the surface of a person's thinking, and you interest him. He will listen to what you say.

Although specific wants are widely varied, a practical classification of them can assist a speaker. A. E. Phillips, in his *Effective Speaking,* listed the so-called impelling motives as self-preservation, property, power, reputation, affections, sentiments and tastes. Another list, that offered by V. A. Ketcham, was life, home, property, humanity. Similar classifications in great numbers have been made. We believe that a good working list of the wants of people in general is as follows: self-preservation, profit, recognition and authority, love, ideals, and recreational-cultural tastes.

SELF-PRESERVATION. We recognize this as the "first law of nature." People want to preserve their lives. They want to be healthy. They want to avoid injury, pain, and fatigue and to have as much physical well-being and comfort as possible. They want to be safe from accidents and other perils. That this is usually the strongest of all wants seems certain. A speaker utilizes this motive when he points out that his proposal, such as a chest X-ray, a periodic health examination, or safe driving is related to self-preservation.

PROFIT. This involves income, the accumulation of property, the making of a living, the chance of increased value in one's investments, the saving of money: it is the economic motive, which causes us to study for our future business or profession, to plan insurance programs for retirement purposes, to bargain for better wages, to take self-improvement courses, to try to follow a household budget, to try to please those with whom we are associated in business—these, and a thousand other things. We want to keep our jobs, to avoid loss, to insure our property against theft or fire, to buy at prices as low as possible. Clearly profit, or the avoidance of loss, and increase in net worth motivate us strongly. Thus the speaker may persuade, by showing that financial or other economic welfare will be enhanced by what he proposes; and he may *dissuade* by showing that profit will be reduced, expenses increased, savings threatened.

RECOGNITION, AUTHORITY. These closely related wants involve the standing of the individual as shown by the approval of his fellowmen and by his influence or power over them. Recognition by the boss for a piece of work well done is gratifying to a worker. The winning of awards in business and public life, involving an expression of appreciation for achievement, is one way in which the desire to be appreciated is fulfilled. A sincere compliment by a speaker or by an acquaintance in conversation is treasured. Praise for past accomplishments, whether directed to an individual or a group, satisfies the desire for recognition. Sharing credit for achievements with those who have been "on the team" is a tactful and motivating thing to do. Thus praise, sincere and honest, is something that most people desire.

A phase of the desire for recognition, related to it at any rate, is *the desire for authority*. Even though the tax structure may make the added monetary return negligible, many men want high executive posts in business and in government. In part, the desire for power and responsibility motivates them. The authority to direct the activities of others, to make important decisions, and to influence the course of events on whatever scale, is attractive indeed. Other motives, such as patriotism or profit, may be involved, but for many, distinction, fame, and influence are the driving urges.

The advertisements urging people to learn to play the piano and "be the life of the party," to take commercial courses and become the boss, to learn to dance and become popular, are all based on appeal to this desire to be recognized. If a speaker can show that what he is talking about is important in that sense, he can get interested attention. From the elementary appeal of self-improvement courses to the desire to have a fine residence or to occupy an important position, the notion of prestige has strong appeal.

LOVE AND AFFECTION. Just as in our public and semi-public life we desire approval, recognition, authority, prestige, so in our more intimate circle of family and friends, we give and desire in return love and affection. This want, as nearly as any a universal one, may combine with other motives, such as self-preservation, profit, or prestige, in the sense that we will do certain things, or abstain from doing them, because of the effect such actions might have on those in our intimate circle. Often any one of these motives may be superseded by a greater, even more basic desire, to protect and cherish those whom we love.

We improve our appearance, or our speech, or our manners, perhaps with the wish to be more attractive to the opposite sex. We make sacrifices for, and in moments of personal crisis unselfishly aid, our close friends. We build homes and take out life insurance policies to protect our families, and often give up lesser wants to see to it that our children get the benefits of education. We thus are deeply motivated by love and affection. And we are repelled by actions which outrage the code of friendship and family. A speaker or other oral communicator who wishes to interest the hearer, therefore, will consider what he may say that will appeal to the deeprooted desire to benefit, cherish, and protect our family and friends.

IDEALS AND SENTIMENTS. The highest level appeal, that of ideals and sentiments, can often be the most motivating of all. Religious conviction, patriotism, dedication to some cause that is greater than the individual or the group: these are typical of the sentiments which cause men to act in great moments of their lives, or which form a pattern of action throughout their careers. The ideals of freedom, democracy, fair play, community or national welfare, the "square deal," charity toward those who are unfortunate, the rights of free speech and assembly, equal treatment for all, regardless of race or national origin: these are but a few of the appeals that may lift men above selfish or personal considerations.

One has but to scan great speeches of the past and present to realize the strong appeal on this highest of levels that dedication to a cause or an ideal can give. Webster's personal sacrifice in his Seventh of March speech in 1850, when to preserve the Union from secession he endorsed Clay's proposed compromise, is an historic example. The noble words of Woodrow Wilson in his speech asking for a declaration of war in 1917, "We shall be fighting for those things that we have always held most dear . . . to make the world at last safe for democracy," is another. And there are many, many more.

When it is justified, a person speaking on subjects other than the great themes can show that in addition to selfish gains, his proposals serve worthwhile causes, can make use of the higher ideals. Richard Cobden, speaking in nineteenth century England for free trade, after pointing out the economic advantages involved, expressed his conviction that through free intercourse between nations mutual understanding and even world peace could result. Thus he elevated legislation of a commercial kind to the higher level of the promotion of one of the great aspirations of humanity.

Speakers should therefore consider whether their pro-

posals involve the potential of the high-level appeal of sentiments and ideals; and if they can honestly do so, should base
part of their persuasion on such an appeal.

RECREATIONAL-CULTURAL TASTES. Obviously people are
motivated in many of their actions by the desire to do the
things they enjoy. This enjoyment may run all the way from
hiking, golfing, playing tennis, attending sports programs of
one sort or another (and listening and watching via radio
and television) to the enjoyment of great music, fine painting or sculpture, or the drama. It may be the desire to travel,
or to meet distinguished people, or to read great books.

A speaker, then, if he can show that his proposal will enable people *to enjoy* that which appeals to them in the wide
range of culture or recreation, can add to his persuasiveness.
We are always interested in that which we enjoy doing, or
would like to have the opportunity to do.

Summary on want-appeal. The many and varied wants
of people must be a constant subject of study by the speaker
or converser. Unsuspected wants on the part of a prospect
in a sales interview often determine the sale. People will act
if shown with sufficient force that by so doing they can satisfy
some of their wants. For purposes of classification, we have
discussed briefly self-preservation, profit, recognition and
authority, love, sentiments and ideals, and recreational-cultural tastes. The specific wants of an individual, or of an
audience in a given sort of situation, must be studied.

Attention and interest can be gained by linking the topic
with known desires or wants of the hearer. Thus a speaker
before a city audience, speaking on the activities of the 4-H
clubs, pointed out that his hearers would find most of their
future employees among young men and women with a farm
background, who would become part of the city's labor force.
Thus, he said, they had an interest in the training these
young people received before coming to the city. He then
talked about the programs of 4-H, stressing the skills developed, the cooperation that the various projects involved, and
the character training received by the individual.

Identify your topic or proposal with one or more of the vital interests of people, and your presentation automatically becomes interesting to them. The appeal must, practically as well as morally, be an honest one. False motivation is, in the long run, self-defeating. Be genuine and honest in using want-appeal.

INTEREST IN THE FAMILIAR, THE UNUSUAL, THE SPECIFIC

In discussing the Speech Details in Chapter 3, the point was made that *comparison* gains its interest by likening the subject or thought at hand to something that is familiar to the hearer. Thus Lincoln's "house divided against itself" metaphor made his speech interesting, because people saw the similarity between his idea and their own experience of poorly-constructed houses. Pitt's comparison of America to "the fountain of our strength" and "the nursery of our naval power" had similar value.

Such comparisons are interesting because they employ several well known principles: the *familiar*, the *unusual*, and the *specific*. The observation of home construction, fountains, and nurseries is part of common experience. The comparison of them to the more abstract ideas of the speaker not only made the ideas more readily understandable, but caused the audience to think along with the speaker. These comparisons were unusual because they combined in each case two things not ordinarily treated together. They were specific, in that definite mental pictures were evoked.

Examples may utilize one, two, or all three of these principles of interest. Since they are actual cases, happenings, incidents, they have the quality of being specific. So far as the cases cited are known to the hearers, they may involve the familiar. To the extent that they have vividness, dramatic quality, or some other unexpected characteristic, they may involve the unusual. The same is true of statistics and testimony, the other Speech Details. Reiteration may gain these three qualities by virtue of the language employed.

WHY THEY ARE INTERESTING. The familiar, the unusual, and the specific make one's speech "come alive" in the minds of the audience. When Victor Hugo, in his famous description of the Battle of Waterloo, likened the disposition of troops to a capital "A," he was employing that which was familiar to that which he wished to make clear. It was relatively simple, once this comparison was established, to fill in the details of the explanation. In general, if you wish to sustain interest in an explanation, compare that which you want to make known to something the audience already understands.

Beecher, in his famous address at Liverpool in 1863, argued that a market composed of free workers would be more profitable to English manufacturers than one including a slave population. The farther civilization and education advance, he continued, the greater the demand for fine products. "A savage is a man one story deep, and that the cellar," he said, "a civilized man is many stories high." This *unusual* comparison also involved the *familiar* in its reference to low or high buildings. And the mental image it produced was a definite, specific one.

The familiar, unusual, and specific may appear, not only in the Speech Details, but in the language used by the speaker. When Roosevelt proclaimed a "New Deal," he used a familiar term in an unusual and definite way. Truman's "Fair Deal" and Kennedy's "New Frontier" involved the familiar, unusual, and specific. "All that I can promise you is blood, sweat and tears," Churchill's famous phrase, involved familiar concepts, stated in an unusual way. "Ask not what your country can do for you; ask what you can do for your country," President Kennedy's inaugural slogan, had all of the qualities we are discussing.

An example of how the familiar, unusual and specific may be used in persuasion may be found in Henry Grady's historic speech, *The New South*. Facing at best an unreceptive if not hostile audience, the young editor of the Atlanta Constitution in 1883 won a persuasive triumph that equals any other in American history. This speech is printed in full, beginning on Page 249 of this book.

He began by reference to a familiar man and place, Benjamin H. Hill speaking at Tammany Hall. His stories, that of the minister perplexed by a misread text, of the man falling downstairs with a pitcher of milk, and so on, dealt with familiar types of happenings. But at the same time, they had "surprise endings," and their application to his theme of faith in his mission involved the unusual. Their nature was highly specific. Just what happened was recounted. He used the unusual and vivid again in his description of the "tall white shaft" which commemorated his father; yet reverence for the dead and pride in their achievements strikes a familiar note. He evoked thunderous applause by his glowing tribute to Abraham Lincoln—a passage involving the familiar and the unusual in that he, Grady, a Southerner, picked Lincoln as the embodiment of the American. And his reference to Webster, the idol of the North, at the climax of his speech, applied again all three principles of interest. Humor, pathos, high-level appeal and vivid word-pictures all contribute to the fascination of this great speech. It is no wonder that it completely won over the audience of New Yorkers, and became a sensation all over America when reported in the press.

VARIETY OF APPEAL. A good speech does not linger too long on any one thought, nor depend upon any one principle of interest. It has movement and change—variety in mood and constant forward movement from detail to detail and idea to idea. This is illustrated in the speeches in Part Three.

Summary on principles of interest. Informally, we have reviewed basic principles that should be added to clearness and logic in order to gain and hold the interested attention of the hearer: the appeal to wants, plus the familiar, the specific, and the unusual or vivid. We have shown how in words, and in the use of the various Speech Details, these principles may be applied.

THE SPEAKER-AUDIENCE RELATION
AND INTEREST

If the speaker is to interest his particular audience, it follows that he must adapt what he says to the wants, attitudes, and general character of the group he addresses. On the other hand, an audience will respond favorably to a speaker for whom it has respect, and who, through his personal characteristics, makes a good impression on them when he appears before them. This two-way relationship likewise is important in interviews, conferences and discussions. Effective communication takes place when there is a mutually interested, understanding, and sympathetic relationship. In the event that at the beginning of a speech such a relationship doesn't exist, it is the speaker's problem to create it.

Thus the preliminary analysis by the speaker of his hearers becomes important. Likewise, what the audience knows of him prior to the speech, and the personal impressions gained during the speech, become a big factor. We shall briefly discuss each of these.

The audience—Its interests. A good beginning point for the analysis of an audience is to ask, "What are the general or special interests of this group?" If the hearers are of one occupation or profession, or are alike in that they have assembled as members of a particular organization, as parent-teachers, or labor union members, or physicians, or architects, or federal employees, it is not too difficult to answer this question. An able speaker will choose his topic, and select subject-matter, that falls within their sphere of activity. The special interest of such groups will be obvious from the nature of the meeting and of the expectation they have of the speaker. The writer, for example, has spoken on sales techniques to widely diverse groups. In speaking to real estate salesmen, the illustrative material about salesmanship is properly drawn from the situations involved in listing property for sale, in showing the property, and in closing sales of property. In speaking to hotel executives, for another example, the ideas and illustrative material are drawn from the situations involving contact with patrons, and with the general public. This adaptation of the speech materials to the occupational interests of the group aids interest. Their wants, their experiences, and their problems provide the motivation, the use of the familiar, the unusual, and the specific.

When meeting as members of a social, business, professional, political, or religious group, people tend to have much in common because of the nature of the meeting. This is true although they may differ considerably as individuals. Likewise, when an otherwise mixed audience gathers to pay tribute to someone who has died, is retiring, or is moving to another city, *the idea in mind at the moment* is a unifying factor. Similarly with audiences assembled for commemorative occasions, such as the Fourth of July, Memorial Day, or a centennial celebration. A partisan political rally has an automatically united audience for much the same reason.

In 1933, when President Roosevelt addressed the nation in his memorable Bank Holiday speech, he had an audience whose concern at the moment was its economic welfare, and whose special interest was the closing of the banks which the administration had decreed as a depression-checking move. Everyone had the same primary want at the moment: to be reassured that effective steps to restore the nation's economy would be taken.

"Why has the audience assembled? Why am *I* to speak?" Such questions go a long way in determining what will interest the hearers.

Audience characteristics. Aside from social, occupational, business, professional, or religious backgrounds, and the special interest created by the nature of the occasion, one can delve more deeply into general audience characteristics that may reveal a basis for his use of ideas and materials. Some of these are age, educational level, intelligence, knowledge of and attitude toward the speaker's subject, quickness or conservatism in adopting new ideas, activity level, and the physical conditions under which the speech is to be given.

AGE. Traditionally, young people and old differ in their reactions to a speaker. The extremely young, lacking a background of experience, may require a simpler treatment, and more elementary details, than the mature. The old, on the other hand, may be more skeptical of ideas, and require a greater amount of logical proof before giving favorable consideration. The young, as a class, may react more favorably to broad humor and to emotional persuasion. Yet these general notions are often upset in practice. In the 1960's, there was a growth of conservatism among college students, at least in a political sense. And one has only to remember the excited, emotional reaction of some "senior citizens" to the Townsend old-age pension plan, and to later proposals for their benefit, to realize that age often is not a dependable basis for analysis of an audience. But if it is true that youth is in general forward-looking and open-minded and that age is conservative and even reactionary, the speaker should give consideration to this fact. Actually, other factors usually are dominant, although the tastes of different age groups and their interests do vary.

EDUCATIONAL LEVEL. Whether the hearers are college graduates, high school graduates, or people who have had a minimum of education must be considered. With the warning that a speaker should not "talk down" to an audience, it is true that a simpler set of ideas and simpler language should be employed in talking to the relatively uneducated. Examples and illustrations from everyday life should be used; usually an intricate argument fails to "get across." Of high school or college graduates—and these today probably make up a majority of most audiences—more knowledge on their part of history, of current events, and of various social, political, and economic ideas may be assumed. If the audience is of mixed educational levels, the speaker will have to combine utmost simplicity of ideas with details that will be of interest to all groups. It is usually a mistake to gear everything in a talk to the lowest 10 per cent of hearers.

INTELLIGENCE. Educational level and intelligence do not necessarily coincide. Verbal intelligence, the range of vocabulary and the ability to follow spoken statements, usually goes with the higher levels of education. But mechanical intelligence, the ability to understand how things work and how devices operate, is often high in those who may not have much formal education. Mathematical intelligence may not coincide with one's level of education; artistic or esthetic intelligence, social intelligence—the sensitive awareness of such things as courtesy and tact—all of these may or may not depend upon the amount of formal education. Some derive from occupational interests or recreational-cultural activities. At any rate, intelligence enhances or detracts from the ability of hearers to understand a speaker's ideas. It merits his careful consideration.

VIEW OF THE SUBJECT. The hearers' knowledge of the subject of the speech and their attitude toward it are probably as important as any of the other considerations we have mentioned.

Nothing can be more frustrating or boring to an audience which has a good knowledge of the speaker's subject than to be treated to an elementary, repetitious treatment of ideas already well known. They dismiss it as trite and undeserving of attention. For instance, a group of people engaged in social work is thoroughly familiar with the concept that delinquent parents are usually the cause of delinquency in children. A speaker who belabors this general point would be insulting their intelligence and "talking down" to them in assuming that this point needed explanation. On the other hand, if he had specific examples to report bearing on how delinquent parents may be trained to assume their responsibilities, or original suggestions to make, the audience would be interested. Of course his suggestions would have to be adjudged valid in reference to their own experience as social workers.

Opinions about the speaker's subject are almost certain to exist. This is true whether the audience is well informed, uninformed, or *misinformed.* Such opinions might be represented by the following diagram:

Minus 2	Minus 1	0	Plus 1	Plus 2
Strongly Opposed	Slightly Opposed	Neutral	Slightly Favorable	Strongly Favorable

A knowledge of the state of mind of the hearers enables the speaker to decide upon his Specific Purpose, Ideas, and Details. In other words, he can determine his task and his strategy.

With a neutral audience, he will make a balanced presentation as between logical proof and appeal to wants and interests, with the hope of rendering the hearers slightly to strongly favorable.

With a slightly or strongly opposed audience, he will perhaps be forced to limit his objective to conciliating opposing views and removing opposition rather than creating strongly favorable opinion. He will attempt to stress common ground of interests and aims, to remove or correct misinformation, and to offset reasons for their opposition with reasons on behalf of his proposal.

With an audience predisposed in his favor, he will have a nucleus of logical arguments to reenforce their views, but will aim rather to appeal strongly to wants and desires with the purpose of increasing enthusiasm and getting positive favorable action.

The more a speaker can find out in advance the state of mind of his hearers, and why they hold the opinions they do, the better he is equipped to make a persuasive presentation.

ATTITUDE TOWARD NEW IDEAS. The quickness or the slowness with which an audience is likely to adopt new ideas will be a factor in the design of a speech. If the audience is of a type that acts quickly or even impulsively, one will stress wants and interests; if it is of the conservative or reactionary type, he will use a greater proportion of logical argument and will limit the action he seeks to get to what he deems attainable.

ACTIVITY LEVEL. The emotional tone of the audience may vary considerably, from indifferent to passive to enthusiastic. In terms of activity level, it may be low, middle, or high and even excited. This is a prevailing mood which the speaker can often observe before being called on at a meeting, or even during the progress of his speech. He has a problem of interesting an indifferent, passive audience by showing them that their interests are affected by his topic, and by being as emphatic and vivid in his language and manner as possible. With an audience that is already "stirred up" and eager for action, he has but to channel the enthusiasm into the execution of his ideas. The state of feeling which prevails may be the result of convictions long held, or of what previous speakers have said, or of the pressing nature of the problem before the audience.

PHYSICAL CONDITIONS. Although sometimes unfavorable surroundings, such as a stuffy room, or one that is too cold or too noisy, must be *combatted rather than corrected* by the speaker, he often can do something to improve them. If a loudspeaker system, for example, is set at too high a volume, he can perhaps get it adjusted, or can modify his distance from the microphone to prevent "blasting." If the hearers are few and scattered, he can invite them to "come down front" with some hope of success. He can observe other conditions and adjust his volume of voice to the size of the room, etc. He can relax an uncomfortable audience by inviting them to stand up and stretch before he launches his speech. These and many other conditions may affect audience-reaction, and the speaker should do what he can to make them as favorable as possible.

The speaker—His reputation. In Chapter 1, we pointed out that logical, emotional, and personal persuasiveness are the speaker's sources of strength. In dealing with speech structure we have treated clarity and have in part dealt with logic as an attribute of effectiveness. In discussing the appeal to wants and the utilization of other interests of people, and also in surveying the characteristics of the audience, we have, of course, dealt with what may be called emotional, or psychological, persuasiveness.

Equally important is one's *personal* persuasiveness. If one has the respect and liking of his hearers, they will respond favorably to him. This element of persuasiveness includes one's reputation, one's basic qualifications, and personal manners and appearance. These, in addition to skill in speech composition and delivery, are factors.

Reputation includes what the audience knows of or believes about the speaker as a person. Is he, for instance, known to be well informed and expert on the subject on which he is to talk? Does he have a good moral reputation? Is he generally popular? Has he a record of success in the enterprises in which he has been engaged? Is he known to be an interesting, forceful, or logical speaker? Is he distinguished for patriotism, contribution to public welfare, or as a member of his own profession? What the audience knows about him goes a long way toward establishing personal persuasiveness; or indeed to detract from it if unfavorable elements exist.

Command of one's subject matter is one means by which a speaker who may not be known to be an authority may quickly establish himself with an audience. On other matters what he does and says early in the speech may assist. In former days the speaker could, without violating good taste, use a large amount of *overt* personal or ethical proof: that is, he could discuss his qualifications to speak on the subject, and also prove his personal disinterestedness. Webster did the latter in the famous White Murder Case speech, when he replied to defense criticism of the fact that he was in the trial as a special prosecutor.

If a speaker is relatively unknown to an audience, he may arrange with the person who is to introduce him to set forth some of his qualifications: position held, past accomplishments, and special knowledge of the subject. Today this is more appropriate than for the speaker to spend time talking about himself, with the only exception being in response to a personal attack upon his character, record, or motives.

That a speaker's reputation or standing with the audience can be overwhelmingly important is shown by the almost universal attention given to addresses by the President of the United States. A prominent senator, a governor, or the head of a prominent college or an important business or industry commands in lesser but still great degree the interest and attention of the audience.

Outstanding achievements in any field, especially when widely publicized, lead to audience acceptance. A famous war hero, aviator, astronaut, or athlete will benefit from his known feats.

Some basic traits. One bears a good reputation with audiences, and thus enjoys acceptance by hearers, because of his accomplishments, positions held, character, and his record in general. In this sense, the famous dictum of Marcus Cato, that "the orator is a *good* man, skilled in speaking," has been brought to the attention of people for many centuries.

Therefore such traits as morality, honesty, fairness, industry, public spiritedness, liberality or conservatism, idealism, practicality, and many more universally regarded as desirable affect one's personal persuasiveness. Education, when not revealed by an obvious sense of superiority to the less educated, plays its part. All of these, and others, help to qualify a speaker for audience acceptance. Sometimes age and experience tend to establish the prestige that the speaker wishes to have. Yet the "elder statesman" who commands respect from many may be regarded by others as past his prime, or old-fashioned in his thinking. The relatively young person may overcome the impression of inexperience by showing competent knowledge of that which he is discussing.

Personality factors. One's record and basic characteristics, as sketched above, enhance or detract from audience acceptance. *There are, in addition, traits of attitude and personality that operate during contact with the audience,* and these are vital to one's immediate effectiveness.

Foremost in these point-of-contact traits, perhaps, are the fundamental qualities of delivery: a strong sense of *communication, animation,* and an *enthusiastic sincerity.* These will be treated in detail in the following chapter because of their direct connection with the presentation of a speech. Suffice it to say that one who possesses them in high degree will not only get the attention and interest of his hearers, but will very likely succeed in influencing them, provided, of course, that he has a worthwhile message stated with at least minimum clarity, logic, and interest. They are among the qualities that make a person an effective and interesting communicator. Taking into account all of these as the *special qualifications of a speaker,* let us say that *competence in speaking* is a strong personality factor.

Confidence on the speaker's part, unless shown in a manner that indicates undue egotism, is a great asset. Confidence rests, let us emphasize, on *competence,* and this suggests that it is best developed by intelligent practice. This applies to one's speaking skills; it also applies to the need of knowledge and experience about subject matter.

FRIENDLINESS. A confident speaker can build up his personal persuasiveness by cultivating a friendliness toward people. "Like begets like" is a principle that applies here, and one that can earn dividends in audience responsiveness. Superficially, a friendly smile creates a better impression than a sour or depressed-looking expression. Act as if you were glad to speak, and glad to talk to the particular audience you face—not as if it were a boring or painful thing to do. *It can be as simple as that!*

Out of friendliness comes *tact,* the ability to say things without giving offense. Out of friendliness comes *fairness* toward those who don't agree with you 100 per cent. Out of friendliness comes *toleration* for the views or mannerisms of others. Out of friendliness comes a *sense of appreciation* for the good traits and worthwhile deeds of others. Out of friendliness comes the *willingness to compliment* or praise good things done by others.

Whether one is inclined to look for the good in people rather than the bad and to appreciate them; or whether he is hypercritical, sarcastic, overbearing, conceited, given to exhibitionism, sarcasm, "talking down" to people, cynicism and argumentative combativeness ("I'm right, you're wrong"; "Our side, your side"; "Our *honorable* opponents"; etc.) depends largely on his friendliness or lack of it. *Do you like people?* If not, make a drastic change in your attitude! Like does beget like, and it's nowhere truer than in our relations with audiences and individuals.

And we might add, "What you are speaks so loud I cannot hear what you say." *Make what you are speak in your favor.*

COURAGE. There are occasions in private and public life when courage, the willingness to espouse an unpopular cause, or to attack abuses, is both necessary and admirable. Elijah P. Lovejoy, speaking out for abolition in a territory that was strongly pro-slavery, is a case in point. The crusading of Theodore Roosevelt against trusts and monopolies is another. When one is willing to risk his life or his livelihood for a worthy cause, or to court political or social unpopularity in order to advance it, he commands genuine respect. On the other hand, to bristle and denounce without due justification and to look for things to criticize and condemn, is unnecessary and dangerous to the reputation of the speaker. There is a difference between true dedication to a cause and carping criticism.

APPEARANCE, HEALTH, BEARING. We mention these obvious things because they do importantly affect the audience's reaction to a speaker. Sloppy, unkempt people are simply not at their best. A person who dresses appropriately and neatly adds something to his stature. Health and strength are everywhere greeted responsively. Bearing, not only in a comfortably erect, self-respecting posture while speaking but in every circumstance, adds or detracts. The person who sits slumped down in a chair while being introduced or while listening to other speakers apparently does not pay alert attention; he discounts himself. These matters are so important that we insert this reminder. Why not, in appearance, health, and bearing be as nearly at your best as possible? Blue jeans, spotted sweatshirts, and tousled hair may be what some like, but unfortunately they don't seem to build prestige with audiences.

HABITS CAN BE CHANGED

In this chapter, we have tried to treat briefly what might be called the psychology of effective speech. Perhaps what has been said about the interests of people, the nature of audiences, and the personal characteristics of the speaker may seem like "old stuff," trite, to be read and forgotten. Yet if trying to be as interesting as possible, and as persuasive as can be, is foreign to your habits, the chances are very good that you could improve greatly by trying to change them.

If you are the "debater type," and depend primarily upon logic and evidence, you may find that consideration of *what audiences want* might give you greater persuasive power. As you begin to word your ideas so that they appeal to self-preservation, profit, the desire for recognition and authority, for love and affection, ideals, and recreational-cultural tastes, you may get a much better response from those whom you want to persuade. Greater use of the familiar, the unusual and the specific may begin to pay you further dividends.

Going deeper, you can study your actual or potential hearers and find out what their interests may be, what their attitudes and other characteristics are, and thus be enabled to establish much greater communication with them. And finally, you can, perhaps, change some personal characteristics of yours for the better. If you have the humility to do this, the results may be gratifying indeed.

All of the points discussed in this very elementary survey

of audience-speaker psychology may suggest to you that *change* in some of your habits of thought and of conduct is desirable. Personality, for instance, is not a mysterious, intangible thing; it is described by Overstreet in his great book, *Influencing Human Behavior*, as "simply *the sum of our habit-systems.*" And he adds the tremendously important words, "Habits can be shaped and changed." Willingness to change where it is desirable is the mark of an open-minded, forward-looking person. *You can improve.*

5

How to Be Effective in the
Way You Talk

*But all these parts of oratory succeed accordingly as they
are delivered. Delivery, I say, has the sole and supreme
power in oratory. . . . To this Demosthenes was said to have
assigned the first place, when he was asked what was the
chief requisite in eloquence; to this the second, and to this
the third.*

CICERO

"To SAY the right thing, at the right time, and *in the right
way*" is an oft-repeated statement of the task of the effective
speaker. The picture of a man or woman standing before an
audience, speaking with confidence, with poise, with enthusiasm, and conveying an idea to the hearers with force and
conviction, is what flashes into our minds when we think of
public speaking. *What* the speaker says is important: equally
important is *how he says it.* "All these parts of oratory succeed accordingly as they are delivered," said Cicero—who
certainly knew whereof he spoke! Clearly, then, the study of
effective presentation, or as it is frequently called, delivery,
deserves the best efforts of the novice and of the master.

In everyday conversation, whether merely social or more
purposive, *how you say it* is as important as in making a

public speech. This chapter is written mainly from the viewpoint of the speaker, but the qualities of effectiveness that it discusses apply with equal force to the conversationalist.

The fundamental qualities of delivery. Just as in any other art, there are certain basic qualities which enable the speaker to convey his message to the audience, to interest his hearers, and to move them to action. It is these qualities to which one should first give attention. Later, he may add some of the technical excellences of expression, voice, and action that are essential to the finished master of public address.

These qualities are: *a sense of communication, animation,* and *an enthusiastic sincerity.* To develop and strengthen them, from the very beginning of practice, ought to be a constant aim of the student. They are not *technical* qualities which can be reduced to mechanical rules and procedures. Rather, they demand of the student of speaking a determination of purpose, and a clear understanding of their importance.

Instead of being beset by worry about *negative* things in connection with delivery, or of being too concerned about mechanical precision in following some artificial pattern, the beginner should focus his attention upon the attainment of these *positive* characteristics. Try in your first speech—perhaps the talk introducing yourself to the class—to gain the attention of your hearers by the way you talk, by looking at them, by conversing naturally and animatedly, and by feeling and showing enthusiasm and sincerity. Don't make this speech, or any later one, a merely perfunctory performance. Be interested in doing it: enjoy doing it! Ask yourself, "Am I communicating with each individual in the class? Am I alive and active? Am I showing enthusiasm?" Try each time you speak to show improvement in these fundamental qualities.

If you will do these things, you will be making the right start. This *functional* approach to delivery is the sound one: it emphasizes the *purposes* for which you speak.

Not only will the development of the basic qualities of communicativeness, animation, and enthusiasm best aid the speaker in influencing the audience favorably, but it will solve many "problems" for him. Concentration upon these qualities brings about a growth in confidence and poise, improved physical bearing, ease, freedom of manner, informality, and better expressiveness vocally, facially, and bodily; in general, a more pleasing and forceful personality.

A discussion of each of the fundamental qualities and suggestions for its development follows.

How to be more communicative. First of all, remember that the whole purpose of speaking is to "get an idea across" to the hearers: to reach them with it, to interest them in it, to influence their thought or conduct. Be sufficiently prepared so that you can devote all your energies to that task.

Second, realize that you are talking to *individuals*, not to an intangible entity called "the audience." Your task is to reach each individual, to see that he is giving you *his* attention. If individuals are slumped down in their seats, looking vaguely off into space, reading something, or giving other indications of inattention, it is your responsibility—by what you say and how you say it—to win their attention. To do this, you must *speak to individuals.*

The determination to communicate, backed by your preparation and your belief in the importance of your subject, will give focus and purposiveness to your manner of speaking. Remember a speech isn't an exhibition, nor is it merely an outline or a manuscript: it is essentially a two-way conversation, the speaker expressing ideas and the hearer responding! Until this two-way communication is set up, *there simply isn't a speech.*

Communicativeness, then, is essentially the product of the right mental attitude: the understanding by the speaker of his purpose and of his relation to the members of the audience. It results in, and conversely, may be increased by, certain physical and vocal actions. Among these physical and vocal indications of communicativeness are:

1. *The speaker looks at his hearers:* not beyond or above or vaguely past them but directly. He establishes and maintains eye contact with persons in all parts of the room.

2. *The speaker is facially expressive.* Obviously the "poker face" or the "frozen features" have no place in the communication of thoughts and feelings. A highly communicative speaker smiles, frowns, and otherwise varies his facial expression because it is natural to do so.

3. *The speaker leans toward his hearers.* He doesn't stand stiffly erect, weight back on his heels, but rather leans forward, especially at emphatic points in his talk, to get physically closer to his audience.

4. *The speaker uses vigorous but conversational tones and inflections.* He doesn't "orate" nor "bellow" at the hearers, but on the other hand he sees to it that he is heard and understood and that his tones are sufficiently strong and emphatic to convey meaning effectively.

5. *The speaker uses physical movement.* He realizes that change in posture, descriptive and emphatic movements of the whole body and of hands and arms, are just as important in conveying meaning as are words and tones. "We speak with our whole body"—Woolbert.

6. *The speaker varies his manner during the speech.* By observation of the audience, he knows that "change of pace" in intensity, in movement, in vocal expression is necessary if attention is not to lag. So he keys his manner in all respects to the audience reaction: he's highly "audience-conscious."

Please note that these physical and vocal actions are at once *results of a highly communicative attitude* and a *means of increasing communicativeness.* Because the way we feel is influenced and conditioned by *the way we act,* the beginner should use the physical and vocal suggestions made above in order to increase his communicative power.

If such actions are not *habitual* to the beginner, it doesn't follow that they are undesirable! On the contrary, the way to improvement is through the formation of habits that are communicative and that increase communication.

Excessive use of notes—or in fact almost any use of notes, hanging on to a speaker's stand, reading lengthy quotations, looking down at the floor, mumbling, keeping the face impassive, clasping one's hands behind the back, and a thousand and one other habits that appear in classrooms are obviously hindrances to communication. Get rid of them!

Anything that aids communication is good: anything that hinders communication is bad. Apply that simple yardstick to your speech habits, and go "all out" for habits and actions that are communicative.

How to be more animated. "Dead men tell no tales." Dead speakers communicate no ideas!

For truly effective communication, at least 90 per cent of all student speakers need to become more animated, more alert, more alive. The beginner may take it as a personal suggestion that in all probability he needs to use more animation, mentally and physically, to attain his highest effectiveness as a speaker.

There are important reasons why there is a general need of greater activity and energy in speaking.

One is the strangeness of the platform situation. In spite of the fact that speaking is merely effective conversation with a group of persons, the newness of the experience tends to make beginners "freeze" physically. This tightening up, which is similar to what happens in any new and strange situation, restricts communicative power.

Another is the fact that natural physical expressiveness has been restrained by the "don't's" of parents and teachers, to the point that the individual withdraws within a mental shell and seeks to conceal his feelings. It is necessary to break that shell and to restore normal, natural physical activity.

A third is the fact that audiences need stimuli that are stronger than ordinary ones. There is a tendency on the part of hearers to resist, unconsciously, the suggestions and statements made from the platform, to assume a blasé attitude of half-attention. To gain attention, then, it is necessary to be forceful and alive. This applies to the speaker's ideas, facts, and words as well as to his manner.

So to gain confidence and ease, and to become sufficiently

forceful to command audience attention, the speaker needs to emphasize animation: mental, physical, and vocal.

If it is true that we all have a *normal* level of activity, a *depressed* level, and a *high level,* in the last of which we are active, enthusiastic, confident, and persuasive (and ordinary experience confirms the truth of this), then it is the task of the speaker to attain his highest and best level *at the moment of speaking.* Being "yourself at your best" is another way of expressing this idea.

Some specific suggestions on the development or improvement of animation are:

1. Be sufficiently rested and thoroughly prepared so that you can be at your best physically.

2. Be dressed neatly and thus enabled to appear with confidence.

3. Remember that *mental* aliveness—a degree of enthusiasm and fervor—is basic.

4. "Warm up" physically before the speech, if possible, just as a baseball player warms up before going into the game. Swing your arms, walk briskly, put energy into your movements.

5. Begin properly by walking smartly and energetically to the front of the room when called on to speak.

6. Keep free and easy physically—don't permit yourself to "freeze."

7. Force yourself to use head and hand gestures, whether it is habitual or not. Describe things by motions; pantomime or "act out" different ideas; use the index, open hand, and fist gestures for emphasis; don't forget facial expression.

8. If you find yourself freezing or experiencing tremors, DO SOMETHING about it: go into vigorous action. Take a deep breath and increase your vocal volume and force. Fight through!

9. If the audience "goes to sleep on you," remember it is your fault—and turn on more power!

10. Bear in mind that for almost all beginners, it is good to overdo action. So "cut loose" and be active! It is an easy matter to tone down at the suggestion of a teacher, if that becomes advisable.

You will achieve one of the great objectives of the study of effective speaking when you attain high-level activity, physical freedom, and poise. The aliveness and force of your delivery will then return to you in the greater response of your audience. Free yourself—for vigorous, active speaking!

How to increase enthusiasm and sincerity. The magic of enthusiasm, the compelling power of deep sincerity, ought to be the allies of every speaker. To overlook them is to deny one's self the very basis of persuasion.

Classroom speeches, in particular, may suffer from lack of any motivation on the part of the speaker. This should not be. The student should be so interested in his subject matter and so desirous of interesting or persuading his hearers that he forgets he is in a speech laboratory and imagines he is before an actual audience, dealing with real and vital things. And there is actually no reason why it can't be true! So make every speech as *real* as you can.

It has been said that if you make a man angry enough about something, he will make a tremendously effective speech whether or not he has had any special training or ability. Why? Simply because he is *sincerely* and *enthusiastically* angry! He forgets his inhibitions: he gestures, shouts, makes faces, and in general becomes forceful and effective. He may overdo it or become too impassioned for best results; but at least he makes a forceful speech, and such things as stage fright never occur to him.

A college student who in class is indifferent, bored, or inert in manner goes to a football game. His team scores on a brilliant, quick, opening play or a dazzling forward pass; he leaps to his feet and shouts and gestures and grimaces. He's become enthusiastic!

Evidently, if one *cares* enough, or if he acts as if he were enthusiastic, it is possible for him to be so. And that is the key to the problem.

> Speak about subjects about which you care.
> Speak as if you cared.

There is no reason why one should be indifferent to his subject, merely because his is a classroom speech. In the first place, one should take subjects about which he has convictions, or in which he is interested. If he has a subject which at first hand doesn't seem interesting, he may find that study of the subject, and a growing knowledge of it, will increase interest. We are interested in what we know and in what we learn.

In the development of his subject, the student should seek to interpret it in the light of his past experience and observation: what it means to him, what it means to the group to which he belongs, why it affects their interests. If he will do this, he will find that there is no conflict between having "worth-while" subjects—that is, topics of general social, economic, and political importance—and being sufficiently interested in them to speak with conviction.

Enthusiasm may be built, sincerity deepened, if the speaker reflects upon the importance of his topic.

For example, there is no more boring topic, as handled by most speakers, than the common one of safe driving. Yet by visualizing the results of automobile accidents, by thinking what it would mean to you if a dear friend or relative were maimed or killed, by imagining the crash of the collision, the cruel injuries, the crushed bodies of the victims, and applying all this to one's own everyday life, a vivid speech can be made. To increase and deepen sincerity, *live the subject mentally.*

Then remember that you must also *act as if you cared.* "Act enthusiastic and you'll be enthusiastic" is a popular way of stating this idea. The James-Lange theory of the emotions, which is that emotions may be produced or deepened by acting out their symptoms, is applicable here. One of the reasons for freeing ourselves for action, as discussed under the heading of animation, is that we may better express our feelings.

A sincere, enthusiastic speaker is almost always effective. Enthusiasm is contagious. The audience will react almost precisely in proportion to the sincerity and enthusiasm of the speaker.

Exercises for improvement in delivery. To improve in the use of the fundamental qualities, one should:

1. Practice them in all his speeches, in the classroom and elsewhere.

2. Commit to memory and practice selections from masterpieces of public address; these offer greater opportunity for expression, in most cases, than one's own speeches.

3. Practice short exercises, either in company with his classmates or alone, which stress the use of the basic qualities.

In the assignments described in Part Four, Lincoln's Gettysburg Address, an excerpt from Conwell's "Acres of Diamonds," and Roosevelt's "War Address" are suggested as good material for practice in delivery. Any other speech masterpiece in this book may be used similarly.

In class, and in private rehearsal, the use of short exercises and selections from speeches for the purpose of improving delivery and stressing fundamentals is desirable. Following are some which have been used by classes in recent years:

1. Speak in concert, with freedom of physical and vocal action, with enthusiasm: "I will communicate. I will illustrate. I will motivate. I will activate myself and my audience."

2. Speak in concert: "I'm free and easy. I enjoy speaking. I will be at my best when I speak. I'll make my audience enjoy it."

3. Try these sentences for directness. Emphasize eye contact with audience, and direct gestures.

> "Compare the two. This I offer you is plain and simple; that complex."
> "Ladies and Gentlemen: this is your cause. What will you do about it?"
> "This is up to you, and you, and you."

4. Try these sentences for forceful utterance:
"Force compelled the signature of unwilling royalty to the great Magna Charta; force beat with naked hands upon the iron gateway of the Bastille, and made reprisal in one awful hour for centuries of kingly crime; force waved the flag of revolution over Bunker Hill, and marked the snows of Valley Forge with bloodstained feet; force marched with Sherman to the sea, rode with Sheridan in the valley of the Shenandoah, and gave Grant victory at Appomattox."

"I know not what course others may take, but as for me, give me liberty or give me death."

"With confidence in our armed forces, with the unbounding determination of the American people, we will win the inevitable triumph, so help us God."

"If ever I get a chance to hit that thing, I'll hit it hard."

5. Try these sentences for enthusiastic and sincere emotion:

"The name and the fame of Washington on this gracious night will follow the silver queen of heaven through sixty degrees of longitude, nor part company with her till she walks in her brightness through the Golden Gate of California, and passes serenely on to hold midnight court with her Australian stars. There and there only, in barbarous archipelagoes as yet untrod by civilized man, the name of Washington is unknown, and there, too, when they are peopled with enlightened millions, new honors will be paid with ours to his memory."

"I shall enter upon no encomium upon Massachusetts. She needs none. There she stands. Behold her, and judge for yourselves. The past, at least, is secure. There are Boston and Lexington, and Concord, and Bunker Hill, and there they will remain forever."

"This is my own, my native land."

6. To "break the shell" and develop positive force and freedom from self-consciousness, try some of the following:

Describe a football game with appropriate gestures and pantomime. *Overdo it.*

Make a speech, "My pet peeve," pounding on the table and silencing those in the audience who shout at you.

Act out with another person the *Acres of Diamonds* scene beginning "Next morning, very early, Al Hafed went to the priest and awoke him."

Do an impersonation of any stage or radio character using exaggerated mannerisms and action.

7. Take a sentence or a few sentences of a speech and try to bring out the full meaning by emphasizing key words. Discover the emphatic points, the key words, and give them special stress. Note the value of changes in rate, pause, and in vocal force. For example:

"We are now engaged in a great Civil War, testing whether that nation, or any nation so conceived and so dedicated, can long endure."

"If you work for a man, in heaven's name work for him! If he pays you a salary that supplies your bread and butter—work for him—think well of him—speak well of him—stand by him—stand by the institution he represents."

" 'Thus,' said the guide, and friends it is historically true, 'were discovered the diamond mines of Golconda, the richest, the most productive of the ancient world.' "

Repeated practice will enrich your delivery and give you added self-confidence. Exercises like the above, or others that the instructor may suggest, should be a part of your daily program of self-improvement. These, used in conjunction with memorized passages from some of the great speeches in Part Three, will help you when you come to the delivery of your own speeches.

THE FUNDAMENTAL QUALITIES IN CONVERSATION

Communication, animation, and sincerity—the fundamental qualities of good platform delivery—become even more urgently necessary in conversational speech.

Practice directness, or comunicativeness, in your conversations and interviews. Not only the desire to communicate, but the assisting mechanics, help greatly. Look "the other fellow in the eye." Note carefully his reactions to what you are saying. Adapt your manner and rate of speech to his. Try to adjust to his mood, although maintaining your own animation. *Don't* talk down to the floor, or past him, or out the window! Without "staring him out of countenance," *do* be direct and communicative.

Animation, alertness, "spark," are a responsibility of yours if you are to arouse interest and get responses in conversation. Therefore "be alive," and *don't slouch, slur, and mumble! Sit* erect. Lean toward your hearer. Be active both in your general attitude and in your movements. *Vary* your vocal presentation: don't be a "flatland" talker. Use change in rate, volume, pitch, and quality to keep the conversation alive.

Enthusiastic sincerity, the third fundamental quality, is a necessary one in an interview or conference, just as it is in a speech. Real interest in what you are talking about and the vital quality of enthusiasm will do as much to make you interesting in every speech contact as it will in your formal speechmaking.

Summary on fundamental qualities. Give a speaker a highly developed sense of communication, a lively activity, and a positive sincerity and enthusiasm, and he will go far toward influencing his hearers. These are the essential qualities of good speaking, and they ought to be the constant objectives of the student. Refinements in technique, details of vocal-physical expression, can be added later, but the first task is to master the fundamentals. Moreover, these are *affirmative* characteristics; there is nothing of "don't do this and don't do that" in them, but rather they suggest positive actions that will make one increasingly interesting and persuasive.

Because these fundamental qualities are within the reach of any normal person, it follows that anyone who desires it sincerely and deeply can become an effective speaker.

BODY AND VOICE IN SPEAKING

The more practical and less mechanical trend which both public speaking and conversation have taken during recent decades has deemphasized the elocutionary training which prevailed during the period before 1915. Many of the mechanical "rules" about posture, gesture, tone production, and vocal expression have been discarded. The emphasis is now —and happily so—on the *fundamental qualities* of communication, animation and sincerity. Their development leaves every speaker free to express himself in his own way; whereas the elaborate codes of elocution tended to straitjacket people, and to divert their attention from communication to the mere formal observance of what were thought to be "rules." Thus a somewhat artificial and "oratorical" manner often was produced. *Virtuosity*, the expertness of the speaker in conforming to the code, tended to be the result. Speaking was a "performance" to most of those trained in this manner, rather than a realistic, sincere communication of ideas. The concept of the "boy orator" or the "declaimer" often resulted. And such concepts, where they may survive, have almost nothing to do with the real purposes of speech.

It is true, of course, that the actual presentation is made by use of the whole body, including the vocal apparatus. Such things as posture, relaxation, action, breathing, tone-production, and vocal expression therefore enter into the over-all task of communication. But if a speaker considers these as ends in themselves, rather than as physical aids to communication, he tends to become so conscious of them that the primary aim of communication is missed.

Posture and action. In exercises suggested earlier in this chapter, we have implied that posture and action will assist in communication. And poor, slouchy, unbalanced posture and either "frozen" action or awkwardness will detract. What, then, can we say about posture and action that will be helpful?

First, posture should be comfortably erect. One who downgrades himself by an indifferent or unbalanced way of standing detracts from his personal effect on the audience. Therefore, stand erect, not in the military position of "attention," but in a relaxed and balanced stance. Hold the chest comfortably high. Distribute weight fairly evenly between the two feet. Let your arms hang relaxed at the sides, not "tied up" in a "wristlock" or folded. *Stand tall.* You'll look better; you'll feel more confident.

Second, move about a bit. Walk erect and poised. Don't stand rooted in one place, like a marble statue.

Third, use eye-directness and facial expression. Look at individuals; note their reactions. This helps communication. Don't have a blank, "poker face" countenance. Smile, frown, express others of your ideas by being mobile facially. This, too, helps convey meaning.

Fourth, go into action! At emphatic points, cut loose with emphatic movements of your whole body, including hand-

and-arm movements. Use your hands and arms to describe things, and to reenforce meaning. Such movements may be classified as those which describe or locate things, as on a chart; or those which emphasize, as the open-hand, index finger, and fist gestures. Generally, the open-hand gesture conveys moderate emphasis or appeal. The index gesture singles out a particular point for emphasis. The fist gesture implies strong conviction. Your whole body, of course, must be in action with these hand-and-arm movements, or the latter look awkward and "tacked on." But action *is* desirable, and perhaps 90 per cent of those beginning the study of speech need to force it a bit at the beginning. Get free for vigorous, over-all physical action.

Practical vocal aims. To be *heard,* and to be *understood* are the obvious minimum goals so far as your use of the voice is concerned. Some reach a beginning course in speech without the ability to achieve these necessary ends. Being *heard* is a matter of using the organs of breathing with sufficient skill to produce an easily audible tone. Being *understood* depends, not only upon sufficient volume, but upon enunciation, the distinct sounding of consonants, so that the words may reach the hearer clearly.

Beyond these minimums, *vocal expression* becomes your concern. By changes in volume, rate of speech, vocal quality, and in the pitch used, meanings and feelings can be given effective expression. Usually they cannot be artificially produced, but when the speaker is enthusiastically sincere and animated, "tone color," or expression, is the natural result.

It is with these minimum goals, and with the bases of expression, that we shall deal briefly here.

Tone production. The raw material out of which voice is made is breath. When you inhale deeply, the lungs fill with air and the diaphragm, the muscular partition between the chest and abdomen, flattens out. When you exhale, the diaphragm rises and aided by abdominal and chest muscles, expels air from the lungs. This can be illustrated by inhaling

deeply and expelling a whispered "Hah." You'll feel the diaphragm rising and the muscles contracting in the upward
movement. Deep breathing of this sort is necessary to adequate tone production.

When the air is expelled from the lungs and through the
larynx, or voice-box, in the throat, its passage causes the so-
called vocal cords, or vocal lips, to vibrate. This resulting
tone, amplified by the oral and head cavities as by a sounding-
board, produces tone. Inhale as before, and vocalize the
broad "A" sound as a sustained note—"*aaaaaa*"—or the long
"E"—"*eeeeee*." Volume depends upon the amount of air, the
vibration of the cords, and amplification. Sound any of the
vowel sounds in this way, and by repeated practice build up,
or increase volume. Avoid throat strain. Keep the mouth well
open, like the opening of a loudspeaker. Deep breathing, plus
open and relaxed tone passages, thus can produce sufficient
volume to be heard. Your instructor will doubtless elaborate
on this basic explanation.

Enunciation. What you have produced are basic vowel
sounds, which make up the foundation of every word. Enunciation is the formation of the consonant sounds necessary to
turn the vowel sounds into words. This is done by means of
precise use of the so-called organs of articulation: the jaws,
teeth, tongue, lips, and hard and soft palates. Usually a beginner *under-enunciates*, this is, he does not use the organs
that form consonants actively and precisely enough.

Analyze how various consonants are formed: the *v, p, f,
m, n, g, t,* etc. Some are labial, or lip-formed; some are tongue-
and-teeth; some are palatal, as the "k"; some are tongue-and-
palate, as the "l," which also has some basic vowel quality.
Precision and activity in their utterance is the guide to clearer
speech, and thus will help in being understood. This will be
sufficient, along with practice, for the average person to attain distinctness. For those with unusual difficulty, a study
of phonetics, or individual corrective work, may be necessary.
Let it be noted that over-precision produces as undesirable
an effect as under-precision. The person who sharply enunci-

ates ev-er-y syl-la-ble in a me-chan-i-cal man-ner is clearly overdoing it! Most of us, however, need more precision than has been our habit.

For practice in tone production plus distinct enunciation, take any spoken sentence or line of poetry and speak it with sufficient volume and with good enunciation:

"Roll on, thou deep and dark blue ocean, roll."
"Fourscore and seven years ago."
"My own, my native land."
"The title of this lecture originated away back in 1869."

Check with your hearers for sufficiency of volume and for proper clarity of enunciation. The instructor will no doubt add comments and suggestions.

Vocal expression. From a mechanical standpoint, vocal expression rests upon changes in four elements: *quality, force, pitch,* and *rate.* Quality refers to the timbre of the voice: fully resonant, or lacking in complete richness because of failure to use the natural sounding boards: the oral and nasal cavities, or because of obstructions in them. The *whisper* is practically all breath and no resonance, for example. Then there is the so-called "nasal" quality, which is produced when there is nasal obstruction or when nasal resonance is cut off voluntarily. Harshness, fullness, and the like are due to proper or improper vocalization, or to an emotional mood which creates them. So we speak of full, rich *orotund* tones, "chesty" stentorian tones, rough, throaty ones, and so on. Obviously through variations in *quality* one may give expression to various feelings.

Force has to do with volume and with the intensity with which tones are uttered. A sharp "attack," producing a staccato, driving impression; or a smoothness of utterance, producing a pleasant, relaxed but not necessarily forceful effect, may be used. Changes in volume, from low to high, may express changes in thought or feeling, as can the difference between an incisive, staccato utterance and a smooth, relaxed one.

Pitch has two aspects: the normal position on the scale,

ranging from bass to high tenor in the case of men; and the changes in this respect which take place in the utterance of words or sentences. These changes are often called *steps,* when between two words or phrases one goes from a low pitch to a higher, or a higher to a lower. Other changes are called *slides* or *inflections,* which involve pitch changes within one syllable or word. In asking a question, for instance, an *upward slide,* or rising inflection, usually marks the final word. On emphatic words within a phrase, on the other hand, a *downward slide,* or falling inflection, indicates definiteness, certainty, strength of meaning. And there is a combination of the two, called the *circumflex* inflection, which indicates doubt, uncertainty, or gives a twist of irony to what is said.

To illustrate these:

Do you think this is a good thing? (Rising on "thing.")
I have no *doubt* that this is *good.* (Falling on "doubt" and "good.")
Could this *really* be *good?* (Circumflex, conveying doubt.)

Rate is the speed, or slowness, of utterance, including the use of pauses between words or phrases. Changes in this can of course convey emphasis or give added expression. Let it be said that many, if not a majority of beginners tend to talk too rapidly, and thus need primarily to slow down and to learn the value of the pause. By slowing down, the speaker gives an opportunity for the hearers to assimilate what he has said, and himself the chance to "think ahead." Pauses, punctuating one's talk, serve a like purpose. In over-all rate, the minor words and thoughts are often given rather rapidly, but emphatic words and phrases are given stress by a markedly slower delivery.

"**Think the thought.**" Through changes in quality, force, pitch and rate, much expressiveness may be developed. The question is, however, whether *excessive attention to these mechanical details produces valid expression.* It is true that by practice in changing these qualities, one can attain greater flexibility, and thus be able to add variety and emphasis. Overdone, it can produce the worst sort of artificiality.

Although we have briefly reviewed these elements of vocal expression, we believe that the best advice is to "think the thought" and "feel the feeling." Allowing for inhibitions, one who understands clearly what he is saying, and who is emotionally "back of it," that is, sincere and enthusiastic, will tend to give effective expression to his ideas. The fundamentals of delivery: the desire to communicate, animation, and sincerity, are thus the best springboards for development. In some individual cases, drill in the mechanics will help.

Summary on "how you say it." "How you say it"—one's manner of talking—is a very individual and personal thing. Much depends upon one's attitude toward the task of becoming effective. Much depends upon one's mood at the moment of speaking: serious, friendly, humorous, or what not. You communicate, essentially, what you are, and what your attitude is toward occasion, subject, and hearer. This is true of public speaking, and it is equally true of conversational speech. "Be at your best" is perhaps the most valuable advice one can give.

We have tried in this chapter to indicate what one should try to develop in the way of fundamental qualities that make one's presentation most effective: communicativeness, animation, sincerity; and in addition we have summarized some of the physical and vocal considerations involved. These, considered not as ends in themselves, but as means to the end of better communication, are worthy of attention.

So much of the success of one's speech depends upon *how it is said* that lifelong attention should be given to it. Something poorly said is better not said at all. Something well said is given importance and persuasiveness. Attitudes, manner, manners, and mannerisms all enter into this vital act of communication. A constant evaluation of strengths and weaknesses will lead to improvement, and thus to greater success in dealing with your fellow men.

Part Two

BUILDING PROFICIENCY
IN PUBLIC SPEAKING

6

The Process of Speech Preparation

Gentlemen, I have been preparing that speech all my life.
DANIEL WEBSTER

In this section of the book, we are to treat of the preparation of speeches. Time will be saved, and efficiency promoted, if a systematic, orderly procedure is adopted. This is true, not only of the composition of the speech itself, but of the rehearsal which should precede its presentation.

Related to the method of preparing a speech in advance of delivery is the method that may be employed for impromptu ("off the cuff") talks. It is an important speech skill to be able to talk without specific preparation on a topic under discussion by a group. Suggestions on this phase of speaking are, therefore, given in this chapter.

In succeeding chapters, we shall treat the informative, persuasive, commemorative, and entertaining varieties of speeches, with specific suggestions on the choice of Specific Purpose, Principal Ideas, and Speech Details. In each of these chapters, further, we shall present *added techniques* that apply especially to each type. Thus each chapter will contain (1) directions for the planning of the specific type of talk and (2) the special means by which it may be made more vivid, interesting, or persuasive.

Finally, we present a chapter designed to aid the student in meeting his obligation for good topics and good subject-matter.

We have said before—and it is important to bear this in mind—that the planning of a speech is similar to the planning of an interview, discussion, or conference, and that many of the procedures apply even in informal conversation. A salesman will plan his presentation with all of the forethought that the speaker uses when he plans a persuasive talk to be given to an audience. The best way to approach the many problems of conversational speech is to become thoroughly grounded in the principles of speech structure and technique. Their application to serious conversation will become obvious.

GENERAL PROCEDURE

Let us recur to the basic speech structure, which is diagrammed below:

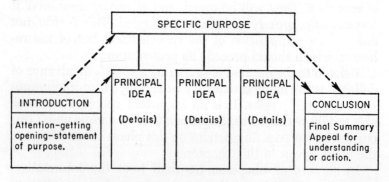

This structure, already explained in Chapters 2 and 3, can assure clarity and coherence in any type of oral communication. The order of planning is:

1. Determination of the General Purpose, which may be to inform, to persuade, or to entertain.

2. Selection of the Specific Purpose, which must be definite, limited in scope, and appropriate to the General Purpose.

3. The selection and phrasing of the Principal Ideas, which must support the Specific Purpose, be interesting, provocative, logical, few in number, and adapted to the General Purpose.

4. Support of the Principal Ideas by the Speech Details: comparisons, examples, statistics, testimony, and reiteration.

5. A review of the structural elements with a view to what interests people: want-appeal, the familiar, the unusual, the specific, and variety.

6. Planning—*after* the above steps have been taken—an appropriate opening, or introduction, designed to arouse interest and to reveal the specific purpose.

7. Planning a conclusion, directly or indirectly repeating the main points and purpose, and perhaps adding an appeal for understanding or action.

This is the proper order for preparation. During the process, the factors that make a speech interesting—the appeal to wants, the use of the familiar, the unusual or striking, and the specific—will affect the choice of ideas and details. And the speaker-audience relation will be borne in mind, affecting each decision about what to say.

Diagrams or outlines? An enlarged copy of the diagram given above can be used effectively for the written preparation. The Principal Ideas can be stated briefly, and the details under each sketched in by "key words." About all that would be needed additionally would be the summary or summary-transition sentences between points. The diagram, since it sharply defines speech structure, has some advantages over the outline.

Formal outlining, with its traditional introduction-body-conclusion form, may be employed. This method is perhaps familiar to most students. How much detail, and whether the full-sentence or the catchword system is used, can vary greatly.

Directions for outlining. The following directions are for making a full outline.

CONTENT. The outline consists of four main parts: heading, introduction, discussion, and conclusion.

FORM. Use 8½″ by 11″ paper, writing only on one side. Leave wide margins, indenting each subordinate point at least ½″. Type if possible.

The heading. The heading identifies the outline and indicates at a glance the subject, speech type, and other necessary information.

CONTENT. A standard heading should include (1) the student's name, (2) course and section numbers, (3) the instructor's name, (4) the title of the speech, and (5) the general purpose (informative, persuasive, or entertaining).

FORM. The student's name, course, and section number, and the instructor's name should be written in the upper right-hand corner of the page; the title of the speech and the designation of speech type should be centered near the top of the page.

The introduction.

CONTENT. The content of the introduction consists of two or more divisions:

1. The *approach*. This is designed to arouse the interest of the audience in the subject by the use of definite elements of interest, such as the vital, the specific, or the striking.
2. The *partition*. This may be a simple statement of the specific purpose, coupled with a statement of the principal ideas; or it may omit either *(a)* a mention of the specific purpose or *(b)* of the principal ideas.

FORM. The word *Introduction* should be written in the center of the line, and underlined. Each of the main divisions of the introduction should be indicated by a Roman numeral, I, II, III, etc. Subdivisions should be indicated by capital letters, A, B, C, etc., and speech details by Arabic numerals, 1, 2, 3, etc.

The discussion.

CONTENT. The content of the discussion consists of the Principal Ideas, each indicated by a Roman numeral, and each outlined in detail. This outlined development should be carried out in sufficient detail to indicate the subordinate ideas (if any) and to state *briefly* the comparisons, examples, statistics, and testimony the speaker intends to use.

FORM. The word *Discussion* should be written in the center of the line, and underlined.

All principal and subordinate ideas should be written in brief sentence form, not as phrases, nor single words.

The following system of symbols and indentations should be used in outlining each principal idea:

I. (Principal idea, stated in full sentence)
    A. (Division of idea, in full sentence)
        1. (Speech detail, in phrase form)
            a. (Division of speech detail, in phrase form)
            b. (Division of speech detail, in phrase form)
        2. (Speech detail, in phrase form)
            a. (Division of speech detail, in phrase form)
            b. (Division of speech detail, in phrase form)
    B. (Division of idea, in full sentence)
                .etc.

The conclusion.

CONTENT. The conclusion may include two or more parts: (1) a restatement of the main ideas; (2) a brief summary of the *appeal* which the speaker intends to use.

FORM. The word *Conclusion* should be written in the center of the line, and underlined. Symbols to correspond with those of the introduction and the discussion should be used.

Marginal notations. Marginal notations should be used to indicate the intended use of elements of interest and of such other principles or devices as the instructor may designate, such as the names of speech details.

The name, or an abbreviation thereof, of each element of interest should be placed in the left-hand margin, opposite the place in the outline containing it. In the case of want-appeal, the specific motive appealed to should be named, as, "recognition."

If requested to do so by the instructor, the student should proceed similarly in the case of the speech details, imagery, or activation.

A SAMPLE OUTLINE

In order that directions for detailed outlining may be understood fully, we print here an outline of "Spun Logs," by Dr. E. E. Slosson, the complete text of which is given in Part Three. We shall assume, for illustrative purposes, that this is a student's speech.

> *John Smith*
> *Speech 1, Section A*
> *Mr. Brown, Instructor*

SPUN LOGS

GENERAL PURPOSE—Informative; expository type.
SPECIFIC PURPOSE—To make clear to my audience the manufacture and characteristics of rayon.

Introduction

Striking . . . . I. (Approach.) Science learns from nature how to surpass nature.

A. The chemist has competed with nature in dyes for textiles.

Concrete, 1. He competed with the indigo plant, and won.

Familiar . . . . 2. He competed with the snail, and produced royal purple out of coal tar.

B. In the field of textiles, he has challenged the silkworm.

Concrete,
Striking, 1. He makes a silk-like thread out of logs
Familiar . . . . of wood.

2. It is fascinating to watch the process of rayon manufacture.

Concrete ......
    a. At one end, spruce logs go in.
    b. At the other, synthetic silk comes out.

II. There are two interesting facts about this synthetic product:

Concrete ......
    A. It is widely used, constituting about two-thirds of such fabrics as are associated with the term "silk."

Striking ....
    B. There is no accepted name for the product.
        1. It is offered as "near" or "imitation" something.

Concrete,
Familiar ....
        2. "Rayon" has been adopted as a trade name by most manufacturers.
        3. Some use such trade names as "celanese" and "lustron."

III. (Partition.) Four different processes are used for making this product, but the general steps in manufacture are easy to understand.

    A. All processes use the same fundamental material, cellulose.

Familiar ......
        1. Some get it from timber, some from cotton linters (short bits of cotton that stick to the seeds).

Familiar ......
        2. Cellulose is the same stuff that paper is made of.

Discussion

I. (Principal Idea.) The first step is to get the cellulose into liquid form. This is difficult,

Familiar ......
Concrete ......
for wood does not dissolve easily.

    A. Nitric acid was first used as a solvent, in 1884.

Familiar ......
        1. This forms, first, nitrocellulose, or guncotton.
        2. The nitrocellulose is dissolved in alcohol and ether, forming collodion, like "new-skin."

3. The nitric acid is eliminated after the spinning process.

Familiar ...... B. The second process uses strong ammonia with copper dissolved in it.

Concrete ...... C. The third process uses another alkali, caustic soda, plus carbon bisulfide, a vile-
Olfactory image smelling liquid.
Visual image .. 1. This produces an orange-colored viscous liquid, called viscose.

2. Four-fifths of the synthetic silk is made this way.

Familiar ...... D. The fourth process employs acetic acid, which in dilute form is vinegar.

II. (Principal Idea.) The solution is then forced into fine filaments, which are spun into threads.

Concrete ...... A. The filaments are produced by forcing the solution through glass tubes, in the end of which are 10 to 50 minute perforations.

Familiar ...... 1. The thin streams of liquid are coagulated by running into water containing something to neutralize and wash away the solvent.

B. The filaments are then caught up by revolving reels, twisted into thread, and dried in skeins.

Concrete ...... C. They are packed in 10-pound bundles, containing 150,000 or 300,000 yards of yarn.

1. Each spinning machine turns out 45 yards a minute.

III. (Principal Idea.) Rayon has many valuable characteristics, which make it widely useful.

A. Although chemically the same as cotton, it has the sheen of silk, and takes dyes even more brilliantly.

1. Two colors are secured by weaving artificial and natural fibers together.

Familiar ...... 2. Velvet brocades have been made by this method.

Familiar ......

Concrete ......

Familiar
  (examples) .

Concrete,
  Familiar ....
Striking
  (Humor) ...
Auditory
  image ......

Self-
  preservation

Concrete ......

Familiar,
  Concrete ....

B. All of these synthetic fibers are weaker and less elastic than natural silk.
  1. Their strength is from half to two-thirds of the natural when dry, and much less when wet.
    a. Rayon is only a half or a quarter as strong when wet as when dry.
    b. Cellulose acetate does not weaken so much on wetting.
    c. The relative advantages of different water-absorptions are in dispute.
C. Manufacturers made several mistakes early in the days of rayon production.
  1. They made it too glossy, a mistake that is now corrected.
  2. They even put "scroop" into it to make it resemble silk in sound.
    a. "Scroop" is the rustling of a lady's silk petticoat.
    b. This was given up when styles changed.
D. Cellulose acetate is more transparent to ultra-violet rays than wool or silk.
  1. This is significant from the standpoint of health.
E. (A digression.) The United States now leads the world in the manufacture and use of rayon.
  1. Of the 185 million pounds, about a third are produced in this country.
  2. Next year our anticipated production is 74 million pounds.
F. Rayon is used for many purposes.
  1. About half of the production goes into knit goods, especially hosiery, in combination with cotton, wool, or natural silk.
  2. It is used for braid for dress trimmings.
  3. It appears as cellophane, in wrappers, etc.
  4. It substitutes for horsehair, lace, rugs, lace curtains, and fur of various kinds.

Conclusion

I. (Summary: omitted.)

Striking ...... II. Sometime we may not need to skin animals for fur coats and collars, or to steal the silk from the worm.

Extemporaneous or memorized? It is possible, after outlining or diagramming, to write out the speech in full, and memorize it, or indeed, to *read* it to the audience. *Except in a very few situations, however, writing and memorizing or reading are both unnecessary and relatively ineffective.* Only where extreme accuracy is mandatory, as in a pronouncement by the President or other high official, should such systems be used. Writing out in advance, except in the hands of a highly skilled person, leads to a "literary" or "oratorical" style which lacks communicative power. Reading effectively is likewise more demanding than any other form of presentation, and rote memory can create an unnatural and uncommunicative kind of delivery, not to mention the ever-present risk of forgetting.

Good speaking, except in the few situations alluded to, should consist of spontaneous, though planned, communication. The so-called *extemporaneous method,* with well-planned ideas, but with the actual wording of details left to the moment of speaking, should ordinarily be used. This method not only permits more direct, communicative delivery, but develops the sort of fluency that enables one to express ideas effectively in impromptu talking, both on the platform and in conversation.

To develop extempore skill, begin with the diagram or outline before you. Talk through the entire speech aloud, expressing the ideas and details as accurately as you can. Fix the Principal Ideas and their best wording in mind. Relate the details to each of them. Perhaps visualize the whole presentation as a journey across the "bridge of thought." Then try again, going through the whole talk, consulting the diagram or outline as little as you can. On a third try, dispense with these, and, with the Principal Ideas in mind, go through the presentation again.

If you follow such a procedure in rehearsal, you will have the basic plan for your talk well fixed in mind, and will be able to talk to the class or other audience *without the use of notes*. This practice should be followed in most classroom talks. *Notes or manuscripts are barriers to direct, effective communication.*

Mixed methods. Some speakers memorize exactly the opening and closing of their talks, or the "key sentences" of each part, leaving the rest to be extemporized. Again, some learn their speeches extemporaneously, and then write them out in full, *without* committing the manuscript to memory. Writing aids them to get their ideas in mind, and to achieve better expression. Each student of speaking should follow that method, or combination of methods, which he finds best fitted to his particular case. For most purposes, however, extemporizing is the most efficient method.

Reading from manuscript. Broadcast speeches, by studio rules, are practically always read from manuscript or teleprompter. In many cases, this reduces expressiveness and communication. The problem is to be as direct, as emphatic, and as expressive as possible, regardless of the immediate surroundings in the studio. Careful rehearsal ahead of time, for expression, is desirable. Many speakers mark the manuscript to show emphatic words, pauses, etc. This is helpful if the resulting expression conveys the spontaneity of normal speaking conditions.

The principal limitation on broadcast speech is that the volume used by the speaker should not change too abruptly. Keep the general degree of force relatively uniform. Develop your vocal expression by changes (not too sudden) in rate, pitch, and tone quality, rather than in force.

Keep your mind on the audience, unseen though it may be. Try for the intimate, conversational, yet forceful manner which made President Roosevelt's fireside chats memorable. Listen to successful speakers and announcers and note how a communicative, conversational quality assists them in getting results.

A tape recording of your voice, made at home or in your office, will let you know how well you read a speech. In fact, it is a helpful device for discovering and correcting faults of quality, pitch, force, and rate in all speaking.

COLLATERAL HINTS. Some of the collateral suggestions usually made to broadcasters are: [1]

1. Preserve a reasonably uniform distance from the microphone.

2. Avoid background noises as much as possible, such as those caused by crackling paper, sudden intake of breath, coughing, etc.

3. Remember that any parenthetical remark that you might make will broadcast! Be careful.

4. Keep enunciation clear but relaxed. Be careful not to overdo *s, v, k* and other consonant sounds which involve an expulsion of unvocalized breath.

5. Avoid "uh's" and "and-ers" between words.

6. Have your speech timed to the second, and watch the lapse of the minutes as you talk.

Summary on general preparation. In beginning this chapter, we have reviewed methods of preparation that should be used in getting ready for any sort of talk, informative, persuasive, or entertaining. We have emphasized the use of the basic speech structure: Specific Purpose, Principal Ideas, Details, and short introductions and conclusions; and have pointed out that the elements of interest and the speaker-audience-occasion relationship must always be borne in mind. Finally, we have advocated diagramming or simple outlining as means of getting "something down on paper," and the use

[1] Public address microphones should be tested by the speaker in advance of delivery. The suggestions about expressive speaking, and those included in the first five collateral suggestions given here, apply similarly to "Public Address" speaking. But with a P.A. system the speaker has his audience in front of him, and he should practice directness, animation, and enthusiasm regardless of the fact that he has a microphone. He should not let the "mike" kill his animation and his sense of contact with the audience.

of the extemporaneous method of learning and practicing the talk for delivery.

QUICK PREPARATION AND IMPROMPTU SPEAKING

By adherence to the basic structure of a speech, one may meet the demand for an impromptu speech, or may quickly organize a good talk upon short notice. Those whose position makes them liable for such speaking will find the suggestions below especially helpful.

"Preparation" for impromptus. In real life, one is almost never called upon to talk upon a subject about which he possesses no information. For instance, if you as a parent were attending a meeting of the Parent-Teacher Association called to discuss the acquisition of playground equipment, you would know a great deal about the subject under discussion. You would know what the present equipment is, what has been suggested for better facilities, and perhaps how it is proposed to obtain the new articles. When called upon unexpectedly, you would have at least this general preparation. Similarly, you may feel assured that if you are asked to speak impromptu at any meeting, you will not be without information on the topic.

The first thing to do, when attending a meeting, is to have in mind what your opinion is, or what information you possess, about the topic under discussion. Ask yourself, "If I were called on now, what point would I make?" Attend to what speakers are saying. From their remarks, you will gain suggestions for a possible speech of your own. You may be either for or against what a speaker is saying, or you may possess specific information that might supplement a previous speaker's remarks. As you listen to the program, *keep preparing* for a possible speech.

Make an organized talk. If called upon, do not be hurried nor flustered. Rise slowly from your chair, in the meantime mentally outlining what you will say. Do not begin by apologizing for lack of preparation, nor for lack of information, nor for lack of ability as a speaker! Begin either by stating your point, or by referring to what a preceding speaker has said.

Have an organized talk. Your point or purpose, developed by whatever examples, statistics, testimony, or comparisons you can call to mind, followed by a brief summary sentence, is a sufficient outline. You can formulate such an outline easily.

Be brief. After you have made your point, conclude and sit down!

Your point or specific purpose may be supported by one or more main ideas, plus the speech details. The procedure is simply this: organize a talk quickly, stick to the simple outline that you have developed, and follow it! Do not try to make a "great speech." Deliver your talk directly, simply, forcefully. Meet the challenge of the situation calmly and competently.

Remember the basic formulas. In organizing either an impromptu talk or one which must be made on short notice, remember that for the different general purposes of speech there are basic formulas which are applicable.

If it is an informative speech of explanation, for example, if the people at a Parent-Teacher meeting asked you to explain how the Howard Street School P.-T.A. raised funds for its playground equipment, your formula would be that of explanation:

> *Purpose:* To explain *how* the funds were raised.
> *Principal Ideas:* To define, or to name the steps included in the process.
> *Details:* Comparisons, examples, etc., to clarify each step.

Perhaps you would be asked to describe the conditions on the playground at present. You would use the informative formula again, but probably you would stress one characteristic of the situation, for instance, that the playground is overcrowded. Each of your main ideas would deal with one phase of the "overcrowded" situation.

For a persuasive speech, your basic formula is:

Purpose: What audience should believe and/or do.
Principal Ideas: Reasons why they should believe or act.
Details: Examples, comparisons, statistics, testimony to support the main ideas.

This would apply if you were asked to give your opinion of the problem and whether the organization should proceed to raise funds.

Thus the basic speech patterns can be applied simply and easily to meet the needs of the impromptu or quick-preparation situation.

"Ready-made" ideas. Professor V. A. Ketcham, a number of years ago, suggested that certain "ready-made" ideas may be useful in the impromptu situation. They are so-called stock ideas, which are general enough to fit almost any subject, and which are valuable as "self-starters" in case the speaker is unable quickly to determine more specific ones as the framework of his talk. Some of these stock ideas, applicable to a wide range of subjects, follow:

1. Who, when, where, what, why, how.
2. What is the problem? What are the possible solutions? What is the best solution?
3. Past, present, and future.
4. Theoretically; practically.
5. The right way; the wrong way.
6. Necessary, beneficial, and practical (or just).
7. The individual; the group.
8. Local, state, and national (and other geographical divisions).
9. The employer, employee, and general public (and other group divisions).
10. Mentally, morally, physically.
11. Socially, economically, politically.
12. (The Borden action formula) "Ho-hum; why bring that up, for instance, so what?"
13. "What shall we do first, second, third?" (For a speech calling for immediate action.)
14. The general principle (legal, moral, religious, etc.) involved; its specific application to the subject at hand.
15. The probable results if we take this action; if we do not.

These "ready-made" or stock ideas ought to be at the instant command of every speaker, and he should work out more formulas of his own. They are useful in that they furnish a least a reasonably logical division of a topic for instant use. It is good practice, in working to develop skill in impromptu speaking, to apply one of them to your topic and to attempt to build a speech accordingly.

Use illustration. It is highly desirable in an impromptu or hastily organized talk to use at least some illustration. After determining the main ideas that you will follow, try to draw out of your memory some comparison, example, testimony, or statistics that will serve this purpose.

Develop impromptu mastery. The student of speaking should seek mastery of impromptu and quick-preparation speaking as one of his principal goals. The ability to organize one's thoughts quickly and to present them effectively will bring many rewards. Many of the most important speeches and statements in conversation that one is called upon to make during his life must of necessity be impromptu.

SUMMARY

In this chapter, we have drawn together the discussion in Part One of the structural and psychological aspects of a speech, and have shown how to apply them in the process of planning the talk. We have presupposed a knowledge of General and Specific Purpose, Principal Ideas, and Speech Details. We have suggested the diagram or the outline as a means of written preparation, and have warned against the practice of writing out in full and memorizing, except in unusual circumstances. The *extempore* method, of learning by *ideas*, with diagram or outline in mind, is far more efficient. Finally, we have shown how one may best meet the challenge of impromptu speaking: use the basic speech plan, and be conscious of the ready-made ideas that are available.

7

How to Plan Informative Talks

When a speaker addresses himself to the understanding, he
proposes the instruction of his hearers.
GEORGE CAMPBELL, *Philosophy of Rhetoric.*

THE informative speech seeks to convey information *as such*, not to persuade nor to entertain. It succeeds if the information is understood by the hearer, if he *comprehends*. Please note that the words "understood" and "comprehends" are used here in their accurate sense. No change of opinion, no persuasion of any kind is sought. It is important to grasp this fact: if one says he wants to make you "understand" why you should vote for Jones rather than Brown, he is using the word in an inaccurate way. The informative speech deals, not with opinions, but with *facts*. Its aim is simply to make those facts clear to the hearer. As George Campbell, the great Scotch rhetorician quoted at the heading of this chapter says, "When a speaker addresses himself to the understanding, he proposes the *instruction* of his hearers."

Such a purpose of instruction is dominant in many sorts of speeches and interviews in all phases of our contacts with others. Issuing orders to subordinates; teaching; training new employees in their jobs; making clear a process of manufacture or repair; explaining how a piece of machinery works or how to operate it; making clear the nature or functions of an organization; describing or characterizing an historical or current situation; reporting on activities of a past period in one's business or other organization; summarizing the results of research or other investigation; reporting a news event; interpreting current social, economic, political, or military developments or trends; evaluating the significance of men, movements, or events—all of these and more are, in most cases, instructional. They deal with facts, and do not seek to change existing opinions, although, through stressing the importance of *admitted facts*, they seek to deepen the knowledge or understanding already possessed by the hearer. For instance, in explaining the function of a computer, one might seek merely to show for what purposes it can be used. But equally *informative* (and *not* persuasive) would be a talk on the rapidly-growing adoption of computers in American businesses. The object in this case would be to deepen the understanding already possessed by the audience, *to wit*, that the use of computers is widespread.

Two degrees of instruction. From the above examples, it is clear that there are, broadly speaking, two main sorts of informative speeches: one is the simple, factual explanation, the other the talk stressing the fact of a known and admitted characteristic of the subject. The first is called the speech of explanation or instruction; the second, the informative-impressive speech. Both deal with matters of fact as understood and agreed to by the hearers. Both are essentially instructional in character.

Examples of the Specific Purposes of some speeches of explanation and instruction might be:

1. To explain the duties of a desk sergeant in the police department.
2. To make clear the method of driving onto a freeway from an access road.
3. To explain the process of manufacturing space capsules.
4. To describe the functions of a chamber of commerce.
5. To show the organization plan of the United Nations.
6. To explain how to construct a bomb shelter.

7. To make clear what the "law of diminishing returns" is.
8. To report on progress in slum clearance in the city.
9. To explain allowable deductions in Federal income tax returns.
10. To report the results of a money-raising campaign.
11. To explain the term, "conflict of interest."
12. To explain how public opinion or customer-reaction investigations are conducted.

These examples will perhaps indicate the scope of the speech of explanation or instruction. We may sum it up by saying that the object is to make clear the nature of any process, device, organization, or term: what it is, how it is done, what its function or meaning is, or what results have been attained. Clear, objective facts are required.

The informative-impressive talk, likewise dealing with known facts, *assumes some understanding of the subject,* but seeks to emphasize or stress the existence of some known characteristic or attribute which it possesses. Some typical Specific Purposes might be:

1. To impress upon the audience the *patriotic significance* of the Fourth of July.
2. To stress the *complexity* of the Federal income tax return form.
3. To make the audience realize the *grandeur* of the Grand Canyon.
4. To impress the hearers about the *stirring eloquence* of Winston Churchill.
5. To stress the *achievements* of medical research.
6. To impress upon the hearers the *importance* of the legal profession (or any other vocation).
7. To stress the *impact* of the invention of the electronic tube (or any other device).
8. To impress the audience with the *"team spirit"* of the astronauts.

The italicized "key words" in these examples of informative-impressive Specific Purposes perhaps best illustrate the nature of this sort of talk. A known characteristic of the subject is selected—*one that is not controversial* in the view of the hearers. Information is given to make more complete the audience's realization of the existence of this characteristic. Facts are used, not to explain, but to make more vivid, the selected trait.

The question may occur, "Suppose the audience doesn't agree, for instance, that Churchill's eloquence was stirring?" In such a case, of course, we would have a problem of persuasion. But in view of the occasion, the hearers, and the nature of the subject, it is obvious that the Specific Purpose would deal with known, agreed-to, non-controversial matter. People wouldn't likely attend a tribute meeting in honor of Churchill who wouldn't tacitly agree that he possessed the trait of stirring eloquence. Nor would an audience gather to hear a speech on the patriotic significance of the Fourth of July if its members questioned its generally accepted importance.

We shall now deal with these two broad types of the informative speech, in respect to the selection of ideas and details.

TALKS OF EXPLANATION OR INSTRUCTION

Determining the purpose. In the section just completed, we have suggested a number of typical Specific Purposes for speeches of simple explanation or instruction. Stated in the infinitive-phrase form, they indicate exactly *what* is to be explained. A caution to be observed is that the *scope* of the Specific Purpose must be limited, in view of audience and time limits, to what is possible of achievement. "Organization and achievements of the United Nations" would obviously be too wide in scope, unless almost unlimited time were available. In explaining a process, such as the manufacture of a space capsule, a sharp limitation of scope would be in order. Details of the procurement of materials, the steps in the design of the product, and the like, would probably have to be excluded in favor of an explanation of the actual manufacturing process. The technical or other information already possessed by the audience would in this, as in any other case, operate to determine just how much could be achieved.

One of the reasons why some attempted speeches of instruction or explanation never "get off the ground" is that so much allegedly necessary "background material" is given that the speaker has no time left for the actual giving of the information. So don't try to explain too much!

Bases for idea-selection. The Principal Ideas in explanatory speeches support the Specific Purpose, in general, by defining or describing the subject. They answer the questions: "What?" "How?" "In what way?" Etc.

These are, of course, statements of fact, not of opinion, as we have repeatedly defined those terms. Beyond these general principles, however, is the problem of finding the right basis for the explanation of whatever process, device, organization or other type of subject we are striving to make clear. There are many possibilities, depending on the nature of the topic.

Time-order—chronology. A natural basis for the selection of Principal Ideas for the explanation of a process, a "how to do it" talk, or an historical report of the activities of an organization may be the *chronological,* or *time-order* one: what is done first, second, third. For instance, on "how to enter a freeway from an access road," one might tell, first, what the "yield" sign means; second, how one determines when it is safe to drive onto the freeway; third, how to "merge" with the principal traffic.

In a talk on "how to administer a hypodermic," the Principal Ideas might be as follows:

1. The instrument to be used should be sterilized.
2. The patient's arm should be cleansed before the needle is inserted.
3. The needle should be inserted after making sure that no "air bubbles" are present in it.
4. It should be withdrawn and the area again cleansed. (We do not guarantee the medical accuracy of these ideas!)

In explaining a process of manufacture, the ideas might well consist of a statement of the raw materials to be used, the fabrication of the materials, and the finishing process. A caution to be observed here is to limit the Specific Purpose in scope, so that only the essential steps in the process will be covered. "How steel is made," could cover too wide a range of subject-matter if one went back to the mining of the ore. It would be better to start with its actual processing.

The time-order basis could be used in explaining the count-down process in the launching of a missile or space capsule. It applies to the explanation of such a process as registration at a college, or to the giving of instructions to a night watchman on his regular rounds of duty. It might be used in reporting on the progress of a slum clearance and rebuilding project in a city, or on the development of a drive for funds for a charitable purpose. In short, the chronological order lends itself to explanations, instructions, and reports. Beside limitation of scope in the Specific Purpose, as suggested above, it is important that the Principal Ideas *be principal*—that they are so selected that they deal with *major steps in the process* and not with minor ones.

Division or departmentalization. Perhaps you are called upon to explain the structure or functions of an organization, such as the United Nations or a chamber of commerce. Division or departmentalization obviously furnishes a good basis for the choice of Principal Ideas. The General Assembly, the Security Council, the Secretariat, and the various organizations for social or economic welfare could be taken up in turn. The function of each could be related to the over-all purpose of the organization. Similarly, the various divisions of a chamber of commerce could be taken up, and the nature and function of each explained. Often such a division or departmentalization may be developed with reference to a *general definition* of structure or function, as for example, "The United Nations is an organization devoted to the promotion of better relations among countries." Each department could then be explained in terms of the contribution it is expected to make toward this general aim.

In making reports on past activities the procedure of division or departmentalization may be superior to the chronological method. Costs, revenues, net profits, and the like might be used in a financial report. Production, sales, and market conditions might furnish another type of division. In a sales manager's report the division might be by products or by territories. Thus the principle of division may be employed in many situations.

Definition and Details. We have indicated above that the method of division or departmentalization may employ also a general definition of function or aim, as in the case of a talk on the United Nations. The use of the method of explanation by definition and details thus relates to that of division. It consists of first giving a concise statement of the meaning of a term, and then taking up the parts of that statement as Principal Ideas; for example, in explaining the term "conflict of interest," one might begin by the general definition: a situation in which an office-holder in government might have private interests which could improperly affect his decision on matters of public policy. Details might consist of a listing of examples of private interest and of cases in which a conflict of interest existed. The legal and ethical matters which might be involved could be listed. The extension of the principle of conflict of interest to cases involving non-governmental positions might be included.

Legal concepts, social or economic principles such as the law of diminishing returns, the population explosion, Gresham's law of currency, and, in general, technical or difficult terms—all lend themselves to the method of explanation by definition and detail.

Comparison and Contrast. The application of comparison and contrast not only utilizes reference to familiar things already understood, but enables the speaker to show merely how the subject explained *differs* from that which is already familiar. This is often employed in the details of explanations following the chronological or other order, but it may itself constitute the basis for the selection of Principal Ideas. An example would be a talk explaining how to operate an electric typewriter, to an audience familiar with the use of the manually operated type. The comparison of the two procedures would point out similarities: the placing of the paper in the machine, the identical arrangement of the keyboard, etc. The contrast would consist of an explanation or demonstration of the different sort of stroke employed by the operator, and of other operating differences.

Where this method can be employed, the speaker is wise to use it, because his explanation is based on that which is already known and understood: it is only the incidental differences which need to be developed in detail. For example, this method would be useful in a talk explaining the difference in functioning between the government of the United States and of some Latin American nation whose constitution is essentially similar to ours. Beginning with the similarity in basic law, the differences which exist could be pointed out. For instance, the greater role of the military in Argentina could be explained, and contrasted to the civilian control of the armed forces which prevails in the United States.

Typical of the topics which lend themselves to the comparison-contrast approach are these: the explanation of rugby football, the voting eligibility laws of a specific state, the nature of preferred stocks, bonds, or common stock, staff organization in business (compared and contrasted to line organization), requirements for degrees in British universities, modern method of manufacturing steel pipe, etc.

In concluding these suggestions about the choice of Principal Ideas for the speech of explanation, let us remind the reader that by whatever approach they are chosen, they must in general describe or define the topic. They must be statements of fact, not of opinion. They must answer such questions as "Who, what, where, in what way, how and when."

THE SPEECH DETAILS IN EXPLANATION. With well-selected ideas, the development of the talk by the use of Speech Details next confronts the speaker. If the ideas are properly chosen and worded, *they suggest their own development,* as we have pointed out before. Comparison, because it likens the subject at hand to that which is already familiar, is perhaps the most valuable detail in reaching the understanding. Examples are necessary to make the explanation or instructions specific. These details should make up the bulk of the supporting material. Where an authority has phrased the meaning of a point with unusual clarity, the use of testimony may help considerably. Statistics may be appropriate. And, of course, ample use of reiteration, by way of repetition of ideas in summation as well as by clarification of points through the use of synonyms, is requisite. It will repay the student at this point to refer to Chapter 3, in which each of the Speech Details is treated. A sufficiency of them, and variety in their employment, are necessary in all speeches.

Visual-auditory aids. Because of the special value of the "exhibit"—whether it consists of charts, models, demonstrations, films, or other devices—it is appropriate here to consider briefly the use of visual-auditory aids. Explanation and instruction usually are presented with some sort of exhibit. What is *seen* and *heard* through visual-auditory aids will be more quickly understood and more thoroughly recalled.

In practice speeches of the explanatory or instructional kind, including reports, at least an elementary use should be made of charts or other forms of visual or auditory aids. We do not intend here an exhaustive treatment of the subject, which has been the subject of many extensive treatises. Rather we wish to point out simply some of the ways in which exhibits may be utilized by a speaker.

Displays involving presentation before the audience of actual articles, models, pictures, charts, maps; the use of demonstration; the use of moving pictures, slides, slide-films, and recorded sound; and the use of living dramatizations, in which skits are presented to illustrate ideas—these visual and auditory aids may help the speaker. Audiences enjoy *seeing* things and they enjoy something that resembles a play. The ideas thus illustrated are likely to get attention and to be remembered.

"Showmanship" is almost a *must* in some types of speaking. In preparing almost any talk, the speaker should consider the possibilities in audio-visual demonstration. We shall treat some of its forms briefly.

Exhibits. If a sales manager were introducing a new model of a washing machine to his staff, he would naturally have one or more samples on hand. The actual article itself, if it is large enough to be seen, is the first possibility of visual appeal.

A second type of exhibit is an enlarged or reduced-size model of the actual article. A new locomotive, for instance, might be represented by a small reproduction, preferably one which could be taken apart to show its mechanism, and possibly could be operated. A new watch might be shown by an enlarged model.

A third type of exhibit is an enlarged photograph, which can be displayed in lieu of the actual article. Or, instead of having one large, "blown-up" picture, the speaker might have a number of ordinary-sized prints, which he could distribute among his hearers. Or illustrative printed matter such as promotional circulars might be used.

In showing new products or models to meetings of dealers or salesmen, an elaborate stage setting, with background scenery and lighting effects, is often provided. The student of speaking would do well to visit such meetings to study the possibilities of visual appeal.

Demonstrations. The possibility of actually *demonstrating* an article before an audience should be considered. In sales and promotional speaking, this is customary.

In a college class, linoleum block printing, reduced to its simplest terms, was well explained by a young woman who had equipped herself with a large block, some ink and paper, and a brush to apply the ink. She inked the block, placed the paper on the floor of the platform, put the block on it, and using her own weight, stepped on the block and produced a good example of printing. No amount of oral explanation would have been as effective.

A fountain pen, some lumps of sugar, and some powdered

sugar were used by another student to demonstrate why the soil is cultivated. He took one lump and dropped ink on it from his pen. The ink speedily went through the entire lump, showing how moisture runs through the soil when it is not thoroughly plowed and pulverized. Then he covered the top of the other lump with powdered sugar and repeated the dropping of the ink. It ran very slowly through the top layer of powdered sugar, thus demonstrating retention of moisture as an aim of cultivation.

Students should plan such demonstrations. A Varityper might be explained best by actually typing different kinds of lines before the audience and then passing around samples.

There are a few considerations about demonstration:

1. Practice the demonstration enough to be skillful.
2. Be sure that nothing can go wrong during the actual demonstration: that it "works."
3. Be sure that your articles are large enough to be seen.
4. Go slowly enough so that the audience can see and understand each step in the process.

Charts and diagrams. Various kinds of sketches, charts, diagrams, and maps are important means of visual appeal. In general, be sure when presenting charts and diagrams that the drawing is large enough for its details to be seen, simple enough to be understood; and in presenting it be sure to maintain contact with the audience. Stand at one side of your chart or diagram, using your hand or a pointer to call attention to various points and, for the most part, look at the audience!

Whether the chart, sketch, or diagram is placed on the blackboard, drawn on paper in advance, or done with crayon or other marking device during the speech depends upon its amount of detail and the preference of the speaker. One who can do a good chalk talk while carrying forward his speech has a certain advantage, but obviously he cannot do anything very complicated. For classroom purposes, inexpensive paper and one's own drawing abilities may be employed. For public or business use, the services of a good artist or sign painter are needed.

Forms of Charts. Among the more commonly used kinds of charts are the following:

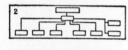

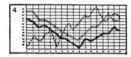

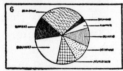

1. The simple table of figures or list of points.

2. The diagram showing, for instance, how an organization is divided into various departments.

3. The map, on which locations may be plotted or areas of different kinds shown by shading and coloring.

4. The graphic chart, showing by means of lines and curves such things as the rise and fall of retail prices during a given period.

5. The mass or comparative area chart showing by symbols, such as soldiers of different sizes, the relative strength of the armies of different countries; or the production of automobiles in different years; and similar comparative facts by relative bulk.

6. The "pie" chart, showing by different-sized slices of "pie" the relative size of various items: for instance, the share of the national income going to taxes, to salaries, to wages, etc.

7. The "bar" chart, showing by bars of different length such things as comparative sales.

8. The cartoon-type chart, bringing out one salient idea by extreme simplification. One form of this is the popular "stick-man" cartoon, which can be drawn before an audience to portray graphically almost any mood or reaction.

9. Mechanical drawings, architects' floor plans, architects' elevation of buildings, etc.

Any of these types of chart may be shown from slides as well as being presented in the usual manner.

Recorded sound. Extensive use of recorders has made it possible to add these to the means of illustration. Not long ago a student made a recording of a scene from a play. He talked about the play in his speech, and to illustrate it turned on the recorder, thus bringing an actual dialogue before the group.

Recordings are often used in business meetings to bring the voice and words of some official to the group. The speaker should not overlook this technique.

Moving pictures and slide-films. Moving pictures, with or without sound, are used extensively in business and industry. They are an aid to explanation and serve as a means of bringing much illustrative material vividly before the audience. They are widely used in sales promotional work.

Slide-films, or more properly, strip-films, consist of a series of "stills" linked together into a story. Usually they are accompanied by a record of synchronized sound. They are highly regarded as an instructional medium. A number of organizations in the educational field produce film series on a wide variety of topics. Compared to moving pictures, the strip-film is inexpensive and easily produced, in addition to possessing flexibility in presentation. It is easy to turn back the film to repeat or re-emphasize a particular scene.

Living dramatization. Highly effective as a means of emphasizing ideas, and combining visual and auditory appeal, are living dramatizations, acted by the speaker or by two or more aides. These are based on scripts, written and practiced in advance, which present the point by means of dialogue. For example, instead of the speaker telling the audience what services his company would render them, the script might call for presentation of a family scene in which the services described are actually being given and used.

The attention value of a well-dramatized skit is high. The writer recently made a convention speech on salesmanship.

He was advocating "selling by explanation only," under certain conditions. The audience gave good attention, but when four short dramatized skits were presented the attention and the positive reaction of the hearers increased sharply. In a letter from the official in charge of the program, the following statement appeared: "While you were speaking, several men behind me were expressing dissent from your views, *but when the well-timed and interesting demonstrations had been presented, their talk was to the effect that 'we've probably been wrong in our approach to this selling problem.'*" Evidently the skits were more effective than the speech!

This is just one case of the illustrative value of dramatizations. The skits themselves were very simple: (1) a man using "high-pressure" methods was "turned down" violently by his prospect; (2) a man who hemmed and hawed and apparently feared to come to the point was impatiently dismissed by his hearer; (3) a man well qualified to explain the proposal interestingly was given attention and succeeded in making his sale without even directly asking for an order; and (4) a similar salesman encountered some objections but tactfully answered them and closed his sale. The series was presented, over all, in sixteen minutes. The points illustrated were: (1) be able to discuss and explain your product in a friendly but expert fashion; (2) assume throughout that if you are able to make your proposal interesting enough, action will follow.

In making a persuasive or instructional talk, it is most desirable to consider such dramatization. This is true not only because such skits can be written to illustrate a point vividly, but because their presentation provides a "change of pace" from ordinary speaking. People are interested, entertained, and often persuaded by them.

Summary on visual-auditory aids. Modern conditions practically demand the use of visual and auditory aids. Exhibits, models, pictures, charts, diagrams, recordings, films, and dramatizations—all may assist the speaker in his task of holding attention and getting a favorable reaction from the audience.

Even the speaker who wears costumes, or uses gags such as tossing cigars to members of the audience, or who, like a speaker of the writer's acquaintance, used a set of trick false teeth to enliven a talk to a dental association, adds something in the way of showmanship to what he says. Such things, when overdone or done in inappropriate circumstances, can of course produce an unfortunate reaction. But they illustrate a realization of the need of visual and auditory appeal.

We remember what we see. We like dramatization. A good speaker takes advantage of these facts.

Although especially needed in informative speaking, visual-auditory aids are used in many persuasive speeches.

Beginning and ending well. With the Specific Purpose and Principal Ideas well selected and phrased, and Speech Details and some visual-auditory aids planned, the informative speaker has only to plan his introduction and conclusion. Let us reemphasize that *this, not an earlier time,* is when the beginning and ending should be planned.

The introduction usually may consist of a statement of the subject, or of the Specific Purpose, coupled with a short indication of why the topic is of interest or importance. *Do not* make a long, rambling beginning.

The conclusion simply reiterates the main points of the explanation, and perhaps expresses a willingness to clear up any point that may not have been understood. It does not urge action!

Keep these subsidiary parts of your talk short. As Taft, McDermott, Jensen, and Yeager say in *English Communication,* "The introduction and the conclusion, comparatively unimportant parts of any theme or paper, should not be overemphasized or given a disproportionate amount of space. Careless writers find that their formal introductions and formal conclusions are so elaborate that they have nothing left to say in the main part of their papers." This applies, not only to written composition, but to speaking.

Taft and his co-authors offer these suggestions about the introductions and conclusions of written compositions, and they are equally valuable to the speaker:

"An introduction may forecast the discussion to follow, or may limit it; an introduction may establish the mood or tone of an essay, or may use any one of several devices—a paradoxical statement, a quotation, or an anecdote—to arouse the reader's interest.

"Since the conclusion marks the end of what the writer has to say, he should not coast along indefinitely on whatever momentum he may have acquired.

. . . A conclusion may take several forms. It may summarize very briefly what has been said, and prophesy new developments of the subject, or it may draw inferences from the facts that have already been presented."—*English Communication,* pp. 249–250.

We believe that what has been said sums up the essential nature of the beginnings and endings of informative speeches. Variations of these, as they apply in other types of talks, will be considered in the appropriate places.

INFORMATIVE-IMPRESSIVE TALKS

Earlier in this chapter we have defined the informative-impressive talk, and have pointed out that it is more than simple instruction or explanation: that it assumes a certain knowledge of the subject on the part of the audience, and seeks to deepen the realization of the hearers of the existence of some attribute, trait, or characteristic. This trait or characteristic is not only known, but agreed to, by the listeners. By presenting additional facts and ideas, the speaker seeks to make the audience realize more fully the *importance, greatness, complexity, difficulty, seriousness* or other traits inherent in the topic.

In the examples of Specific Purposes for informative-impressive talks, we illustrated *patriotic significance, grandeur, stirring eloquence, achievements, "impact,"* and *team spirit* as traits that might be emphasized.

As a matter of practice, although there is no difference in underlying theory, we might usefully divide this sort of talk into two classes in regard to subject-matter: first, the talk which deals with the importance or other characteristics of processes, devices, theories, occupations or professions, geographic or other scenes, buildings and other structures, etc. These are all objects which may be treated in such a way as to bring out some existing qualities and to make them vivid. The second class includes many speeches traditionally given on national holidays, anniversaries, and other occasions involving celebration or commemoration; also at meetings designed to pay tribute to distinguished men, living or dead, and at formal dedications of institutions, buildings, scholarships, and the like. Speeches of presentation and acceptance also usually come under this second heading, as indeed do at least some speeches of introduction.

These two areas of subject-matter do not involve, as we have said above, different treatment in principle. The formal occasion address does usually demand greater vividness, and calls for a more eloquent and elaborate style, than the informative-impressive speech dealing with, shall we say, more routine or prosaic matters.

We shall deal here with the design of this talk on the simpler, more everyday topics, reserving treatment of the speech of formal occasion for a later chapter.

Ideas stress characteristics. The Specific Purpose in informative-impressive speeches, we have seen, underlines a characteristic or characteristics of the subject which it is desired to emphasize to the audience. Logically, then, the Principal Ideas *support* or *develop* that trait or traits. *They do not bring in other ideas* about the topic. The following sets of purposes and ideas will illustrate this relationship:

SPECIFIC PURPOSE: To impress the audience with the grandeur of Niagara Falls.

PRINCIPAL IDEAS:
1. The size and volume of the Falls gives it great majesty.
2. The thunderous roar of the falling water is awe-inspiring.
3. The relentless current above, and the whirlpools and

rapids below the Falls, contribute to the splendor of the scene.

SPECIFIC PURPOSE: To make the audience realize the impact of the electronic computer.

PRINCIPAL IDEAS:

1. It has revolutionized bookkeeping in business and industry.
2. It has saved millions of man-hours.
3. It has made possible many operations hitherto too expensive.
4. It has reached many aspects of our everyday lives.

SPECIFIC PURPOSE: To emphasize the greatness of achievement of our program in outer space.

PRINCIPAL IDEAS:

1. We have orbited the earth with manned vehicles.
2. We have probed the secrets of space with scientific satellites.
3. Instantaneous worldwide communication has now been achieved.

SPECIFIC PURPOSE: To make the hearers realize the extent of the shift of population from rural to urban areas.

PRINCIPAL IDEAS:

1. Statistics of city-suburban population growth reveal this.
2. The movement of the negro from the South to metropolitan areas is a phase of this change.
3. The influx of Porto Ricans and of other national groups into New York is another.
4. The decline in population in rural areas is a correlative development.

SPECIFIC PURPOSE: To show the importance of good communication between groups in our society.

PRINCIPAL IDEAS:

1. Racial groups often have stereotypes about other racial groups, leading to prejudice.

2. There is a lack of true understanding between different religious groups.
3. Labor, business, and government often lack understanding and sympathy for the problems of each other.

These examples show the method of relating ideas to the purpose in such speeches. In general, they answer the questions "how," "in what way," "to what extent," and the like. Let us repeat that they should all support the "key word" in the Specific Purpose directly, not consist of preliminary or "background" material.

The speech details. Quite clearly, all of the Speech Details find important functions in the development and elaboration of such Principal Ideas as those given above. Examples, statistics, testimony, comparison, and restatement would all help, for instance, to develop the ideas in the talk about the impact of computers. Examples might play a primary part in the speech about our space program, but there, too, comparison, statistics, and restatement, as well as testimony, could be used. *Variety* and *vividness* are important here. We are not merely explaining or giving instructions: we are trying to make a lasting impression about the traits or attributes of our topic. We are no longer entirely objective: we are introducing our feelings or conceptions of the subject, and giving the treatment more life and color.

WORKING FOR VIVID DETAIL

Since colorful and vivid treatment of the speech subject is one of the requisites of a good informative-impressive speech, it is appropriate here to consider some of the first steps that can be taken to increase the striking quality of one's Speech Details. Actually, this material is applicable in all types of talks. In the chapters that follow, other means of building vividness will be suggested.

It is through mastery of vividness in words and in illustration that a speaker attains a high level of effectiveness. We remember great speakers because of their striking language, dramatic examples and comparison quite as much as for their command of facts and logic and their effective oral presentation. Daniel Webster's "Liberty and Union, now and forever, one and inseparable"; Patrick Henry's "Give me liberty or give me death"; Abraham Lincoln's "With malice toward none, with charity for all"; Franklin D. Roosevelt's "We have nothing to fear but fear itself"—these and many others are part of the American heritage.

Although one may not hope to rival the greatest of speakers in illustration and language, he can at least work for improvement in these respects. This particular type of speech furnishes an opportunity for a beginning.

Let us, then, look at some of these procedures: extended examples, extended comparisons, narration and description.

Extended examples. A speaker on relief work might *cite* several examples: the case of the Jones family, that of the Brown family, etc. From a mere reference to specific cases, the speaker might expand his treatment of any one of them to give the details: to tell of the family history of poverty and unemployment, to describe the plight of the mother and children, perhaps to tell verbatim of the interview with the social case worker, and to give in an explicit way the steps taken to rehabilitate the family. This would constitute an *extended example*. If well composed, it would be specific, vital, striking, and familiar, thus employing the elements of interest. It would be more impressive than the mere mention of the case in a sentence or two. Instead, the case could be painted in vivid colors and given emotional appeal.

The extended example has been a favorite device of speakers. Webster, in the "White Murder Case" speech quoted in the following chapter, did not merely say "Mr. White was stabbed by his assailant as he lay sleeping." Instead, the scene was vividly depicted by description and narration, every detail of the crime being portrayed.

In "A Message to Garcia," Elbert Hubbard used an extended example in recounting how a Major Rowan volunteered to take a message through the Cuban jungle to Garcia, swiftly but vividly summarizing his landing on the coast, his penetration of the jungle, and his final success. He then developed the theme of direct and positive action into a famous preachment about initiative and dependability. The example of Major Rowan served as the "theme song" of the entire article.

Russell H. Conwell, in his "Acres of Diamonds," used the story of Al Hafed and his fruitless search for a diamond mine, the sequel to which was the discovery of diamonds on Al Hafed's own farm, as the first of a series of extended examples, all of which illustrated the point that opportunity usually lies near at hand, not somewhere far away.

Extended comparisons. From the extended example, it is but a step to the *extended comparison.* Here, instead of just saying that "This nation is like a house divided against itself," Lincoln carried the comparison further:

A house divided against itself cannot stand. This nation cannot permanently endure half slave and half free. I do not expect the house to fall; I do not expect the nation to be destroyed; but I do expect that it will cease to be divided.

Aesop's fables use the pattern of the extended comparison, with a conclusion drawn from it at the end of each fable. The story of the fox and the grapes, for instance, is an extended comparison based on the similarity of the human trait of pretending not to want what one cannot have to that of the fox who said, "The grapes were probably sour anyway."

The parables uttered by Jesus are further examples of the extended comparison. Many sermons in modern times use this method of development.

Webster, in the opening passage of the "Reply to Hayne," used an extended comparison when he likened the plight of the sailor lost in a storm to a confused senatorial debate:

When the mariner has been tossed for many days, in thick weather, and on an unknown sea, he naturally avails himself of the first break in the storm, the first glimpse of the sun, to take his longitude and ascertain how far the waves have driven him from his true course. I suggest that we imitate this prudence, and before we float farther upon the waves of this debate, refer to the point from which we departed, that we may at least be able to conjecture where we now are. I ask for the reading of the resolution.

An extended example or comparison may constitute the framework of an entire speech, as in a parable, or it may be used to illustrate some one point in a speech.

Narrating events. The narration of events, or the relating of personal experiences which illustrate the point under discussion, requires careful composition. Usually the speaker, unless he is skillful at narration, tells too much of the preliminary detail of an occurrence, rather than cutting the introductory remarks to a minimum and concentrating on that event or part of an event which actually illustrates his point. The rule is: center on the important parts of the narrative; summarize very briefly the introductory part of it.

In using personal experiences as a means of illustration, many speakers explain painfully and tiresomely, for example, how they decided to take a vacation trip; how they investigated various means of travel; how they bade their office associates goodbye; how they started out; how they camped the first night on the road, etc.—and finally come to the salient point, which may concern an automobile accident! Yet vivid personal experiences, compactly told, with emphasis on their unusual or striking elements, make good illustrative material.

Edward O'Connor, in a speech in class in St. Louis University, used a vivid personal experience effectively in the following terse narrative. He had been a member of a group of the Brothers of Mary, a religious order, engaged in rescue work during World War II along the English Channel. Note how he eliminated preliminaries and explanations and brought out the drama of the incident:

It was a tragically sad vigil and a horrifying experience. One of our classmates, the closest friend I have ever had, was lost in the sea that lay so forbiddingly before us. We had been standing on the beach for several hours, most of us with eyes flooded with tears. Only that morning George had led the choir in singing a

Requiem Mass. Little did he or we know that it was to be his own Requiem. Then without warning of any kind, his lifeless body was thrown on the beach, practically at our very feet. If ever living bodies have become rigid with horror, ours certainly did at that moment. Cold, blue, wounded and bleeding—dead—that was our brother.

His body was anointed there on the beach by his superior, while the rest of us knelt on the sand, forcing ourselves to pray for his soul, even though our hearts were so overwhelmingly despondent. Sorrowfully we carried the body home and, for the last time, clothed him in the habit of his order.

For the next two days and nights we kept a vigil over that lifeless body, a vigil indeed not incomparable to the vigil of Mary under the Cross of Her Son and not lacking in very, very similar sentiments.

How vividly now his words come back to me: "Ed, I'm not going to live very long after my Profession." George died on the exact date of his Religious Profession ten months later. A boyish prophecy? Perhaps—Perhaps NOT.

Description. Description is usually intermingled with narrative in speeches, but occasionally an entire passage of a descriptive type may be used. Ingersoll's famous passage on his thoughts as he stood at the tomb of Napoleon is heavily loaded with description:

A little while ago I stood at the grave of the old Napoleon, a magnificent tomb of gilt and gold, fit almost for a dead deity, and gazed upon the sarcophagus of rare and nameless marble, where rest at last the ashes of that restless man. I leaned over the balustrade and thought about the career of the greatest soldier of the modern world.

I saw him walking upon the banks of the Seine, contemplating suicide. I saw him at Toulon. I saw him at the head of the army of Italy. I saw him crossing the bridge of Lodi with the tricolor in his hands. I saw him in Egypt in the shadows of the pyramids. I saw him conquer the Alps and mingle the eagles of France with the eagles of the crags. I saw him at Marengo, at Ulm, and Austerlitz. I saw him in Russia, where the infantry of the snow and the cavalry of the wild blasts scattered his legions like winter's withered leaves. I saw him at Leipsic in defeat and disaster, driven by a million bayonets back upon Paris, clutched like a wild beast, banished to Elba. I saw him escape and retake an empire by the force of his genius. I saw him upon the frightful field of Waterloo, where Chance and Fate combined to wreck the fortunes of their former king. And I saw him at St. Helena, with his hands crossed behind him, gazing out upon the sad and silent sea.

Quotation. In addition to, or as a part of narration and description, quotations from prose or poetry (or real or imagined discourse) are often used by speakers. Biblical quotations have long been a stock in trade. William Jennings Bryan, among non-clerical orators, is remembered for his apt use of Biblical illustration and quotation.

SUMMARY ON INFORMATIVE SPEAKING

We have distinguished, first, between the two main types of informative speeches: the speech of simple explanation or instruction and the informative-impressive speech. The choice of Specific Purpose, Principal Ideas, and Speech Details has been reviewed for each type. That all such speeches convey *information as such,* and do not seek persuasion, that is, their purpose is not to change opinions nor to get action, is an important point. The use of visual-audio material has been sketched, for it is especially useful in instruction, although helpful in all kinds of talks. As a step forward in speaking power, the use of extended comparisons and examples, and of narration and description, have been presented. These, too, are helpful in all sorts of speeches, as well as in the informative variety.

By the illustrative material used in this chapter, we hope we have indicated the great importance of non-persuasive talks. Explanations, instructions, reports, and informative-impressive speaking not only are greatly in demand; the use of informative material in persuasive and entertaining speeches is an important means to the end of moving or pleasing audiences.

8

How to Plan Persuasive Speeches

Rhetoric is the art of discovering the available means of persuasion in any case.

ARISTOTLE, Rhetoric.

Persuasive speech, whether public or private, demands the utmost skills, and offers, generally, the greatest rewards to the speaker. Historically, the effective speaker has been regarded as the man or woman who could argue effectively for or against a matter of public policy; who could prosecute or defend in the courts of law; who could arouse others to action to vote, enlist, donate, or take whatever other line of conduct the speaker might advocate. To convince men of the rightness of a cause, or to get their active support, has been the aim.

In the field of religion, not only has instruction been given: pulpit speakers seek to convince or to actuate their congregations. In the everyday field of business and professional activity, the persuasive presentation, whether in conversation or in public meetings, deals likewise with advocacy of policies or with the influencing of conduct through seeking to bring about such action as buying, selling, accepting positions, investing, saving, cooperating, working harder or more harmoniously, and the like.

Oral persuasion then may be defined for our purpose as the process of influencing conduct through speech. That there are many other means of persuasion, such as social pressure, compulsion, stark necessity, as in a famine, laws, and so on need not be dwelt on here. In fact, in given circumstances, a speaker may make use of some of these external influences. But we are concerned here with spoken persuasion and its sources: "the available means of persuasion," as Aristotle put it. Naturally, some of these are used in written persuasion as well.

Speeches seeking belief. Through what is said, and how it is said, the speaker seeks to convince the hearer that he should adopt a new or changed opinion about some matter in dispute; or he seeks not only to change opinion but to get immediate action. For instance, one might seek to convince the audience that government ownership of the means of transportation would be desirable. Unless the audience is a house of Congress, the hearers would not be in a position to legislate to this effect, and the Specific Purpose would be to get agreement, rather than direct action. The debater might argue before an academic audience that labor unions should be subject to anti-trust legislation; conviction, or *belief,* is sought. The only action that such an audience could take might be to sign a petition, adopt a resolution, or "write to their Congressman," but these are in reality mere expressions of opinion. A student might argue that oral examinations at the end of the sophomore and senior years are fairer than written examinations each semester. Unless he is talking to a faculty committee, his aim is to *convince,* to get *agreement,* with any action such as petitioning merely an expression of that belief to which he has led the hearers.

Most debate topics, and many other controversial questions upon which the audience cannot be asked to take any really decisive action, come under the heading of what is called the Persuasive-Belief speech. This may deal with questions of *policy,* or with questions of *fact.* Some examples of each follow:

QUESTIONS OF POLICY
   1. Should the United States continue all-out support of the United Nations?

2. Should the State of Ohio adopt the unicameral legislative proposal?
3. Should the sales tax be increased in this state?
4. Should foreign aid by the United States be limited to those nations in the non-Communist bloc?

QUESTIONS OF FACT
1. Has municipal ownership of bus and streetcar lines been successful?
2. Will football replace baseball as the "national sport"?
3. Has substantial progress been made in interracial relations in America?
4. Are we facing a disastrous inflationary wage-price spiral?

In dealing with such topics before a student audience, or one composed of members of the general public, the speaker is actually limited to seeking agreement, conviction, belief. He has succeeded in persuasion if the audience indicates that it has come to agree with his position. Of course, he hopes that eventually some action will occur, as a sufficient strength of public opinion may develop: but the immediate audience, lacking authority directly to put the speaker's opinion into effect, is limited to such incidental actions as letter-writing, petitioning, or eventually voting for candidates who agree with their views.

Persuasive-action talks. Contrasted in degree, at least, with such topics as we have mentioned above, there are subjects on which the hearer *can* act directly. He can join an organization, make a gift or donation, offer his services, buy, or otherwise take observable and concrete action. It is within his immediate or nearly-immediate power to do, or refuse to do, that which the speaker or other oral communicator asks.

In a campaign, he can vote. In a community drive for charitable funds, he can donate, or he can participate as a worker. As a student, he can elect a certain course, or determine to major in a selected field. He can accept or reject a job offer. He can join, or decline to join, a fraternity or special-interest club. He can decide to be a lawyer, doctor, advertising man or teacher. He can apply for life insurance, or refuse to do so. He can attend the church of his choice. He can go to a play, or stay home. He can decide to travel during his vacation, or to take a summer job.

In business, a manager or board of directors may increase an advertising budget or not. The vice-president in charge of sales can engage a sales training specialist or decline to do so. Stockholders can ratify the decisions of management, or vote them down in annual meeting. People can join civic organizations, or refuse. They can participate in P.-T.A. activities or avoid them. They can buy, or refuse to buy, any specific article or service.

Thus there are many situations in which the audience or individual hearer *has the power to act,* and can exercise or refuse to exercise that power. In such a situation, not only agreement or conviction is sought, but affirmative action as urged by the speaker is the goal. This action, usually, is one that it is hoped by the speaker will be taken *soon,* such as starting a savings account, or planning a summer trip, or buying an automobile. The *practicality* of the action desired —that is, that it lies within the power or authority of the audience—and usually the relative *immediacy* of the action, distinguish the *persuasive-action* talk from the *persuasive-belief.* Archtypes of the two might be the formal debate and the mass sales presentation of a television commercial. The one can only seek agreement; the other seeks immediate or early action—buying.

Let us add that the persuasive-action speech may call upon people *to desist* from something that they now do: to quit some undesirable habit; to avoid undesirable moving pictures; to abstain from thoughtless criticism of others; to stop last-minute "cramming" for examinations, etc.

To summarize: the persuasive-belief sort of talk seeks agreement or concurrence, and usually the audience lacks authority for decisive action; the persuasive-action talk calls for early, overt and specific acts, which are practicable for the hearers to take.

The difference between the two is not one of *principle,*

for surely one's belief will in the long run influence conduct, but rather in the possibility of early and decisive, concrete action and to a considerable degree in the relative emphasis on the use of logical, emotional and personal proof. The persuasive-belief speech tends to emphasize logic and an objective attitude on the part of the speaker, while the persuasive-action one tends to emphasize motivation and vividness in its content, and a more subjective approach by the speaker. Yet this is a difference mainly of degree: all persuasion should ideally consist of personal dedication (ethical proof), logical proof, and emotional appeal. It is in the blending of these "available means of persuasion" that the great speakers, business leaders and others excel.

Choosing the ideas. Having determined the Specific Purpose, i.e., the exact belief or action at which the speaker aims, the next step is, of course, to choose strong Principal Ideas: supporting points that when developed by the proper details, will lead to the accomplishment of the speaker's aim.

Briefly to repeat what was said in Chapter 2 the Principal Ideas of a persuasive speech should have a dual nature: (1) they should furnish sound reasons-why the belief or action desired should be had; (2) they should be so chosen and worded as to make a direct appeal to wants, or motives for action. In other words, they should involve both logical and emotional proof. The questions they must answer in the minds of the hearers are "Why *should* I accept this belief or act accordingly," and "Why should I *want* to do so?" In choosing them, let us remember the statement of Overstreet, "No appeal to reason that is not also an appeal to wants is ever effective."

A student advocating comprehensive oral examinations rather than semester-by-semester written ones considered both logic and want-appeal in choosing Principal Ideas in a classroom speech:

SPECIFIC PURPOSE: To persuade the class that oral comprehensives are desirable.

PRINCIPAL IDEAS:

1. Written examinations do not give a true picture of a student's knowledge.
2. Neither objective nor subjective questions permit the tester to evaluate knowledge.
3. Oral comprehensives give both student and tester a fair chance.

The want-appeal here is to the desire of students to have a "fair deal" in proving their knowledge of a subject, and to have that knowledge accurately graded. Each idea also gives a logical reason which, when supported by examples, statistics, and testimony, proves the soundness of the speaker's contention.

The often-used subject, "Give a donation of blood to the Red Cross," can be developed by ideas which appeal both to reason and to wants:

1. Your donation assures you and your family of blood when it is vitally needed.
2. Donation is a painless and non-injurious process.
3. You are helping humanity by giving blood.

These outlines, the first for a Persuasive-Belief talk, the second for Persuasive-Action, illustrate briefly the task of selecting Principal Ideas for persuasion. *Make them logical; make them appeal to wants.*

The speech details. All of the Speech Details are important in persuasion, and vividness and concreteness in their presentation are necessary. *Examples take first rank* in most such talks, because while appealing and sound ideas may get attention, they need concrete support to be effective. Witness Lincoln's painstaking listing of how the "fathers who framed the government under which we live" voted on the federal control of slavery. Without these examples, which were buttressed by statistics and quotations from basic documents, he could not have hoped to establish his point. We have quoted Cummings and Franklin D. Roosevelt in a previous discussion of examples (Chapter 3).

COMPARISON, because it appeals to the understanding and often to the emotions, likewise is valuable. "That is cool," says Lincoln. "A highwayman holds a pistol to my ear, and mutters through his teeth, 'Stand and deliver, or I shall kill you, and then you will be a murderer!'" These references are to The Cooper Institute Address, which appears in full in Part Three.

STATISTICS, being in effect a compilation of many examples, are, when their authoritative nature is established, excellent logical evidence. *Testimony,* when from recognized experts or qualified witnesses, aids in proof; and when a striking quotation from such an authority is used, it adds vividness and color. And such *reiteration* as is needed to emphasize ideas, and to recall them to the audience in summation is necessary.

We have mentioned vividness and concreteness in the use of Speech Details. In persuasion as much or more than in other kinds of speaking, these are essential. Perhaps visual or auditory exhibits will help. Extended examples or comparisons, vividly worded, may be desirable. Narrative and descriptive passages, with the cautions suggested in the preceding chapter, may be useful. In short, the accumulated speaking skills all apply in the task of moving others to belief or to action. They are among the "available means of persuasion."

Openings and closings. In short practice speeches of the persuasive kind, special effort should be made to plan brief but interesting openings, which call the attention of the audience to their concern with the subject, pointing out that it affects some of their interests. The Specific Purpose would follow logically, and usually should be made known. To those who may have the notion that this destroys suspense or kills interest, we might say that on the other hand, knowing what the speaker wants us to believe or do enables us to judge whether his "reasons-why" are good ones. This is in addition to the pressing need of being clear at all points in a talk, which we have emphasized in Chapters 2 and 3.

The conclusion should ordinarily reiterate the Principal Ideas, whether with formal summary or otherwise, and should make a direct appeal for the belief or action desired. The strongest reason-why or the most appealing motive for action should be used. The conclusion, in a word, should furnish a logical-emotional climax, and directly suggest action or belief. It need not be highly wrought in language, nor "eloquent," but it should represent the total dedication of the speaker to his cause.

So much for an elementary "run-through" of the planning of persuasive speeches. Back of such planning, of course, is *audience-analysis*, the survey of the nature, attitudes, and other attributes of the hearers; and of the *speaker-audience* relationship, the opinion and knowledge the hearers have of the speaker, and the qualities he must try to show when speaking. Both of these topics have been explored in Chapter 4, and a review at this time would be in order. Important to the success of the speaker here, as always, is his effectiveness in *the manner of speaking:* his sense of communication, physical and mental animation, and his enthusiastic sincerity, treated in Chapter 5.

We proceed now to a discussion in brief form of persuasive elements as they appear in logical and emotional proof, and to the presentation of some specific persuasive techniques that will aid in attaining mastery.

LOGIC IN PERSUASION

Applied logic furnishes a basis for permanent, long-run persuasion. Although want-appeal is necessary, it must be supported in depth by sound reasoning and evidence, or it produces only a temporary effect. Thus a review of logical principles is in order. We would add that debate training or training in its counterpart, written argumentation, ought to be on the program of every student who really desires to develop maximum effectiveness. One should not be deceived, either by the superficialities of some advertising or by the "dryness" of some debates, about the solid merit of logical argument. One should know its principles, and apply them, both in his own arguments and in defense against the arguments of others. *Logic is basic to real persuasion.*

It concerns, first, the reasoned analysis of subjects under discussion or in controversy, to the end that the speaker may determine the *pivotal points,* or *issues,* upon the establishment or disestablishment of which a rational decision may be made. In other words, the speaker must study the pro's and con's of the subject to find out what the Principal Ideas of his presentation must be. Second, it involves the reasoning processes by which an issue may be established or overthrown. This demands a knowledge of the nature of argument in general and of its specific forms—deductive, inductive, causal, from authority, from comparison, from example, from generalization, from classification, and by elimination.

The speaker should not only understand these formal and informal kinds of argument, but he should know the tests of their validity, so that he can both safeguard his own arguments against faults, and so that he can detect weaknesses or fallacies in opposing contentions. Further, he should understand the nature of evidence: the materials of fact that serve as a basis of proof, and should know the rules governing its validity. This is the field of logic in persuasion; and perhaps this mere statement indicates the necessity of training in it. Here we shall give only a short summary, dealing first with the analysis of the subject to determine proper Principal Ideas, and second with some of the basics of argument.

Finding the issues. In any matter subject to argument, a preliminary analysis to determine the issues is necessary. Issues may be defined as those *principal* points of contention, settlement of which is necessary to a final decision. There may be many points of disagreement, for example, between those who favor or oppose bringing labor unions under the federal anti-trust laws, but the pivotal points—the decisive ones—might narrow down to something like these: (1) Is there real or imminent monopoly power in the hands of unions? (2) Does this, if it exists, constitute a danger to the public welfare? (3) Would this proposal damage unduly the legitimate interests of working people? (4) Is this proposal the best method of coping with whatever dangers may exist in the present situation? Obviously, many pro-labor or pro-management arguments commonly employed would not, in any real sense, be relevant to the discussion of the proposal. It is, then, to determine what the *real issues* in any case are that we first must analyze a proposal.

PROCESS OF ANALYSIS. Here we are in the position of a debater who is confronted with the task of studying a specific proposal and of determining what his main points should be. The usual order of procedure is as follows:

1. *Define the terms.* Just what does the proposal mean? What specific legislation or action is intended? In a debate, the proposal is usually stated as a resolution, as, "Resolved, that the administration proposal for medical aid to the aged should be adopted." In other than debate situations, the speaker should reduce his proposal to similarly definite language.

2. *Exclude irrelevant material.* A case in point would be the Kennedy proposal of 1962 on medical aid, which did not include direct compensation to doctors.

3. *Survey the origin and history of the topic.* The story of how the controversy arose, and what has been done about it here or elsewhere, reveals much of the nature of the arguments involved.

4. *List the principal arguments of proponents and of opponents of the proposal.* Determine points agreed on or conceded; consolidate others into principal points of contention; eliminate irrelevant or unimportant ones.

5. *From the steps taken above, determine the issues,* which are pivotal points of controversy. Affirmatively or negatively, these form the Principal Ideas of a speech.

The "stock issues." A valuable means of checking on the ordinary process of analysis is through use of what are called the "stock issues," which, though general in their statement, may serve to assure the speaker that he has considered at least the most important points upon which he must be prepared when he advocates a proposal for a new policy:

1. Is there a need for a change?
   a. Are there serious evils in the present policy?
   b. Are these evils due to defects in the *policy,* and not remediable without a change in policy?
2. Is the proposed policy practical?
   a. Will it solve the existing problems?
   b. Will it create new and worse evils?
   c. Does past experience indicate that this policy would succeed?
3. Is the proposed policy the best available solution?
   a. Is it better than any revision of the present policy?
   b. Are there other, better alternative new policies?

In general, the *burden of proof* is on a person who advocates a new policy, and the above points indicate the extent of that burden. One who opposes a new policy may deny any of the points under need or practicality, or may concede the point of need and advocate a "counter-plan," that is, an alternative policy. In advocating a counter-plan, he must show that it is superior to the proposal which he is opposing. This list of "stock issues," therefore, is valuable as defining what an advocate must establish, and of indicating the possibilities for successful opposition.

Applying logic to arguments. Once a speaker, or a group organized as a debate or discussion team, has determined what the Principal Ideas for advocacy or opposition should be, the next task is to gather evidence for the support of each argument, and to test each for its logical validity. The assertions made above in the discussion of "stock issues" are all statements of fact, which must be proved. This depends upon the use of valid reasoning and authoritative evidence. Following, then, is a skeletonized review of the kinds of argument of the tests for their validity.

Deductive argument—formal. Essentially, all argument is deductive, that is, it proceeds from accepted principles to specific conclusions concerning individual cases. Its formal statement is the *syllogism,* which consists of a *major premise,* a *minor premise,* and a *conclusion.*

The major premise is a statement of a general truth, applicable to an entire class of objects.

The minor premise is a statement of specific truth, to the effect that the specific case at hand is included in the class of objects referred to in the major premise.

The conclusion is a statement applying the characteristic of the class of objects mentioned in the major to the specific object mentioned in the minor.

To illustrate:

> All men are mortal. (Major premise.)
> Socrates was a man. (Minor premise.)
> Therefore Socrates was mortal. (Conclusion.)
>
> That which creates international ill will brings about war. (Major premise.)
> Russia's policy creates international ill will. (Minor premise.)
> Therefore Russia's policy brings about war. (Conclusion.)

All arguments may be put into this form for the purpose of discovering their major and minor premises, and for testing the validity of the conclusion. Seldom are both premises and the conclusion formally stated in actual argument. Usually one premise or the other, or the conclusion, is "suppressed," i.e., left to be inferred.

TESTS OF THE SYLLOGISM. All arguments may be tested for logical validity by being put into complete syllogistic form and being tested from two points of view:

1. The test of the major premise: Is the general statement made universally true of all objects of the class referred to, is it accepted as true, and are there any important exceptions?

2. The test of the minor premise: Is the statement made concerning the specific object true, and is the specific object wholly included within the class of things covered by the major premise?

These two tests include, in a broad way, all the technical criteria which logic involves. Applying them to the first syllogism above, we see that the major premise, "All men are mortal," is universally true, accepted as such, and without exceptions; and the minor premise, "Socrates was a man," is true, and that Socrates is wholly included in the general class of men. Therefore we may conclude that the argument is sound, and that the conclusion, "Socrates was mortal," is true.

The second syllogism given above is deficient logically. Applying the test of the major premise, we see that it is *not universally true* that "that which creates international ill will brings about war." There are many important exceptions, which certainly created international ill will, but which did not lead to war.

These tests of the major and minor premises are broad and elementary, but they will be useful to the student until his study of argument has replaced them with more detailed rules for gauging the value of arguments.

Deductive argument—informal. As stated above, most arguments are not stated in syllogistic form but appear with one of the three parts eliminated. In every case, the tests of the major and minor premises may be applied after the missing part has been replaced. There are certain easily recognized types of informal argument, however, which have specific tests of their own:

1. The argument from authority. This depends for its validity upon the tests for expert evidence.

2. The argument from example (or "literal analogy"). This depends upon the tests for inductive argument, given later in this chapter.

3. The argument from comparison (or "figurative analogy"). Test: Is there any essential similarity between the two things compared? Example: Is there any essential similarity between a "house divided against itself" and a nation divided on the slavery issue?

4. The argument from generalization or classification. "Jones is a good student, because he is a member of Phi Beta Kappa"; "Delta Sigma Rho is composed of good speakers, for Jones, Black, and Smith are good speakers." The tests of the major and minor premises apply to both of these arguments, and the tests for inductive argument to the latter.

5. The argument by elimination. "There are four possibilities: A, B, C, and D. A, B, and C cannot be the solution, therefore D

is true." In this type of argument, the possibilities enumerated must be exhaustive, i.e., there must be no possibility which is not named; and all but one possibility must be entirely eliminated.

6. The argument from causal relationship (cause to effect; effect to cause; effect to effect).

> *a. Cause to effect:* Observing a cause, the arguer predicts a given effect:
>
>> "Weather conditions are good, therefore we shall have a good crop."
>>
>> "The federal government is spending billions, therefore taxes will be high for many years."
>
> *b. Effect to cause:* Observing an effect, the arguer reasons that it was produced by a certain cause:
>
>> "This field is flooded, therefore there have been heavy rains."
>>
>> "We have better business, therefore the reduction in taxes has been beneficial."
>
> *c. Effect to effect:* This consists of an argument from effect to cause, followed by an argument from cause to effect:
>
>> "These two nations are at war, therefore the United Nations will lose prestige."

Reduced to its two component arguments, this argument follows:

"These two nations are at war, therefore the United Nations must have failed to arbitrate the dispute." (Effect to cause.)

"The United Nations failed to arbitrate, therefore it will lose prestige." (Cause to effect.)

Mistaken causal relationship is probably responsible for more fallacious argument than any other logical error, therefore it is important that the rules governing it be well understood:

> *a.* Tests for argument from cause to effect:
>> (1) The observed cause must be capable of producing the alleged effect.
>>
>> (2) The observed cause must not be prevented from operating.
>>
>> (3) There must be no intervening factor which could change the result.

For example, "good weather conditions" might be capable of producing a good crop, but standing alone, they would not be sufficient. They might be prevented from operating by lack of adequate tillage and cultivation. An intervening factor, such as the boll weevil or chinch bug, might operate to change the result.

b. Tests for argument from effect to cause:
   (1) The alleged cause must have been capable of producing the observed effect.
   (2) The alleged cause must not have been prevented from operating.
   (3) Other causes must not have intervened.
       For example, failure of the United Nations to arbitrate may not have contributed in any way to the fact that two nations are at war. They may not have been members of the United Nations.

c. Tests for argument from effect to effect. These are simply a combination of the two sets of tests given above. To test such an argument, divide it into an argument from effect to cause and one from cause to effect, and apply the appropriate criteria.

Inductive argument. This consists of reaching a general conclusion from the observation of a number of specific instances; in appearance, therefore, it is argument "from the particular to the general":

Municipal ownership and operation of public utilities has succeeded in cases A, B, C, D, E, and F;

Therefore municipal ownership and operation is a success.

It will be seen that actually this is an incomplete syllogism, of which the major premise is: "If a given type of utility ownership succeeds in six cases, it may be called successful in general." Consequently, the tests of the major and minor premises may be applied to inductive argument.

There are, however, special rules for this type of argument, as follows:

1. The instances cited must be true.

2. The instances cited should be typical of all existing cases.
3. All, or a sufficient number, of the existing cases must be presented.
4. There must be no important exceptions.
5. The instances cited must all be of the same kind, and drawn from comparable situations. (To cite examples of municipal ownership of businesses other than utilities, or to draw examples from cities in which conditions are greatly different from the city under discussion, would be unsound.)

USES OF LOGIC. A knowledge of the rudiments of logic will enable the speaker to test his own arguments, thus avoiding possible flaws in reasoning. It will also enable him, in argumentative speaking, such as formal or informal debate, to detect weak points in the reasoning of his opponents. The sketch of the principal types of argument which we have given in this section will be useful in both respects.

EMOTIONAL AND PERSONAL PERSUASION

Logic is a foundation of persuasion. But the old saying, "A man convinced against his will retains his old opinion still," must be borne in mind by every oral or written communicator. Unless people are *willing* to believe or act, and unless not only what the speaker *says*, but what they think he *is*, makes them willing, logical argument will not of itself succeed. *It is the blending of logic, want-and interest-appeal, and personal persuasiveness* that leads to favorable results.

Chapter 4, on want-appeal, together with the familiar, the unusual, and the specific, presented with vividness and variety, should have a thorough review at this time. What is said, further, in that chapter about the speaker-audience relationship should be restudied. The general and special interests of the hearers, their age, their educational level, their intelligence, their attitude toward the subject, their approach to new ideas, their activity level at the moment, and the physical conditions under which they are addressed, all should have consideration. The speaker should consider what the audience knows or thinks about him: his reputation, his basic traits as known to the hearers, his point-of-contact traits such as communicativeness, animation, and enthusiasm, courage, confidence, and competence. All of these enhance or limit his ability to persuade.

Thus the speaker should take positive action in preparation, and during the speech, to make use of emotional and personal persuasiveness. We shall not restate our discussion of these points here; they have been treated in detail in Chapters 4 and 5, and elsewhere when discussing the use of Speech Details, including description, narration, and extended examples and comparisons. All are among "the available means of persuasion."

We *supplement* our explanation of these basic principles here by outlining additional techniques that make for greater audience response to ideas and facts; that *activate* the hearers toward willingness and desire to believe or act. We wish to refer the reader for additional material of this sort to Overstreet's *Influencing Human Behavior* and to Sandford's *Speak Well and Win*.[1]

Audience-responses. An audience which *responds* to the speaker, either silently or by overt action, such as applause, laughter, or cheers, is an audience which is being conditioned to favorable action on the speaker's proposal. The number, as well as the quality or intensity of such responses, creates a feeling of accord, or *rapport*, between speaker and hearer. A cumulation of such responses, especially when brought about by statements that are relevant to the speaker's purpose and subject, almost invariably leads to successful persuasion. It is therefore to the speaker's interest to work and plan for such audience responses.

As simple examples, you have heard a political speaker predict enthusiastically, in a very early part of his speech, that "We will win! The people of this city will vote for progress and constructive achievement." The applause, because of

[1] *Influencing Human Behavior*, by H. A. Overstreet, Peoples Institute Publishing Co., New York, 1925; *Speak Well and Win*, by W. P. Sandford, McGraw-Hill Book Co., New York, 1944.

the nature of occasion and audience, is automatic! Or you
may have heard a speaker pay a glowing tribute to some
distinguished person, present or absent, with the sure response that followed. Again, an early humorous reference, or
story, may "bring down the house." All such things, whether
directly related to the topic or not, build a mood for additional responses. We call this process of seeking—and getting
—audience responses, *activation*. Some call it suggestion,
some call it "getting audience participation." Whatever its
name, it is a result-getting technique.

Users of activation. Great speakers generally have been
masters of activation. In Chapter 4, we reviewed Grady's
New South, and a study of it will show the varied methods
he used to get favorable responses: the vivid quotation from
Benjamin Hill's Tammany Hall speech, the unforgettable
humorous stories, the compassion-arousing description of the
"footsore Confederate soldier," the glowing tribute to Lincoln, the eloquent quotation from Webster, the challenge to
New England. All of these built a pattern of activation that
accounts for the brilliant success that Grady scored. Laughter, cheers, applause, and vibrant emotional response combined as this masterpiece of persuasion unfolded.

Beecher's *Liverpool Speech* is another classic of audience-
activation. Facing boos, catcalls, and a determined effort on
the part of some of the audience to prevent him from being
heard, he appealed to British fair play, challenged his opponents to listen, painted vivid pictures to portray economic
ideas, made overt appeals to self-interest, and gained a hearing. He ended with an eloquent hands-across-the-sea tribute
to England and to America.

Bryan, in his triumphant *Cross of Gold*, which won him
three presidential nominations, appealed to the emotions of
western farmers and of working people, challenged the opposition, predicted victory for the "free silver" people, and
climaxed his appeal with the famous "You shall not crucify
mankind upon a Cross of Gold."

Webster, in the great American speech, *The Reply to*

Hayne, not only used challenge, reproof, appeal to lofty sentiments, and even a highly humorous passage in addition to his solid constitutional and historical arguments; but he capped each section of his speech with passages of glowing eloquence that stirred emotion: the tribute to South Carolina and Massachusetts, and the "Liberty and Union, now and forever, one and inseparable" peroration among them. He, by the general verdict of contemporaries and critics the leading American orator, used activation in many of his speeches: the plea in the Dartmouth College case, The White Murder Case, the Plymouth oration, the address at the laying of the cornerstone of the Bunker Hill monument, the Eulogy of Adams and Jefferson, the Seventh of March speech, and others. They should be studied for this and other elements of persuasion.

Activation is not the sole property of great speakers, effectively as they have used it. The accomplished salesman employs it by asking questions which suggest a "yes-response," and by asking, not whether the prospect will buy, but which of two models he would prefer; also by asking questions which lead the prospect to talk, and by suggestions that involve some physical action by the prospect, such as climbing into the driver's seat of a new car, operating a new electric typewriter, etc.

The means of activation. To list all possible ways in which the speaker can get silent or overt reactions from the audience would require a compilation of thousands of items. However, we may classify them as follows: the activation of the speaker himself; the participation of the hearers in some overt physical action; and the creation of definite emotional reactions in the audience.

THE ACTIVATED SPEAKER. Enthusiasm, vitality, determination, sincerity, aliveness: these are contagious. The speaker with "spark" and sincerity will get reactions of the same kind from his hearers. His dedication to his cause, his knowledge and competence: these and other characteristics and attitudes will in turn make the audience willing to respond to him. Undesirable traits, such as a sense of superiority, disdain, sarcasm, "know-it-allness," of course have a reverse effect. One should be at his best in appearance, communicativeness, animation and sincerity, remembering the doctrine that "like begets like."

GETTING PHYSICAL ACTIONS. An audience is made more responsive if its members can be induced to take some observable physical action. If appropriate to occasion and subject, an invocation by a clergyman unites them in feeling as they rise together for it. The singing of a patriotic or other appropriate song is another group action that can be utilized when fitting. The speaker may ask, "How many have given blood to the Red Cross?" or some other question involving the lifting of hands. He can vary such questions by asking for a voiced response, as "Aye." He can suggest that they get out their programs and read them, or that they take notes, or that they pass an exhibit among them.

Sometimes in a long program, a speaker may get action by having the hearers "stand up and stretch." He can have them look at a portrait or exhibit—and so on through a long list of possibilities. He can ask them some question on which he is sure of a majority agreement, and ask those who agree with him to stand. He may pay a tribute to some person present, and suggest that the hearers "give him a hand." All such tactics, if well done, tend to create that sense of unity among the hearers, and of a favorable disposition toward the speaker, that lay the groundwork for persuasion.

GETTING EMOTIONAL RESPONSES. Motivation—the appeal to wants—is of course the basis for emotional responses. The wording of appeals to wants so that they are direct, dramatic, vivid adds to their moving quality. We have already discussed the point that vague or indirect motivation is not especially effective. Vivid language and specific want-appeal are needed, as when Beecher said to Britons, "Your great need is customers, not cotton!" or in 1961, when Kennedy said, "Ask not what your country can do for you, ask rather what you can do for your country."

On the side of personal persuasiveness, the speaker can

affirm his belief or willingness to act, or to assume leadership, or he can defend his attitude against charges or complaints that may have been made. Webster did the latter in pleading the White Murder Case, when he replied to complaints of the defence that he was "brought in" to assist the prosecution. In so doing he identified himself with the cause of justice and of community protection against crime.

Raymond Robins, a famous Chicagoan who supported the Progressive Party in 1912, got tremendous emotional responses by two tributes to Theodore Roosevelt, at the same time affirming his own dedication to the movement:

I was once a Democrat—I followed Bryan through the wilderness for twelve long years—but when I heard that Theodore Roosevelt had founded a new party based on social justice for all, I said, "I'll go with you, Theodore Roosevelt, to the end of the road."

You will observe that in addition to his announcement of personal sincerity, Mr. Robins used humor in the reference to Mr. Bryan, and also the device of apostrophe—an imaginary direct address to Roosevelt. Another tribute to Roosevelt by Mr. Robins was this:

I would rather have known, and loved, and worked for, and been trusted by—Theodore Roosevelt—than any other man who has lived in my day.

You will note the periodic structure of this sentence, leading up to the climactic announcement of Mr. Roosevelt's name, and the rhythmic final phrase which balanced it. These passages, heard personally by the writer, demonstrated Mr. Robins' tremendous ability to get emotional responses.

Woodrow Wilson's first inaugural address concluded with a highly effective call for support of his leadership:

I summon all honest men, all patriotic men, all forward-looking men, to my side. God helping me, I shall not fail them, if they will but counsel and sustain me.

Franklin D. Roosevelt's speech calling for a declaration of war in 1941, after the Pearl Harbor attack of December 7, contained many stirring passages. He identifies himself as "Commander-in-Chief of the army and navy," and later says

With confidence in our armed forces, with the unbounded determination of the American people, we will win the inevitable triumph, so help us God.

This combines an assumption of leadership with a confident prediction of victory, another technique of activation.

These are but examples of the ways in which the speaker can assert the rightness of his cause, his own sincerity, or his rightful claim to leadership. All help in audience-response.

Other means of activation. Aside from strengthening personal appeal as just explained, there are many other means of stirring the emotions of the hearers. Each emotional response, shared by the audience, increases the willingness to act. Sometimes there is not a logical connection between the feeling aroused and the speaker's subject, although it is better if such connection exists, both practically and ethically. But it must be admitted that many appeals are made to tradition, prejudice, custom, and to audience-vanity, and that these are often effective. The honorable speaker will not abuse his position in this manner, but will seek legitimate emotional response. Here, briefly, are suggestions for this purpose:

1. Connect your subject with commonly held ideals, sentiments, and desires. Indicate that it carries out, or is in accordance, with them.

2. Where ethical to do so, use symbols that have deep emotional associations: the flag, democracy, Washington, Lincoln, home, America, etc.

3. Use humor to illustrate your points; laughter is actually an emotional thing.

4. Stress points of agreement—common ground between you and a perhaps opposed or cynical audience.

5. Praise the audience's past accomplishments or progress.

6. Use the "yes-response" technique by asking questions that you know will get an affirmative answer.

7. Challenge the hearers to meet a responsibility or to win in a contest. (The "putting-it-up-to-you" technique.)

8. Use dramatic parallel examples, vivid quotations, etc.

9. Use language that assumes and suggests action: "we," "our," "your," "let us," "when we have done this"; the imperative mode—"look at this," "make your decision," "stand up and fight," etc.

10. Sloganize your key ideas or purpose: "Make the world safe for democracy"; "Let us go forward, with strong and active faith"; "The only thing we have to fear is fear itself."

11. Predict success or victory and add the "bandwagon technique"—that we should all join in the movement toward victory now.

12. Use the shock technique if necessary: the dramatic prediction of undesirable or tragic results if we do not take certain action.

13. Provide a way to "take the first step," that is, an *immediate* action that will involve or commit the hearers to further action.

14. Change your "pace," both in manner of delivery and in the type of Speech Details used. Furnish recurrent climaxes as you end each Principal Idea and at the end of the speech.

15. Use both selfish and unselfish or idealistic want-appeal. End by the process of *sublimating* your cause by appealing to the highest moral values.

Summary on activation. Remember, it is both the *number* and the *intensity* of audience-responses that you desire to arouse. Good use of the principle of activation will build a pattern of favorable reactions that will make possible the desired belief or action. Without such audience-responses, the best-prepared speech is liable to fail. With them, it gains its full persuasive value. We urge a reading of Overstreet's *Influencing Human Behavior,* already referred to in this chapter. In Part One especially, he has made a lasting contribution to the techniques of influencing people, one that has been generally acknowledged by authors and critics.

CONCLUSION

In this chapter, we have supplemented what has gone before by workable suggestions for planning a persuasive speech. We have called attention to the importance of using all of the means of persuasion—logical, emotional, and personal. Finally, we have discussed the process of getting audience-responses of a physical or emotional kind during the speech, which we have termed *activation.*

In the chapter to follow, we shall set forth stylistic devices for vividness in presentation, such as imagery, figures of speech, figures of thought, and rhythm. Although these are treated as aids to the commemorative speech, they also are important in the great task of persuasion.

Finally, a study of the classic speeches of persuasion in Part Three will show how successful speakers have dealt with this problem of influencing others. Such a study will reveal the use of many of the procedures and techniques that we have presented in this chapter.

9

How to Plan Commemorative Speeches

It is necessary not only to tell your hearers the truth, but to render it vivid, to appeal to the auditors' senses by a striking presentation.

FENELON

W<small>HERE</small> can we get a speaker for commencement? Who would be a good speaker for our civic observance of Veterans' Day? Whom should we select to speak at the dedication of the Jefferson Memorial? What speaker could best express our feelings at memorial services for the great leader who has died? A moment's reflection will indicate to anyone the importance of the commemorative address, and the difficulty of finding men or women qualified to present it. Speeches of tribute, dedication, commemoration, and celebration make up no small part of the total of public address.

In public life, such anniversaries as Independence Day, Flag Day, Armed Forces Day, Memorial Day, Veterans' Day, Constitution Day, Labor Day, and the dates of the birth of great men provide occasions for formal commemorative speeches. In the affairs of businesses and social or other organizations, outstanding achievements, or the annual gathering of members, furnish similar occasions. The presentation of gifts, awards, and prizes, their acceptance, and speeches of introduction and farewell, also come in this category. In some ways, speeches of nomination, although persuasive in their outward form, and inaugural addresses, classify as speeches of formal occasion, and are actually commemorative in their impact.

Appropriateness and vividness. When one is faced with the problem of composing a speech dedicating an important building or paying tribute to a great person, or celebrating a national holiday, he is compelled to think, first, what would be *appropriate?* What would fit the occasion, and satisfy the hearers who have gathered because they deem the dedication, tribute or holiday important? Obviously a speech of simple exposition would not do: the hearers know about the institution, or the man, or the holiday. To recount what the process of raising funds for the building was, or to give a trite biographical sketch of the man, or to tell in detail how the holiday came about, would be to disappoint the hearers and to waste their time. They possess, in general, such information. Not only that, but they also are persuaded that the occasion is important.

On the other hand, they might well be chagrined, or antagonized, by a speech urging them to take some political or other action not related to the specific occasion, or denouncing others for alleged faults. Propaganda of this sort is almost always inappropriate to what, essentially, is an occasion for celebration.

What, then, *is* appropriate? Rather than simple explanation or persuasion, the occasions we have mentioned demand *a well-conceived informative-impressive speech:* one stressing the importance, significance, inner meaning, achievements, characteristics, or influence of the building, the man, or the holiday. What is the real meaning of this institution we are dedicating? Why does the man to whom we pay tribute deserve praise—what traits of character, or what achievements, marked his life? What significance does this holiday have?

Principal ideas. Thus the Specific Purpose of a commemorative speech stresses such key words as *significance, importance, traits, meaning*. And the Principal Ideas each are chosen to emphasize the key word in the Specific Purpose. Then through Speech Details, such as reiteration, examples, testimony, statistics and comparison, aided perhaps by description or narration, we try to make *vivid* the existence of the selected ideas. In short, we use the procedure outlined in Chapter 7, in the section dealing with the informative-impressive type.

Adlai Stevenson, in his masterpiece dedicating the Lovejoy Memorial in Alton, Illinois, selected two major significances of Lovejoy's career: his advocacy of freedom for the slaves, and his stand for freedom of the press. With vivid illustration and quotation, he made most impressive the contribution that the slain editor made to our history.

Wendell Phillips' *Eulogy of O'Connell*, spoken before an Irish-American audience, has the Specific Purpose of emphasizing the *leadership* of the famous lawyer-legislator. He cites his achievement in bringing the question of home rule before the people, his unique method of non-violent, constitutional agitation, and specific characteristics such as wit, courage, and eloquence. Then he develops each idea by numerous details, including striking testimony, comparisons, description and narration. The passage on O'Connell's eloquence shows his power of compact, varied vividness:

Broadly considered, his eloquence has never been equaled in modern times, certainly not in English speech. Do you think I am partial? I will vouch John Randolph of Roanoke, the Virginia slave-holder, who hated an Irishman almost as much as he hated a Yankee, himself an orator of no mean level. Hearing O'Connell, he exclaimed, "This is the man, these are the lips, the most eloquent that speak English in my day." I think he was right. I remember the solemnity of Webster, the grace of Everett, the rhetoric of Choate; I know the eloquence that lay hid in the iron logic of Calhoun; I have melted beneath the magnetism of Sargeant S. Prentiss of Mississippi, who wielded a power few men ever had. It has been my fortune to sit at the feet of the great speakers of the English tongue on the other side of the ocean. But I think all of them together never surpassed, and no one of them ever equaled O'Connell. Nature intended him for our Demosthenes. Never since the great Greek has she sent forth anyone so lavishly gifted for his work as a tribune of the people. In the first place, he had a magnificent presence, impressive in bearing, massive like that of Jupiter. Webster himself hardly outdid him in the majesty of his proportions. To be sure, he had not Webster's craggy face, and precipice of brow, nor his eyes glowing like anthracite coal; nor had he the lion roar of Mirabeau. But his presence filled the eye. A small O'Connell would hardly have been an O'Connell at all. These physical advantages are half the battle.

I remember Russell Lowell telling us that Mr. Webster came home from Washington at the time the Whig party thought of dissolution a year or two before his death, and went down to Faneuil Hall to protest; drawing himself up to his loftiest proportion, his brow clothed with thunder, before the listening thousands, he said, "Well, gentlemen, I am a Whig, a Massachusetts Whig, a Faneuil-Hall Whig, a revolutionary Whig, a constitutional Whig. If you break the Whig party, sir, where am I to go?" And says Lowell, "We held our breath, thinking where he *could* go. If he had been five feet three, we should have said, 'Who cares where you go?'" So it was with O'Connell. There was something majestic in his presence before he spoke; and he added to it what Webster had not, what Clay might have lent—infinite grace, that magnetism that melts all hearts into one. I saw him at over sixty-six years of age; every attitude was beauty, every gesture grace. You could only think of a greyhound as you looked at him; it would have been delicious to have watched him, if he had not spoken a word. Then he had a voice that covered the gamut. The majesty of his indignation, fitly uttered in tones of superhuman power, made him able to "indict" a nation, in spite of Burke's protest.

I heard him once say, "I send my voice across the Atlantic, careering like the thunderstorm against the breeze, to tell the slave-holder of the Carolinas that God's thunderbolts are hot, and to remind the bondman that the dawn of his redemption is already breaking." You seemed to hear the tones come echoing back to London from the Rocky Mountains. Then, with the slightest possible Irish brogue, he would tell a story, while all Exeter Hall shook with laughter. The next moment, tears in his voice like a Scotch song, five thousand men wept. And all the whole no effort. He seemed only breathing.

> "As effortless as woodland nooks
> Send violets up, and paint them blue."

We used to say of Webster, "This is a great effort"; of Everett, "It is a beautiful effort"; but you never used the word "effort" in speaking of O'Connell. It provoked you that he would not make an effort. I heard him perhaps a score of times, and I do not think more than three times he ever lifted himself to the full sweep of his power.

And this wonderful power, it was not a thunderstorm: he flanked you with his wit, he surprised you out of yourself; you were conquered before you knew it. He was once summoned to court out of the hunting-field, when a young friend of his of humble birth was on trial for his life. The evidence gathered around a hat found by the body of the murdered man, which was recognized as the hat of the prisoner. The lawyers tried to break down the evidence, confuse the testimony, and get some relief from the directness of the circumstances; but in vain, until at last they called for O'Connell. He came in, flung his riding-whip and hat on the table, was told the circumstances, and taking up the hat said to the witness, "Whose hat is this?" "Well, Mr. O'Connell, that is Mike's hat." "How do you know it?" "I will swear to it, sir." "And did you really find it by the murdered man?" "I did that, sir." "But you're not ready to swear that?" "I am, indeed, Mr. O'Connell." "Pat, do you know what hangs on your word? A human soul. And with that dread burden, are you ready to tell this jury that the hat, to your certain knowledge, belongs to the prisoner?" "Y-yes, Mr. O'Connell; yes, I am."

O'Connell takes the hat to the nearest window, and peers into it—"J–a–m–e–s, James. Now, Pat, did you see that name in the hat?" "I did, Mr. O'Connell." "You knew it was there?" "Yes, sir; I read it after I picked it up." "No name in the hat, your Honor."

So again in the House of Commons. When he took his seat in the house of 1830, the London *Times* visited him with its constant indignation, reported his speeches awry, turned them inside out, and made nonsense of them; treated him as the New York *Herald* used to treat us Abolitionists twenty years ago. So one morning he rose and said, "Mr. Speaker, you know I have never opened my lips in this House, and I expended twenty years of hard work in getting the right to enter it—I have never lifted my voice in this House, but in behalf of the saddest people the sun shines on. Is it fair play, Mr. Speaker, is it what you call 'English fair play,' that the press of this city will not let my voice be heard?" The next day the *Times* sent him word that, as he found fault with their manner of reporting him, they never would report him at all, they never would print his name in their parliamentary colums. So the next day when prayers were ended, O'Connell rose. Those reporters of the *Times* who were in the gallery rose also, ostentatiously put away their pencils, folded their arms, and made all the show they could, to let everybody know how it was. Well, you know, nobody has any right to be in the gallery during the session, and if any member notices them, the mere notice clears the gallery; only the reporters can stay after that notice. O'Connell rose. One of the members said, "Before the member from Clare opens his speech, let me call his attention to the gallery and the instance of that 'passive resistance' which he is about to preach." "Thank you," said O'Connell: "Mr. Speaker, I observe strangers in the gallery." Of course they left; of course the next day, in the columns of the London *Times*, there were no parliamentary debates. And for the first time, except in Richard Cobden's case, the London *Times* cried for quarter, and said to O'Connell, "If you give up the quarrel, we will."

Later on, when he was advocating the repeal of the land law, when forty or fifty thousand people were gathered at the meeting, O'Connell was sitting at the breakfast-table. The London *Times* for that year had absolutely disgraced itself,—and that is saying a great deal,—and its reporters, if recognized, would have been torn to pieces. So, as O'Connell was breakfasting, the door opened, and two or three English reporters—Gurney and, among others, our well-known friend Russell, of Bull Run notoriety—entered the room and said, "Mr. O'Connell, we are the reporters of the *Times*." "And," said Russell, "we dared not enter that crowd."

"Shouldn't think you would," replied O'Connell. "Have you had any breakfast?"

"No, sir," said he; "we hardly dared to ask for any."

"Shouldn't think you would," answered O'Connell; "sit down here." So they shared his breakfast. Then he took Bull Run in his own carriage to the place of meeting, sent for a table and seated him by the platform, and asked him whether he had his pencils well sharpened and had plenty of paper, as he intended to make a long speech. Bull Run answered, "Yes." And O'Connell stood up, and addressed the audience in Irish.

His marvelous voice, its almost incredible power and sweetness, Bulwer has well described:

> "Once to my sight that giant form was given,
> Walled by wide air, and roofed by boundless heaven.
> Beneath his feet the human ocean lay,
> And wave on wave rolled into space away.
> Methought no clarion could have sent its sound
> Even to the center of the hosts around;
> And, as I thought, rose the sonorous swell,
> As from some church-tower swings the silvery bell.
> Aloft and clear, from airy tide to tide
> It glided, easy as a bird may glide;
> Even to the verge of that vast audience sent,
> It played with each wild passion as it went,—
> Now stirred the uproar, now the murmur stilled,
> And sobs or laughter answered as it willed."

Webster could awe a senate, Everett could charm a college, and Choate could cheat a jury; Clay could magnetize the million, and Corwin led them captive. O'Connell was Clay, Corwin, Choate, Everett, and Webster in one. Before the courts, logic; at the bar of the senate, unanswerable and dignified; on the platform, grace, wit, pathos; before the masses, a whole man. Carlyle says, "He is God's own anointed king whose single word melts all wills into his." This describes O'Connell. Emerson says, "There is no true eloquence, unless there is a man behind the speech." Daniel O'Connell was listened to because all England and all Ireland knew that there was a man behind the speech—one who could be neither bought, bullied, nor cheated. He held the masses free but willing subjects in his hand.

Special openings and closings. Because the commemorative speech, especially when given on occasions of considerable importance, calls for an elevated or "polished" style, special openings and closings are often in order.

To open, to "cross the interest deadline," a vivid quotation, a startling or important fact, or a statement setting forth the importance or gravity of the subject, may be in order. Consider these openings:

"I am here by command of silent lips to speak once more and for all upon the Cuban situation."—Thurston.

"Yesterday, December 7, 1941—a date which will live in infamy —the United States of America was suddenly and deliberately attacked by naval and air forces of the Empire of Japan."—F. D. Roosevelt.

"I am here to do that which the dead often promised he would do for me."—Ingersoll.

Not only do these special openings introduce the subject, but they set the mood of the speech to follow. This technique is applicable in all speeches, but, like Ingersoll's quotation above, especially valuable in commemorative speaking.

In closing. In concluding a commemorative speech, whether about a great man, an important institution, or an important national holiday, the speaker often urges upon the hearers the desirability of applying in their own lives, or in national conduct, some of the principles developed in the speech. For instance, an appeal might be made to give the devotion of a Lincoln to our national cause, or to foster the use of the new library or research facility, or to live by the principles of freedom which the Fourth of July symbolizes. "Let us . . . ," the speaker says, and then briefly urges his hearers to live up to great ideals.

The conclusion of a tribute to a great man may end with an emotional climax dealing with what he stood for, or was. Some examples follow:

"Let us believe that his dying eyes read a mystic meaning that only the rapt and parting soul may know. Let us believe that in the silence of the receding world, he heard the great waves breaking on a farther shore, and felt already upon his wasted brow the breath of the eternal morning."—Blaine, *Eulogy of Garfield.*

"There is not one of us but feels prouder of his native land because of the august figure of Washington presided over its beginning; no one but vows it a tenderer love because Lincoln poured out his blood for it; no one but must feel his devotion for his country renewed and kindled when he remembers how Mc-

Kinley loved, revered, and served it, showed in his life how a citizen should live and in his last hour taught us how a gentleman should die."—John Hay, *Eulogy of McKinley.*

Other occasional speeches. Appropriateness and vividness, which we have stressed in talking about commemorative speeches on important occasions, apply also in less formal situations, such as introductions, greetings, giving awards, acknowledging awards, and the like. The nature of the occasion will determine the degree of formality and regulate the level of style: perhaps sometimes not so eloquent as the speeches to which we have referred, but sincere and appropriate. Significance and importance, likewise, are the keynotes to observe in choosing ideas.

INTRODUCING A SPEAKER. A chairman or toastmaster can make the speaker's path much smoother with a brief, appropriate introduction. Who the speaker is, what his topic is, and why he is qualified to speak on it are the usual ideas. The speaker should not be embarrassed by overly exaggerated praise, nor by a long introduction which, in effect, "makes his speech for him." Cordiality, brevity, and concreteness about name, topic, and qualifications should govern this talk. A word of praise for the speaker's accomplishments is of course in order. On the minor point of when to give the speaker's name, a few prefer to withhold it to the end, others like to refer to it at least once during the introductory remarks, and repeat it in conclusion.

PRESENTING AN AWARD. This is a speech of praise or tribute. A succinct statement of why the recipient deserved the award is necessary. Its importance governs how much detail should be given. If it's a major award, like a Pulitzer prize, the speech of presentation becomes a "major production," but a routine presentation of an athletic letter, speaker's prize, or medal for scholarship can be brief and to the point, a simple statement of achievements.

ACCEPTING AWARDS. This sort of speech calls for a degree of brevity—and humility! Generally, the awardee expresses thanks to the donors, and attributes all or some of the credit for his achievement to those who have worked with him. John Glenn did this admirably in the speaking situations that followed his orbital flight. The talk generally concludes with renewed expression of thanks.

What has just been said about giving and accepting awards applies, of course, to gifts in general. Upon retirement, some employees are honored, and must express thanks. Tact on the part of the speaker awarding the gift is important here: the retiree may be quite unhappy about it all! Usually his services to the company are listed and best wishes for his later years are expressed. In this situation, the emotion should not be overdone. On the part of the retiree, thanks, a brief expression of his regard for his coworkers, and repeated expression of appreciation will suffice.

Annual meeting talks. Usually at the local, state or national annual meetings of organizations, there is one address that may "keynote" the whole affair. (Of course there are many reports, discussions, addresses by guest speakers, and occasionally after-dinner talks.) Usually this is given by the president or other high official of the group. "Past, present, and future" is a good formula for choosing the ideas: What we have accomplished in the past year, or other period; what our present problems are; and what we should strive to do in the future. This formula, incidentally, can be used in many commemorative speeches of the more formal type.

Another useful formula for a speech of this kind is as follows: congratulations on the progress of the past year; "inside information" on current developments and problems; discussion of the organization's stand on important matters; and a plea for continued effort in the future.

GIVING AND ACCEPTING OFFICE. The speech addressed to an incoming president or other officer of an organization resembles that of giving awards or prizes. The speaker stresses the qualifications and achievements of the officer-designate, and ends on a note of congratulation and good wishes. The recipient expresses thanks, and perhaps outlines briefly the policies and goals which he hopes will guide his management of affairs. An appeal for cooperation, and repeated thanks, are in order.

The relative importance of the organization, and the mood of the occasion, will govern appropriateness. A merely nominal office does not call for extended remarks. There is a difference between being president of a luncheon club and governor of a state! Fit your remarks to the occasion.

Speeches in national conventions, nominating presidential candidates, are in essence speeches of tribute. Our candidate is qualified. He can win. This is the framework of ideas.

Inaugural and acceptance speeches by those assuming high political office take on the *form of persuasion,* with ethical, logical, and emotional appeal. Among the greatest of presidential inaugural addresses may be listed Lincoln's First and Second Inaugural; Franklin D. Roosevelt's First Inaugural, and the First Inaugural of Woodrow Wilson.

HOW TO INCREASE VIVIDNESS

Vividness in the development and statement of ideas and details is especially important in the commemorative speech, in order that it may impress hearers with the significance or subject of the occasion. It is in this sort of talk that the elevated and polished style is most useful. We have suggested, therefore, a use of varied Speech Details, and the use of the extended example or comparison, with description or narration. We might add that a reasonable use of activation, explained in the previous chapter, is involved, especially in arousing emotional reactions on the part of the hearers.

We now present additional techniques for vividness, including *imagery, figures of speech, figures of thought,* and *rhythm.* The commemorative speech on an occasion of consequence may well make use of all of these. They are also valuable in persuasive speaking, and in some informative talks.

Imagery. Imagery may be defined as the art of "picturizing ideas," that is, the use of words which have a vivid, pictorial quality, and the use of more or less extended passages of narration and description.

Professor V. A. Ketcham has aptly termed the seven principal kinds of imagery "the seven doors to the mind." He points out that to be highly effective, a speaker should use all of these "doors," for some persons are "eye-minded," while others are "ear-minded," and others respond to other types of references to sense experience.[1]

The following will briefly define and illustrate the seven types of imagery:

1. *Visual*—things seen. The dazzling glare of lights on Broadway; the red, white, and blue of Old Glory; the cigar-shaped dirigible.
2. *Auditory*—things heard. The hiss of steam; the roar of the cannon; the shriek of a woman; the rumbling of trains.
3. *Motor*—muscular sensations. We pushed, shoved, twisted our way through the crowd; we swayed in the rhythm of the dance.
4. *Tactile*—things felt. The smoothness of silk; the roughness of tweed; the dryness of chalk; the stabbing pain of the knife wound; a fly crawling over your face.
5. *Gustatory*—things tasted. The sweetness of candy; the tang of lemon; the bitterness of quinine.
6. *Olfactory*—things smelled. The odor of ether; the aroma of a cigar; the stench of rotting flesh; the perfume of violets.
7. *Thermic*—perception of heat and cold. The chill of steel; the warmth of the hearth fire; the biting north wind.

Although each of the above classes of imagery refers to some sense experience, it will be noted that visual imagery seems to be the predominant form. This is confirmed by research. Most of us are mainly "eye-minded," which means that the speaker can best reach his audience by visual imagery. However, the other forms have their special appeal.

The following excerpt from Webster's "White Murder

[1] V. A. Ketcham, "Seven Doors to the Mind," in Sandford and Yeager, *Business Speeches by Business Men* (McGraw-Hill Book Co., Inc., 1930), pp. 405–17.

Case Speech" uses practically every form of imagery to make the circumstances of the crime vivid to the jury:

Gentlemen, it is a most extraordinary case. In some respects it has hardly a precedent anywhere; certainly none in our New England history. This bloody drama exhibited no suddenly excited, ungovernable rage. The actors in it were not surprised by any lion-like temptation springing upon their virtue, and overcoming it, before resistance could begin. Nor did they do the deed to glut savage vengeance, or satiate long-settled and deadly hate. It was a cool, calculating, money-making murder. It was all "hire and salary, not revenge." It was the weighing of money against life; the counting out of so many pieces of silver against so many ounces of blood.

An aged man, without an enemy in the world, in his own house, and in his own bed, is made the victim of a butcherly murder for mere pay. Truly, here is a new lesson for painters and poets. Whosoever shall hereafter draw the portrait of murder, if he will show it as it has been exhibited where such example was last to have been looked for—in the very bosom of our New England society—let him not give it the grim visage of Moloch, the brow knitted by revenge, the face black with settled hate, and the bloodshot eye emitting livid fires of malice. Let him draw, rather, a decorous, smooth-faced, bloodless demon; a picture in repose, rather than in action; not so much an example of human nature in its depravity, and in its paroxysms of crime, as an infernal being, a fiend, in the ordinary display and development of his character.

The deed was executed with a degree of self-possession and steadiness equal to the wickedness with which it was planned. The circumstances now clearly in evidence spread out the whole scene before us. Deep sleep had fallen on the destined victim, and on all beneath his roof. A healthful old man, to whom sleep was sweet, the first sound slumbers of the night held him in their soft but strong embrace. The assassin enters, through the window already prepared, into an unoccupied apartment. With noiseless foot he paces the lonely hall, half lighted by the moon. He winds up the ascent of the stairs, and reaches the door of the chamber. Of this he moves the lock, by soft and continued pressure, till it turns on its hinges without noise, and he enters, and beholds his victim before him. The room is uncommonly open to the admission of light. The face of the innocent sleeper is turned from the murderer, and the beams of the moon, resting on the gray locks of his aged temple, show him where to strike. The fatal blow is given, and the victim passes, without a struggle or a motion, from the repose of sleep to the repose of death! It is the assassin's purpose to make sure work; and he plies the dagger, though it is obvious that life has been destroyed by the blow of the bludgeon. He even raises the aged arm, that he may not fail in his aim at the heart, and replaces it again over the wounds of the poniard! To finish the picture, he explores the wrist for the pulse! He feels for it, and ascertains that it beats no longer! It is accomplished. The deed is done. He retreats, retraces his steps to the window, passes out through it as he came in, and escapes. He has done the murder.

Other examples of the use of imagery may be found in the complete speeches published in this book. Roosevelt, Grady, and others, both through their choice of words and through narration and description, achieve it.

How to Use Imagery. As indicated above, imagery depends upon appeal to the sense experiences of the hearer, with the visual sense predominating. Therefore, the first step in using it is to choose words which have a pictorial quality: nouns which refer to individuals rather than to general classes of things; adjectives which are vigorous and colorful; verbs which involve motor and tactile sensations.

Consider this sentence by John Bright, famous English orator of the Victorian period:

"This *fair island* became a battlefield; a kingdom was *convulsed;* and an ancient throne *was overturned.*" [Italics ours.]

All the visual and motor imagery could be removed from this sentence by re-phrasing it as follows:

"There was a civil war; the whole nation was involved; the reigning dynasty was deposed."

Second, use ample description and narration. The "White Murder Speech" passage quoted above is an example of this.

Third, use *comparisons.* Great value lies in comparing the

subject at hand to something which the hearer has experienced. Obviously this value depends upon the picture which the comparison creates in the mind of the hearer.

Figures of speech.[2] A review of these follows naturally from a discussion of imagery. We have seen that any use of *comparison* tends to produce vivid images in the mind of the hearer. Figures of speech are based largely upon the principle of comparison. They are not necessarily mere ornaments; on the contrary they contribute importantly to vividness of meaning. Among the major figures of speech are the following:

1. *Metaphor: an implied comparison. Examples:*
   "She (America) was indeed the fountain of our wealth, the nerve of our strength, the nursery and basis of our naval power."—William Pitt.
   "A house divided against itself cannot stand. This nation cannot exist half slave and half free."—Lincoln.
   "International gangsters"—Franklin D. Roosevelt.

2. *Simile:* an expressed comparison. *Examples:*
   The advance of Bolshevism in Russia was like a tidal wave.
   "Like an armed warrior, like a plumed knight, James G. Blaine marched down the halls of the American Congress." —Ingersoll.

3. *Symbolism:* The part standing for the whole, or the whole for the part, or a symbol or characteristic standing for the whole idea.
   "Is life so dear, or peace so sweet, as to be purchased at the price of chains and slavery?"—Patrick Henry.
   The Stars and Stripes waved over Germany.
   Illinois met Michigan on the gridiron.
   "We have caught the sunshine in the bricks and mortar of our homes."—Grady.

4. *Personification:* attribution of human qualities to abstract or inanimate objects.

[2] We use "figures of speech" to apply to figures of a metaphorical type. Ancient rhetoricians called these figures "tropes." The term "figures of speech" was applied by them to stylistic devices affecting phrase and sentence structure. We use "figures of thought" in the classical sense, to cover unusual methods of expressing ideas, such as ironic denial.

"Avarice paints Destiny with a dollar mark; Militarism equips it with a sword."—Bryan.

Panic held our people in the palm of her hand.

5. *Apostrophe:* direct address to persons absent or dead; or to abstract or inanimate things.

O Justice, what crimes are committed in thy name!

Immortal Washington, give us guidance today.

6. *Imaginary speech:* Persons absent or dead, or inanimate or abstract things, are represented as speaking.

And his immortal spirit still whispers from the heavens, "Mortals! Hastening to the tomb, and once the companions of my pilgrimage, take warning and avoid my errors; cultivate the virtues I have recommended."—Eliphalet Nott.

7. *Sound-sense (onomatopoeia):* The rendering of meaning by sound, as in hiss, moo, crackle, rumble, thunder, shriek, twitter, roar, etc.

Figures of thought. The speaker's style may be enhanced further in its attention-getting qualities by the use of *figures of thought*, which may be defined as unusual ways of expressing ideas. Some of them rest upon double meaning, or "reverse English," others upon the conscious use of exaggeration or diminution for rhetorical effect.

Some of the more important figures of thought are as follows:

1. *Simple irony:* stating the reverse of the real meaning.

This is a *fine* class (meaning that it isn't).

We have certainly arrived at a *happy* state of affairs.

2. *Ironic denial:* affirming that which you pretend to deny.

I shall not speak of his many services to the state; I shall not remind you of his generosity; of his heroism in war; or his public-spirited attitude in community affairs.

3. *Ironic hesitation:* pretending to be in doubt, or to hesitate to make a statement:

I hardly know whether this campaign can be called a success; I hesitate to conclude from results already at hand that we have not failed; but I *do* know . . . .

4. *Ironic correction:* Purposive mistatement and subsequent correction for greater emphasis.

   Did I say this would be an easy task? I was wrong. It is full of difficulties. It will require the best that we have to give.

5. *Understatement:* Ultra-conservative language, deliberately chosen to give emphasis.

   I do not claim we have solved this problem. But we have done a few things which contribute toward its solution. These accomplishments may be worth considering . . . .

6. *Overstatement:* Exaggeration for emphatic effect.

   This is the gravest situation with which our company has ever been confronted. We may face bankruptcy. We have only a slim chance to survive.

7. *Rhetorical question:* A question which suggests its own answer.

   Is there anyone here who does not want to win this war? Is not the promise of immortality the supreme gift of the Christian religion?

8. *Anticipating objections:* Stating and refuting real or imaginary objections.

   Now, we may be told that this will cost too much. But . . . It may be objected that democracy is too slow. On the other hand . . . .

Rhythm. This is the principle of metrical regularity in the structure of phrases and sentences. It involves a more or less regular pattern of stressed and unstressed syllables, just as in poetry. The rhythm of spoken prose is less marked than that of poetry, but it is present to some degree in most speeches. It has an important emotional effect.

Just as we enjoy the rhythms of poetry, of dancing, of music, and in fact of all arts, so we are pleasantly affected by the rhythm of speech. This pleasure seems to be quite distinct from the sense or meaning of the words. The orator carries us with him by the rhythmical flow of his phrases and sentences.

Robert G. Ingersoll was one American orator who made great use of rhythm, achieving what has often been referred to as a blank-verse style. The following from his "Speech at his Brother's Grave" illustrates this:

My Friends: I am going to do that which the dead often promised he would do for me. The loved and loving brother, husband, father, friend died where manhood's morning almost touches noon, and while the shadows still were falling toward the west. He had not passed on life's highway the stone that marks the highest point, but being weary for the moment he laid down by the wayside, and using a burden for a pillow, fell into that dreamless sleep that kisses down his eyelids still. While yet in love with life and raptured with the world, he passed to silence and pathetic dust.

In contrast to Ingersoll's slow-moving stately speech is that of Henry W. Grady, which often follows an anapestic pattern, as reference to his speech "The New South" will show. "Let me picture for you the footsore Confederate soldier," is one line which shows his characteristic "swing."

Coming closer to our own time, Albert J. Beveridge and William Jennings Bryan were masters of rhythm. Beveridge was greatly under Ingersoll's influence in matters of style, as perusal of his "March of the Flag," "Opening Speech of the Republican Campaign of 1916," and his "Keynote Speech at the Progressive Convention" will reveal. The conclusion of the last-named speech includes the following passages:

And so, never doubt that a braver, fairer, cleaner America surely will come; that a better and brighter life for all beneath the flag surely will be achieved. Those who now scoff will pray. Those who now doubt soon will believe.

Soon the night will pass; and when, to the Sentinel on the ramparts of Liberty the anxious ask, "Watchman, what of the night?" his answer will be, "Lo, the morn appeareth."

Knowing the price we must pay, the sacrifices we must make, the burdens we must carry, the assaults we must endure—knowing full well the cost—yet we enlist, and we enlist for the war. For we know the justice of our cause, and we know, too, its certain triumph.[3]

[3] G. H. Payne, *Birth of the New Party,* 1912.

Bryan's characteristic rhythm is shown in the well-known passage on immortality from his lecture, *"The Prince of Peace"*:

Christ gave us proof of immortality and it was a welcome assurance, although it would hardly seem necessary that one should rise from the dead to convince us that the grave is not the end. To every created thing God has given a tongue that proclaims a future life.

If the Father deigns to touch with divine power the cold and pulseless heart of the buried acorn and to make it burst forth from its prison walls, will He leave neglected in the earth the soul of man, made in the image of his Creator? If He stoops to give to the rosebush, whose withered blossoms float upon the autumn breeze, the sweet assurance of another springtime, will He refuse the words of hope to the sons of men when the frosts of winter come? If matter, mute and inanimate, though changed by the forces of nature into a multitude of forms, can never die, will the imperial spirit of man suffer annihilation when it has paid a brief visit like a royal guest to this tenement of clay? . . . I am as sure that we live again as I am sure that we live today.[4]

The reading of such excerpts should not mislead the student into believing that orators talk always in such a rhythmical fashion. Usually their cadence is much less marked; but in passages of emotional appeal and climactic emphasis they tend to fall into measured utterance. Rhythm carried out to such a degree through a whole speech would be too artificial for best effect, although in some of Ingersoll's addresses the persistence of metrical pattern seems not to have been harmful.

Rhythmical phrase and sentence structure. It is desirable here to consider some special types of phrase and sentence structure which help produce rhythm.

PARALLELISM. Parallel construction, in which successive phrases are composed in the same form, and which may extend through several sentences or paragraphs, is an important

---

[4] William Jennings Bryan, in R. K. Immel, *Delivery of a Speech*, pp. 187–88. Wahr, 1916.

aid to rhythm. The second paragraph of Bryan's speech, quoted above, illustrates this.

BALANCE AND ANTITHESIS. Sometimes two phrases of similar pattern are set in opposition, so that the one seems to balance the other. Often, these two phrases are antithetical, that is, opposite in meaning. "Man proposes; God disposes," is a brief example of balance and antithesis. The last sentence of the Ingersoll quotation given above is composed of balanced and antithetical phrases. The following quotation from Edmund Burke's "Speech on Conciliation" employs such phrases:

Compare the two. This I offer to give you is plain and simple. The other, full of perplexed and intricate mazes. This is mild; that harsh. This is found by experience effectual for its purpose. This is universal; the other, calculated for certain colonies only. This is immediate in its conciliatory operation; the other remote, contingent, full of hazard.

PERIODIC SENTENCES. The most completely rhythmical sentence pattern is the periodic, in which several phrases, usually all of parallel structure, present a thought, the full meaning of which is not revealed until the final phrase. Thus not only is rhythm accentuated, but suspense is maintained until the climactic or *denouement* phrase at the end completes the meaning. The third paragraph of the Beveridge quotation given above opens with a periodic sentence. Another example is this one from William Pitt:

Since not even severe experience can make them feel, nor the imminent ruin of their country awaken them from their stupefaction, the guardian power of Parliament must intervene.

WORD POINTING. Often, in connection with balance, antithesis, and parallelism of phrases, the choice of words is such as to emphasize, or to "point" rather definitely the beginnings or endings of phrases. Such devices are also used by themselves to make language more striking.

Sometimes several phrases begin with the same word. This is called *anaphora*. Bryan uses this device in his passage on immortality, when he begins several sentences with the word "if."

Again, the phrases, or indeed, words within the phrase, may begin with the same *sound*. This is called *alliteration*. Many English-speaking orators have been fond of this figure. For instance, Pitt says, "I rise, my lords, to declare my sentiments on this most solemn and serious subject."

VARIETY IN RHYTHM. It should be remembered that the rhythm of speech should not be too constant, nor should marked rhythm ordinarily be used throughout a whole speech. Methods of breaking the monotony of cadence are numerous. One may vary the length of his sentences and phrases. Short, driving phrases will furnish contrast with long, rounded ones. Changes in the structure of sentences, through the use of the loose, the periodic, and the inverted order, and through the use of different modes, such as the declarative, the interrogative, the imperative, and the exclamatory, are desirable for this purpose.

SUMMARY ON CEREMONIAL SPEECHES

Occasions for ceremonial speeches (often called speeches of formal occasion, and in some cases speeches of courtesy) are more numerous than most people realize. Dedications, academic occasions, national or other holidays, meetings of tribute, and the like literally fill our calendar. Less formal occasions, too, often call for ceremonial, rather than persuasive talks.

We have examined the nature of ceremonial occasions, and have emphasized that *appropriateness* is a desirable characteristic in speeches at such events. The intellectual or emotional tone of the occasion should be matched by those of the address.

Again, we have pointed out that most ceremonial speeches are, in their nature, of the informative-impressive variety, stressing the existence of known qualities, characteristics, achievements or other significances of the occasion or subject.

Ordinarily, we have pointed out, a more elevated style in ideas and language is called for than in everyday speaking.

Special techniques. Techniques which make for vividness have been surveyed: imagery, figures of speech and thought, and rhythm. These, it has been emphasized, are useful in both informative and persuasive speaking, as well as finding appropriate use in the speech of formal occasion.

In Chapters 7 and 8 we have developed techniques which also are generally useful: narration, description, extended examples and comparisions, and activation. The speaker should master these, in addition to those described in this chapter, if he wishes to be more than "just another speaker."

10

Entertainment: Purpose or Means to An End

*All things are big with jest; nothing that's plain
But may be witty, if thou hast the vein.*

GEORGE HERBERT

Wit and humor, properly managed, can be important
assets to any speaker. We have mentioned in the chapter on
the persuasive speech, the use of humor to get audience-
responses. Informative, as well as persuasive talks, profit similarly from its use. It serves to create a joint reaction which is
essentially emotional; it relaxes hearers; it makes them more
willing to hear what the speaker has to say, and more dis-
posed to react favorably to his serious logical and emotional
appeals: *all this provided that the amount and kind of humor
does not overbalance other means of persuasion, and does
not, by inappropriate subject-matter, antagonize the audience.*

A speaker who "hauls in" alleged funny stories that do not
relate to his subject, or the one who descends to vulgarity,
does little to enhance his over-all persuasiveness. One who
directs many speakers who have a serious purpose warned
about inappropriate or vulgar material by saying, "They may
laugh at such stuff, but at the same time you go down in their

estimation. Avoid it." Humor is a tool to be used with judgment. Thus used, it helps win audiences, no matter what type of speech is under consideration.

Entertainment as an end. There is a very definite place in modern society, also, for the speech designed primarily to entertain. Dinner meetings often include such talks as program features, and there are numerous other occasions in which entertainment *per se* is the end sought. So comparatively rare are really good after-dinner *speakers* that committees frequently hire professional entertainers whose presentations may consist solely of string-of-beads series of humorous stories and topical "wisecracks" bearing little relation to the audience or the occasion. The better entertainers, of course, have the good judgment to connect their scripts in some way with the special nature of the organization addressed.

However, it is possible for the average speaker to design and present a truly entertaining *speech* on a topic reasonably relevant to occasion and audience. And it should be a *speech*, not a collection of unrelated jokes. It should have *speech structure:* Specific Purpose, Principal Ideas, Details. It is in the phrasing and development of these that the speaker finds the opportunity for appropriate humor.

CHOOSING THE SUBJECT

"All things are big with jest," sings George Herbert. There is virtually no topic that cannot be treated in a witty or humorous fashion. It is discovering in a topic *the available means of entertainment,* just as in other types of talks one looks for available means of giving information, impressing, convincing, or arousing action, that the speaker's inventiveness is challenged.

All things are "big with jest." Thus one pitfall to avoid in choosing a topic is to look for one that is inherently funny. The thing to do is to find a subject that, however treated, would be appropriate to the specific audience and occasion.

Thus Chauncey M. Depew, famous lawyer-statesman-raconteur of another day, was to address a meeting of the Lotos Club, honoring outgoing and incoming mayors of New York, and other successful and unsuccessful candidates. He picked the topic, "Honors to the Mayor." This topic might have been developed as a serious tribute to the outgoing mayor or as an inspirational address to his successor, or as an impressive-informative discussion of the nature and responsibilities of the office. Actually, it was developed with high humor. We reprint it later in this book.

The distinguished lawyer, Frederic R. Coudert, speaking at a lawyers' meeting, chose the subject, "Our Clients." Booth Tarkington chose the nostalgic topic, "Where We Come From," for a meeting of the Indiana Society of Chicago, but it turned out to be anything but a nostalgic address. It is reprinted in a later section of this book. "A Husband's Gifts to His Wife," "Landladies," and other entertaining speeches included in this text, did not depend on an inherently *amusing nature* of the topic. Rather they were topics appropriate to a specific audience, and capable of being *made* entertaining.

Topic suited to audience. The topic *must* be one, the humorous development of which rests upon the audience's knowledge and experience. One reason why many highly successful after-dinner speeches do not, when read later, seem to be especially entertaining, is that the reader doesn't understand the allusions to audience experience and to what were at the time of delivery, current events, fads, or styles. Mark Twain's masterful speech, to a meeting of Civil War veterans a few years after the termination of that conflict was entitled "The Babies." It gave a pseudo-military discussion of the invasion and taking over of household command by a newly-arrived infant. Both the military experience and the advent of infants were at the time familiar to his audience; thus the humor. It can be appreciated now mainly by those who in twentieth century conflicts have gained the background that permits amusement.

A Speech Activities banquet, such as is held at many

schools, furnishes a good after-dinner speaker with many topics that would be appropriate because they are familiar to the audience. Similar organizational dinners give other subjects that have the necessary familiarity. Here are some sample topics that could be developed humorously at a speech banquet:

Impression and Expression in Education

The Value of Gestures

What I Learned in Dramatics

The Speaker's Personality

Speech Education for Speech Teachers

I Was a Refugee From Speech Correction

How I will Use Debating in Later Life

The Last Rebuttal

The Use of the Eyes in Speaking

How to Use Speech in Business Life

How to Read Poetry

Activation in Everyday Life

Your Broadway Accent

How to Flub a Broadcast Announcement

BUILDING THE SPEECH

Specific purpose. The skillful selection of a Specific Purpose is important, for in determining the "angle" from which he will develop his topic, the speaker sets guidelines that will determine his Principal Ideas and their supporting Speech Details. The task is, in principle, like the selection of a purpose for the informative-impressive talk, that is to determine the attribute, trait, or characteristic of the subject which is to be emphasized.

Here are a few examples:

1. To entertain the audience by a "military" discussion of babies.
2. To amuse the hearers by a mock-serious discussion of the duties and qualities of a mayor of New York.
3. To entertain by showing how "tough" debate tactics might lead to disaster in personal life.
4. To show humorously what might happen if all of our persuasive-action pleas were to be acted upon.
5. To amuse by outlining some of the consequences of being named Smith.

6. To create enjoyment by advocating that we lawyers treat our clients with the *disrespect* they "deserve."
7. To entertain by an exaggerated discussion of the financial dilemma of "the willing giver" to our numerous "drives."

The principal ideas. It will be noted that in the Specific Purposes listed above, there is, as in the informative-impressive type of speech, a "key word" or phrase which indicates what characteristic of the subject is to be emphasized. This clearly maps the development of the topic both as to Principal Ideas and Speech Details. All must support the point embodied in the "key word." Tough debate tactics-disaster, clients-deserved disrespect, "willing giver-financial dilemmas," etc., govern the selection of ideas. How, or what, debate tactics could be disastrous; in what way clients "deserve disrespect"; and so on, will emerge as Principal Ideas, and the illustrative material of examples, statistics, comparison, testimony, and reiteration will support such ideas.

In short, ideas and details develop, emphasize, and support the point brought out in the Specific Purpose. An entertaining speech so constructed thus has a bit of logic in its structure, and it is a *speech*, not a monologue nor a series of allegedly humorous stories or remarks.

Time spent, then, in selecting for the Specific Purpose the exact combination of characteristics or attributes of the subject that will furnish amusement, is invaluable. From there on, the ideas and details almost automatically come to mind as supporting material. Everything previously said about vividness of details, such as extended comparisons and examples, description and narration, activation, and figures of speech and thought, applies in this sort of talk.

SOME PRINCIPLES OF HUMOR

Incongruity. Incongruity may be defined as the *familiar*, presented in an *unusual way*, or as an unfamiliar combination of two familiar things. It is one of the chief sources of amusement. The fundamental humor of Twain's *The Babies* arose neither from the Civil War nor from infants, but from the combination of these two familiar things: the military command of the household being taken over by the child. In *A Connecticut Yankee in King Arthur's Court*, the essential humor was in the presence in a medieval setting of a modern American. When the late Will Rogers played the leading part in the moving picture based on that book, he awakened from a dream to find a knight in medieval armor above him, and asked, "What dost thou wish?" Later, midget automobiles took to the battlefield against the knights and yeomen of another day: result, amusement.

In a famous after-dinner speech before the New England Society of New York, Joseph H. Choate, renowned lawyer and speaker, talking on the theme, *The Pilgrim Mothers,* combined well known historical facts about the pioneer settlements with familiar domestic scenes that applied to the time of the speech. The wife-and-husband arguments, placed in the Puritan environment, made the speech amusing. The young employee, a former college debate star, using debating phraseology in replying to a criticism by his boss, illustrates the incongruity of two well known settings or situations, and the inevitable result, involuntary unemployment, follows entertainingly. "I proved my point beyond any possibility of contradiction, but he just didn't give me his vote," a speaker on this topic concluded.

Stories and incongruity. The humorous story rests in part, or altogether, on the principle of incongruity. Take a good one apart, and you will find that its components are the common and well known things of everyday experience. It is the way in which they are put together—the originality, novelty, freshness, and unusualness of treatment—that produces amusement. For instance, here is a story based on the theme of "cooperation": a prominent man whose wife was unusually shrewish received an anonymous letter, saying, "Place ten thousand dollars under the great rock by the seventh hole on the golf course, or we will kidnap your wife." The distinguished citizen replied, "Dear Sir: I do not have ten thousand dollars. However, beg to advise that in regard to the suggestion made in the latter part of your letter, I am interested and willing to cooperate." The familiar-unusual combination here is obvious.

Many entertaining speeches are carried in such collections as *Modern Eloquence*. A study of them will reveal how often the technique of incongruity underlies their development.

Other approaches to humor. Exaggeration produces laughter, and if carried to the extreme of being ludicrous, is the basis of slapstick humor. The exaggeration may be in subject-matter, or in the language employed. At the dinner of the National Press Association in Washington, Paul V. McNutt of Indiana named numerous natives of that state who had gained prominence in journalism, and then concluded that all great journalists came from Indiana and that inevitably an Indianian should be president of the club! The Speech instructor who insisted upon clear enunciation was once a victim of an after-dinner speaker who exaggerated this point so that he was portrayed as speaking "with machine-gun explosions of ev-er-y syl-la-ble." And it was amusing.

Inflated or overly-ornate language is a source of amusement, when applied to inappropriate subjects or used by speakers who would not properly employ it. A cartoon of long ago in the *Chicago Inter-Ocean* illustrates the latter point:

Percy and Mickey are standing at the top of a snow-covered hill. Percy is, appropriately, dressed in velvet and has long curls. Mickey is in patched and ragged hand-me-downs. The following dialogue ensues:

Mickey: Wanna slide downhill on my sled, Poicy?
Percy: Why, I can hardly perceive how the brief exhilaration of the precipitous descent can compensate for the indubitably arduous labor of attaining the exalted altitude requisite for the successful inception of each consecutive flight!

"Professorial" language, and the technical jargon of various professions, of the military, and of government bureaus, because of the overuse of "big words" or technical terms, are often productive of amusement. The *New Yorker* frequently prints examples of overly-technical or ornate writing and speaking.

THE SURPRISE ENDING. Some time ago, a southern editor read an article by one of the present authors, in which it was stated that if the words uttered in Congress in a single session were printed in one line on a narrow strip of paper, they would reach from Washington to New York, and seven miles beyond. "Yes," commented the editor, "seven miles beyond, into the Atlantic Ocean, where we hope they will drown." This unexpected ending had its elements of humor.

Chauncey Depew's remark about the qualifications of a mayor used the same principle: "It is expected by every good citizen in this metropolis that its Mayor shall have the fluency of Henry Clay, the solidity of Daniel Webster, the firmness of Andrew Jackson, and the digestion of an ostrich."

Grady's *New South* includes the story of the man who, bidden to take a pitcher of milk to the basement, slipped on the stairway and fell, "with such casual interruptions as the stairs afforded, into the basement," and then heard his wife call out, "John, did you break the pitcher?" "No," said John, "but I'll be dinged if I don't."

FEELING OF SUPERIORITY. Another source of amusement is utilized when the audience, because it is "in the know" while characters in the story are not, feels superiority of status. Again a story from the *New South* involves this situation. Mischievous boys glued together adjoining pages of the minister's Bible. So when he read the lesson from Scripture, he read: "When Noah was 120 years old, he took unto himself a wife, who was . . ." (and then he turned the page) "140 cubits long, 40 cubits wide, built of gopher wood and covered with pitch inside and out."

The minor misfortunes of dignified people, such as a man chasing his hat, or a haughty matron being given a ticket for overtime parking, cause amusement through the same sense of superiority on the part of those observing or being told about them.

JOKES ON ONE'S SELF. Stories or comments which place the speaker himself in the position of the "victim" are often enjoyed by audiences. The radio and television comedian, Jack Benny, routinely and expertly uses these to get laughs. President Kennedy employed this technique in his May, 1962 speech in New York on the medical care proposal, when he said that his father, then recuperating in a hospital, was able to pay his bills, but that if he were not, "they would fall on me." "And," continued the President, "he's much better off than I am."

Father Paul C. Reinert, president of Saint Louis University, used a similar method, that of a joke involving the racial, religious, economic, or social group to which the speaker belongs. He told this story to an audience composed of people of various religious affiliations: A young Catholic priest at his ordination received many gifts, including to his consternation a set of fine towels marked "His" and "Hers." He consulted the priest to whose parish he had been assigned asking what to do with such a present. "Well, son," replied the older priest, "I suggest that you wrap them up securely and store them away—you never can tell what Pope John will do next!" Father Reinert had prefaced the story by remarking that doubtless his hearers knew that the new Pope was making many changes in the Church. The audience response demonstrated the entertaining value of the jest involving one's self or one's group.

R. Sargent Shriver, director of the Peace Corps, and President Kennedy's brother-in-law, used the following story on himself in a commencement address June 2, 1962: Mr. Shriver was urging his son, aged eight, to study harder. He pointed out that Lincoln studied very faithfully as a boy, walked miles to school, and read textbooks by firelight. "Look what Lincoln was at your age," he said, "and look at you." The boy flashed back, "What about you? When Uncle Jack was your age, he was President of the United States!"

JOKES ON OTHERS. Good-humored poking fun at others present is an unfailing source of amusement. This funmaking must, of course, be done with tact: it must not go so far as to be offensive. Generally, it should not refer to racial, religious or other sensitive subjects, nor to any illness or deformity of the person involved, nor to any personal troubles that he may have had. Strickland Gillilan, the famous humorous lecturer, in his *Address at the Rivers and Harbors Convention*, noted that Herbert Hoover, then Secretary of Commerce, had left the meeting. He said, "I know he is somewhere just eating his heart out because he can't hear just one more speech." Mr. Hoover's dislike of long programs—and this had been a very long one—and his probable lack of enthusiasm for listening to speeches, were thus referred to lightly and pleasantly, and in no way offensively. Stan Musial ("The Man"), famous St. Louis Cardinal baseball player, is often teased a bit by speakers or toastmasters who refer to his large salary and successful business enterprises. In a public speaking class, a student who had made speeches indicating his adherence to the conservative movement was referred to as having made "a liberal and forward-looking speech for medical care for the aged," when of course he had argued against this measure. The light touch employed by his fellow-student produced humor without giving offense.

ALLUSIONS TO CURRENT EVENTS. Humor is in part dependent upon "what is going on in the world." The ability to see what is incongruous or ludicrous in current events, and to allude to them humorously, is exemplified by those who write for such a professional humorist as Bob Hope, and for others. This also is a reason why, unless one understands *what was current at the time a speech was given*, it is hard to discern the humor involved. In Russell Conwell's *Acres of Diamonds*, for instance, Al Hafed, the Persian farmer, becomes excited about diamonds, and determines to go looking for them. Conwell observes, "He began his search, very appropriately to my mind, at the Mountains of the Moon." The writer has never known students of the 1960's to laugh at this remark, yet it was a "blockbuster" in the late nineteenth and early twentieth centuries. The "Mountains of the Moon" was associated with a never-never land, where only the extremely foolish would think of going. Today, it's just an area on the map of Africa.

THE MOCK-SERIOUS SPEECH. Two famous entertaining speeches in American history are those of James Proctor Knott on Duluth, and of "Private" John Allen on "A Fish Hatchery for Tupelo." They are examples of mock-persuasion, and in each case the speaker used ornate language and exaggerated ideas and emotional appeals to achieve a slapstick type of humor, "glorifying" the two communities for the amusement of the hearers.

The technique of burlesquing an informative or persuasive speech, if well used, can, as these famous examples indicate, produce great entertainment. Some of the topics suggested for a Speech Activities banquet could be so treated.

Conditioning the audience. It has been pointed out by many writers that an audience should be properly conditioned for an entertaining talk. The toastmaster has a responsibility in this respect. His general conduct of the meeting, if marked by geniality and by *some* humorous comments, can set the proper mood. His introduction of the speaker, tactfully humorous in tone, can assist. On the other hand, the toastmaster who wears out the hearers by lengthy discussions, and by relating endless "funny stories" of his own, or who introduces criticism or argument into his remarks, is doing what he can to discourage responsiveness.

SUMMARY ON ENTERTAINMENT

Every speaker can profit by developing some techniques of entertainment, even though he may not be called upon for after-dinner speaking. If he values his standing with his fellow-men, he will avoid the suggestive, the vulgar, and the overly-critical or embarrassing. This warning seems especially necessary in a time when apparently there is a premium on the distasteful and even on the obscene.

When entertainment is the main purpose, the mood and

attitude of the speaker should involve the informality, geniality and lighter touch that make for a happy talk. Beyond stressing the basic nature of humor, which lies in incongruity, and the specific suggestions made about humorous exaggeration, the surprise ending, the joke on one's self or one's group, and tactful raillery of those present, there is little that need be said. Much depends upon the inventiveness and originality of the speaker. But that an entertaining talk should have a recognizable *speech structure*, with well-defined purpose and ideas, is important. A speech without these is just a conglomeration of remarks.

May we add, brevity is sometimes an aid to entertainment, and it is never inappropriate. Don't wear out your hearers. They came to be amused—remember?

11

The Speaker's Responsibility for
Good Subject-Matter

The orator is a good man, skilled in speaking.

CATO

*The art of eloquence is something greater, and collected
from more sciences and studies than people imagine . . . a
knowledge of a vast number of things is necessary.*

CICERO, *De Oratore*

T HERE is an obligation upon every speaker to tell the truth
as he sees it, and to be well-informed on the subjects upon
which he speaks. This is true, not only on the basis of ethics
or morality, but for the very practical reason that audiences
and critics evaluate *what is said* as well as *how it is said.* Although your training in effective oral communication stresses
principles of clarity, interestingness, persuasion, and the like,
and the methods of presenting ideas orally with maximum
effect, it must not be forgotten that *content, the ideas and
facts contained, must be valid.* We expect a lawyer to be
thoroughly grounded in the general and specific legal principles involved in a case; a political candidate to understand
governmental problems; a lecturer on economics to have a
deep knowledge of his subject. We expect a salesman to know
his product, and a solicitor for a charity to know the facts

about the organization he represents. We expect a teacher to know his field in depth.

In real life, one seldom appears merely as a speaker: he appears as a lawyer, minister, candidate, economist, sociologist, businessman, labor leader, or other. He has been asked to speak primarily because it is assumed that *he has something worthwhile to say.* If, then, he reveals scanty knowledge, or a poor choice of topic, or inaccuracy in factual matters, he is automatically discredited.

"An orator is a good man, skilled in speaking," is the historic saying of Cato. And by that phrase is meant not only a man whose character and reputation are good, but who knows what he is talking about: he is an honest, *well-informed* man. The *combination of knowledge with skill in oral presentation* is what makes an effective speaker.

The student's responsibility. The speaker has, then, a responsibility in regard to the *content of his speech:* what he talks about, and the knowledge that enables him to talk about it with some authority. Although complete mastery of one's subject-matter comes only with longer experience and training than most students have had, the time to begin working toward the goal is now. According to the suggestions in Part Four, the earliest speeches can be based entirely on the personal experience or observation of the student. The object is to get used to speaking. As the course progresses, the need of valid subject-matter, gained from reading, investigation, and personal research, increases.

One should, first, select subjects that are worth talking about to a class of serious students. Second, he should increasingly see to it that his subject-matter is sound and valid. He should at all times, from the very beginning, avoid trivial and frivolous topics. He should respect good subject-matter. He should *learn by doing* how to use library and other facilities for this purpose.

In this chapter, we shall discuss briefly the selection of subjects for classroom speeches, and set forth in summary form suggestions for gathering adequate material for them.

SPEECH SUBJECTS

Subjects must be, or become, interesting to the speaker. He can hardly be effective unless he is initially, or through finding out about his topic, enthusiastically interested in it. We have stated the thought in this way because it is a well known fact that one must become acquainted with, and work on developing a topic before he is genuinely concerned about it, before he really believes it is important.

Naturally, a speaker considers his topic in relation to his prospective hearers. Can he interest them in it? If it's worth-while, and he is interested, he can.

Direct and indirect experience. One way of considering topics is in relation to the speaker's present knowledge of them: his direct and indirect experiences. Direct experiences are those with which he has been in personal contact, and of which he has been a part; experiences gained through seeing, hearing, feeling, tasting and smelling, and through working with them. Indirect experiences are those with which contact has been secondhand: acquired through reading, listening, and discussion with others.

If a student has worked in a factory making autos, he knows a great deal about the process. His experiences of a direct type are vivid to him. He may have interesting information right at hand about autos and how they are made, or about labor-management relations in auto plants. Worth-while direct contact, therefore, will suggest many subjects upon which one may talk, confident that what he has to say will be capable of being made interesting to others.

Indirect experience, however, concerns many things of importance. The materials presented in courses in English, history, economics, psychology, sociology, mathematics, etc. are in a sense indirect experiences, although if supplemented by laboratory or field work they tend to become direct. At any rate, they suggest speech topics of value. There are, too, many questions of the time—state, local, national, and inter-national—upon which there is discussion and debate, and a student must become familiar with their subject matter to get good training. One reason college and high school debating is held in esteem is that it encourages the acquisition of knowledge about current issues. The more one knows about them, the more he may become interested, and able to speak effectively on them. Thus both direct and indirect experiences furnish good speech topics.

Timeliness. Other things being equal, a timely topic is preferable. What can be made interesting to an audience at one time may not be capable of this at another period. If a city's water purification plant is working satisfactorily, a speech advocating a bond issue to get a new system would face difficulties; whereas if the community has been notified that its supply is polluted and the plant obsolete, it becomes almost automatically of interest. This is true on national or international levels, too.

One way that is almost mandatory if one wants to have good subjects for speeches is to keep in touch with events, through reading at least one daily newspaper (and not only the comics and sports!), one weekly newsmagazine such as *Time, Newsweek,* or *U.S. News & World Report,* listening regularly to radio or television newscasts and discussion programs, and by reading at least one professional or other specialized journal in the field of one's major interest. Part of your obligation as a future citizen and potential leader is to be currently informed! Cultivate the habit, and you will have no lack of topics for practice speeches. There is never any justification for the alibi, "I don't know anything to talk about." That's merely a confession of a poverty of ideas.

Your instructor can advise you about topics, and at some point in the course he may *assign* them. But ordinarily you will find, in direct or indirect knowledge, and in current topics under discussion, many valuable suggestions.

Intrinsic merit. One sure way to downgrade yourself with your instructor and *likewise with your classmates,* is to speak on frivolous or trivial topics, that hardly are worth talking about. The 300-pound football player who, when asked to make a speech of explanation, with an exhibit to assist the audience to understand, showed up on the platform and declared, "I am going to explain a bobby pin," was not only *laughed at* then by his hearers, but the basic silliness of this subject hampered him in future speeches (they *laughed at* him automatically). His attitude was one that revealed all too clearly what he thought he was supposed to do in college: play football. (P.S. He lasted one semester!) *And of course, Speech presented no problems to him!*

Self-respect, as well as the vast need of becoming proficient in expressing ideas to others, dictates that the trivial and the foolish have no place. It is your obligation to yourself to find *worthwhile topics:* something worth explaining, or discussing, or making the subject of persuasion. Don't underestimate either your classmates or your instructor. You do that when you "go off the reservation" with nonsensical topics.

Ask yourself, then, "Is this topic intrinsically worthwhile? Am I, or can I become interested in it? Can I make it interesting to my audience?"

Avoiding triteness. Some students complain that "speeches in my class are dull." Usually these are the very individuals who lack interest in subject matter, or who are generally ill-informed. They are the ones most likely to choose wornout, trite, dry-as-dust topics. Or perhaps, having chosen fairly good topics, they merely generalize about them: say the usual things in the usual way, failing to narrow down their Specific Purpose to one phase, or to a manageable segment of a broad topic. Thus speeches occur on the *general* subjects of *communism, democracy, safe driving, systematic study, learn to swim, enter extracurricular activities, obey traffic signals, quit smoking,* etc. Most of these have been "talked to death," in the form in which the topics are stated. None of them is a bad topic, provided the speaker has some specific phase of it to present, upon which he can interest the hearers. *Communism* is too broad a topic, for instance, but might be broken down to "the Soviet tactics about nuclear testing." *Safe driv-*

ing is so trite that it is utterly boring to most hearers, but "install seat belts" might attract interest. *Enter extracurricular activities* as a topic is too broad and general, but might be interesting if the speaker narrowed it down to "join the French club."

On old topics, present a specific, and if possible a new phase. Look for subjects that are important but out of the usual humdrum track. Remember that local, as well as national-international subjects, not only may have immediate interest, but may permit you to gain direct experience about them by interviews or visits to the scene, as for instance, in regard to the topic of community redevelopment.

A footnote of advice. Choose your topic early, give yourself time to select a good one, and time to prepare it thorougly. Last-minute decisions and frenzied eleventh-hour preparations almost certainly are roadblocks on the way to success in anything, and especially in the task of speaking.

Recent topics. To help somewhat with the task of selecting topics, a list of some of those used recently in beginning classes in Speech is as follows. All could be used for any type of talk:

Foreign aid	The space race
Cuba	July 4th
Agricultural price supports	Flag Day
Disarmament	Memorial Day
Nuclear testing	Washington
Unions	Lincoln
Installment buying	Jefferson
Education—all phases	Grant
Inflation	Pershing
Strikes	MacArthur
Athletic policy	Churchill
Science	Labor Day
Crime and criminals	Truman
FBI; other investigative groups	Eisenhower
Television	Kennedy
Radio	The Civil War
Social organizations	Building dedication

Louisiana Purchase
Wright brothers
Lindbergh
The Astronauts
Statehood days
Traffic
How to . . .
Taxes
Russia
How . . . are made
National defense
United Fund
Specific charitable organizations
Medical care
Nursing procedures
Cars
Insurance
Television
Advertising
Propaganda
Integrity in government
Scholarships
Tariff policy
Foreign aid
Latin America
Specific extracurricular activities
Library
Shorthand
Fluoridation
Racial relationships
European problems
Gettysburg
Iwo Jima
Vote for . . .
Buy . . .
Join . . .
Enlist . . .
Reserve Corps
Federal aid to education
Algeria

The Congo
De Gaulle
Adenauer
The United Nations
Organization of American States
Civil rights
Urban renewal
Jobs for graduates
Communist China
Nuclear fallout
Growth of the federal government
Conflict of interest
The movies
The Peace Corps
A great speaker
State universities
Private universities
Prices
Wages
Strikes
World food supply
The water problem
Conservation
Importance of any article, process, business, etc.
Physical fitness
How to play physical games, etc.
Types of city government
The classics
Read (this magazine or book)
Blue Cross
Visit (places, buildings, etc.)
Punctuality
Save
Investment
Commodity purchase
Choosing a vocation
Helicopters

Airplanes—conventional, jet
Space capsules
Logarithms
Chemistry
Building structure
Style
Architecture
Home safety
Unemployment relief
Our old people
Our youth
Trucking industry
Railroads
College expansion
Specialized and liberal education
Reading
Writing
Personality
The theater
Automation
Bacteriology
Geology
Literature
Scouting
Helping young people
The common cold

Specific diseases, prevention of
Budgeting time
Diet
ROTC
The Navy
The Air Force
The Army
Health, Education and Welfare Department, etc.
Redistricting in the states
The Supreme Court
Specific hobbies
Home building and equipping
Do-it-yourself ideas
Specific manual skills
Specific artistic skills
Chain stores
Discount stores
Shopping centers
Mass city transportation
Specific religious topics
Political activities
Specific elections
Marriage and divorce
Population problems
Communications problems

Make it specific. More than one hundred and fifty topics used by students are listed above. All are *general* in their statement, rather than specific, and from each of them many specific topics can be derived. None is a good topic as stated, until narrowed down, adapted to the particular kind of talk you are to make, and to the occasion or audience. Make your topic specific.

GATHERING MATERIAL

Sources of material. Speech material, like speech subjects, may be obtained from both direct and indirect experiences. The sources of material may be classified as follows: *personal* *knowledge* and *observation, discussion, listening, correspondence,* and *reading.* Speeches differ with respect to the amount of material which may be obtained from each of these sources. Sometimes all of it will come from personal knowledge and observation; with others all will come from discussion and correspondence; and, with some, all will come from reading. However, the careful student will make the best possible use of each of the sources of material.

Personal Knowledge and Observation. "Think yourself empty," is sound advice as a first step in the collection of material. The first thing the speaker should do is to find out what he already knows about the subject. Sometimes he will find that he already knows enough to make an interesting talk. Usually, information that the speaker already knows is of more value than information he has to assimilate hurriedly from other sources, because he can present it with much more confidence and sureness.

Speakers should ask themselves: What direct experience have I had with this subject? What have I read on it? What experience or knowledge have I of subjects in related fields? How does it affect me? How does it affect the interest of the audience? These and similar questions should bring to the speaker's mind the knowledge he already has and should be helpful in indicating lines of investigation.

Observation is also an important source of material. As has been noted in our discussion of direct experiences as sources of subjects, a visit to a manufacturing plant usually will give a speaker a much clearer idea of the processes of manufacture in use there than can be acquired through reading. Since the speaker has observed the process, it will be more vivid to him and consequently he should be able to make it more vivid to the audience.

Discussion, Listening, and Correspondence. After examining his own mind and after making the best possible use of observation in gathering material, discussion, listening, and correspondence should be used. Usually when a subject is discussed with others, the speaker will find that his own ideas become clearer because he has expressed them; and frequently he will get some new ones. Perhaps the best use of discussion and correspondence is with those who are recognized experts on the subject. Of course, the speaker should be looking for definite information, and in an interview with or letters to an expert, he should try to ask pertinent questions. Listening to the speeches of experts also is an important source of information.

READING. Our libraries contain a great mass of material on almost every subject. In order to locate needed material, the speaker should know how to use the card catalog, other guides and indexes, and reference books, and how to find periodicals, special publications of business organizations and associations, and government documents.

Use of the Library.

GUIDES AND INDEXES.[1] First, a speaker should know how to use a card catalog, which is an index to all the books, pamphlets, and magazines in a library. Books and pamphlets usually are listed both under the names of the authors and the titles, while only the names of magazines are given.

In order to find material in magazines, unless the citations are known, *Poole's Index*, the *Reader's Guide*, the *Public Affairs Information Service* and the *Industrial Arts Index* should be used. *Poole's Index* is a guide to periodical literature to 1907. The *Reader's Guide* is an index to general periodical literature from 1900 to the present. Material may be found in both, under either the names of authors or titles of articles. The *Public Affairs Information Service* is a guide to the use of special periodicals, the reports and bulletins issued by local, state, and national governments, reports of organizations and special associations, and books on special subjects. This is an especially valuable guide in obtaining

---

[1] For additional information on this subject, including complete lists of all types of reference works, we refer the student to *The New Handbook of English,* by M. McLeod and S. Thompson, New York, The Ronald Press Co., pp. 308–319.

information on public questions. The *Industrial Arts Index* is a guide to special periodicals, books, and reports in the field of industrial arts.

REFERENCE BOOKS. Indispensable for library work is I. G. Mudge's *Guide to Reference Books*. *Guide to the Use of Libraries*, by Hutchins, Johnson, and Williams, and *Bibliography, Practical, Enumerative, Historical*, by Van Hoesen and Walter, are also important books on this subject of reference works.

Among reference books are classified the encyclopedias, atlases, yearbooks, dictionaries, and biographical publications. The encyclopedias include the *Americana, Britannica, Nelson's New Loose Leaf*, the *New International*, and *Columbia*. In the encyclopedias, the bibliography of original source materials is given at the end of most articles.

Atlases are used to obtain historical, political, geographical, and physical information about all the countries of the world. *Lippincott's New Gazetteer of the World* and *Philip's Historical Atlas, Mediæval and Modern* are representative publications of this type.

Among the yearbooks are the *American, Americana, Agricultural, New International, Statesman's*, the *World Almanac, Information Please Almanac*, and the *Statistical Abstract of the United States*. These and many others are excellent sources of material on a wide variety of subjects.

Dictionaries, of course, are sources for determining the meaning of words and their pronunciation.

Finally, there are a great many biographies in the encyclopedias and in standard books. Special publications of importance in this field are the *Dictionary of National Biography* (English), the *Dictionary of American Biography* and the *National Cyclopedia of American Biography*. For material on living men and women of prominence, one should refer to *Who's Who* (English) and *Who's Who in America*. There are similar compilations covering special fields and regions.

In the fields of literature, philosophy, psychology, religion, history, the fine arts, etc., there are numerous publications and guides to material. *The Nelson Handbook of English* is a convenient source for obtaining the names of such reference books.

PERIODICAL LITERATURE. Information in periodicals is located through *Poole's Index*, the *Reader's Guide*, the *Public Affairs Information Service*, and the *Industrial Arts Index*. There are both general and special periodicals. Some of the more useful general ones are: *Atlantic Monthly, U. S. News and World Report, Newsweek, Nation, New Republic, Time, Life,* and *Fortune*. Special periodicals cover only one field. Some of the more important ones are: *Annals of the American Academy of Political and Social Science, American Economic Review, American Historical Review, American Political Science Quarterly, The National Geographic,* and *The Scientific Monthly*.

SPECIAL PUBLICATIONS. The publications of associations and business organizations may be found through the *Public Affairs Information Service* and the *Industrial Arts Index*. A few of the associations whose publications are helpful are: *American Bankers Association, American Bar Association, American Federation of Labor,* and the *International Law Association*.

Among business organizations issuing publications are: *The American Telephone and Telegraph Company, The National City Bank,* and *The Federal Reserve System*.[2]

GOVERNMENT REPORTS AND DOCUMENTS. Many local governments, all state governments, the national government, and the United Nations issue reports on their varied activities. Frequently, these are valuable sources of information.

Let us examine briefly those published by the federal gov-

[2] For additional sources of debate material, see the following publications of the H. W. Wilson Company, 973 University Avenue, New York City: *The Reference Shelf Series, The Debaters' Handbook Series,* and *The University Debaters' Annual*. In the first two will be found outlines, bibliographies, and extracts from articles on a wide variety of subjects. In the last one there are college and university debates, bibliographies, and briefs.

ernment. They are of three kinds: congressional, executive, and judicial.

Congressional documents include the *Congressional Record*, which is a record of the business transacted on the floors of the houses; and reports of the hearings held by the committees of both houses on matters referred to them by their respective bodies. In both the *Congressional Record* and the committee hearings, both sides of questions are discussed.

Judicial documents are the records of the cases tried in the federal courts. They are valuable sources of information about laws and court decisions.

In general, the documents issued by the executive departments are the most valuable for the average speaker. Some of the most useful are those issued by the various divisions of the *Department of Commerce*, the *Department of State*, the *Department of Agriculture*, the *Treasury Department*, the *Department of the Interior*, the *Department of Labor*, and the *Department of Justice*, the *Department of Health, Education and Welfare*.[3]

Recording Material.

MEMORY. For very short speeches, a speaker may safely depend on his memory for the information he has found. For long speeches, however, he should not depend on his memory, for, usually, speakers find it impossible to remember each fact as it is found. Therefore, it is a safe procedure to adopt some systematic way of recording speech material.

NOTEBOOKS. A loose-leaf notebook is much more satisfactory than a bound one because material recorded in a bound notebook cannot be rearranged with the ease possible with the loose-leaf type. Loose-leaf notebooks should be small, and only one item of information should be recorded on each page, thus making quick rearrangement possible.

FILES. Clippings from newspapers and magazines are also valuable sources of information. Many speakers habitually

---

[3] Information about all publications of the federal government may be obtained from the Superintendent of Documents, Washington, D. C.

clip material which they expect to use, classify it, and keep it in files where it is readily available.

CARDS. The use of cards is the most satisfactory method of recording speech material. Small cards, 3 x 5 or 4 x 6, are convenient. Only one item should be recorded on each card, and the subject, author, and source should be indicated.

When all the speaker's material for a speech is recorded on small cards, it is a simple matter for him to arrange it. First, all the cards may be divided into several groups; perhaps according to the topics involved. Then the speaker may arrange each group in the way in which he believes the information will be most effective. For instance, he can in the discussion separate his material under each idea and decide on its order. The adoption of this method of recording material will make the speaker's task of disposition or arrangement easier.

SUMMARY

Care in the selection of speech subjects is necessary if the speeches are to be successful. Subjects may be selected from either direct or indirect experience. In selecting a subject, the speaker should take into consideration his own interest in it, the probable interest of the audience, and his ability to make it interesting. When students have difficulty in finding suitable subjects, our list of those used by our own students should be helpful. After the selection of the subject, there is the problem of gathering material. It may be obtained from personal knowledge and observation, discussion and correspondence, and reading. In the use of a library, familiarity with the card catalog, guides to periodical literature, reference books, special publications, and government documents, is necessary. Speech material may be recorded in notebooks, in the form of clippings, or on cards. For most purposes, cards are most satisfactory.

12

Utilize Your Speech
Opportunities

*If all my powers and possessions were to be taken from me,
save only one, I would choose to keep the power of speech,
for by it I could soon recover all the rest.*

DANIEL WEBSTER

THE late James A. Worsham, outstanding lecturer, said in
an address to a graduating class, "Use it, or lose it." He was
speaking of the techniques of business speech of which the
course had consisted.

Perhaps, in this closing chapter, we should repeat his advice. "Use it or lose it" applies in no small degree to the speaking skill that you may have developed during your period of
study.

One never stands still in this matter of oral communication. He improves, or declines. Obviously no one course can
guarantee to you that your skill will stay at whatever peak
may have been reached. This in spite of the claims made for
at least one commercialized course in speech.

PUT PRINCIPLES INTO PRACTICE

The first thing that you can do to retain present proficiency, and to keep improving it, is to put into everyday

practice what you have learned. Remember, for instance, that *to be understood* is a primary requirement. Keep your conversation clear. Avoid rambling. "State your idea, develop it, restate it." Prepare your more serious interviews or conference statements in just the way that you have learned to prepare speeches. Practice clarity of statement and detail in your classroom recitations, and in every oral contact with others.

TRY TO BE INTERESTING. And that means showing an interest in "the other fellow," in his wants and desires, and adapting what you say to them. It means being specific, using familiar ideas, and sometimes the unusual or vivid illustration.

TRY TO BE PERSUASIVE, as a person, in your logical reasoning, and in your consideration of the feelings of others.

A great dividend that a good course in oral communication can give you is increased clarity, interestingness, and persuasiveness in conversation.

Take speaking opportunities. While you are still in college, and throughout later life, take advantage of opportunities for public speaking. They are all around you in college: you may join the debate squad, take part in the discussions of student organizations, and become a member of the student speakers' bureau, if there is one, and get the priceless experience of speaking to civic clubs, luncheon groups, and other organizations. Later, in the organizations to which you belong, speaking opportunities will arise. In your professional or business group, similar chances will occur. Do not shun them—they are a "way to thrive" in business and public life, and they help you to improve the skills that you may possess.

FURTHER TRAINING IS DESIRABLE

There are advanced or specialized courses in most college departments of speech, that can add a great deal to your stature as a speaker. It should be possible for you to elect some of them.

Following a basic course, for instance, you usually have available courses in oral argumentation, discussion, conference, and business speech. There are, very likely, courses in persuasion, in the forms of public address, and in parliamentary procedure. Each of these, by whatever title it may appear in the college catalog, has something of value for you.

On the upper undergraduate level, you may find courses in the study and appreciation of great speeches, British, American, European, and classical. By analyzing and reporting on speech masterpieces, you not only add to your background information, but gain a greater grasp of principles. Whether in a course or otherwise, the reading of speech masterpieces of the past and present can be helpful and inspiring.

There are courses in the special fields of radio and television in many schools; and in the related areas of phonetics, speech correction, and dramatics. Generally, there are upper division courses in speech theory and pedagogy.

While you have the opportunity, and we hope the desire, to get added training in communication, by all means consider the election of such courses.

Related courses. In the general field of effective communication, you should consider such courses as creative writing, business letter writing, marketing, management, applied psychology, and others that may be directly applicable.

Almost every "content" or subject matter course may be useful to you in your future, inasmuch as it will give you a knowledge that applies in your future business or professional life. History, political science, economics, sociology, human relations, and similar subjects are especially important to the future public speaker, but all liberal arts courses perpare you for the specific task of communication in one way or another. If your future work is in a scientific or technical field, courses of that type function in the same manner. In fact, any subject-matter may be important to the speaker.

OBSERVE GOOD SPEAKERS

Television, radio, and the countless meetings at which good speakers appear, constitute a gold mine of information for you. Not only those who appear as speakers or members of discussion groups, but the men and women who earn their living by being able to talk well—announcers, moderators, news reporters and analysts—give you hundreds of opportunities every week to observe and to profit.

We do not imply that all those who talk over the mass media are excellent speakers or talkers, but there is a great deal of merit in what the better ones do. With the background of theory and practice that you have, you can analyze their talking—both what is said and how it is said—to great advantage.

A fine teacher, a successful executive, a national leader or a clergyman may illustrate for you, in a new way, some of the qualities of effective speech. Listen—and learn.

GOOD SPEECH CAN HELP YOU

Always bear in mind that "you are judged," not only by what you know, but "by what you say and how you say it." Because this is true, a sincere, continued effort to be effective in oral communication can be most rewarding. This applies, no matter what your future vocation.

Opportunities in a business or professional way for the person who can say "the right thing, at the right time, in the right way" are more numerous than ever before. Teaching, marketing, radio and television, supervisory work, public relations, and advertising are just a few of the areas in which there is a premium on good oral communication. This is in addition to the traditional fields of the law, the ministry, and public life.

You have had a sound training in the basics of effective speech. We repeat, with Worsham, *"Use it."*

Part Three

SPEECHES FOR ANALYSIS
AND APPRECIATION

Informative Speeches—Explanatory

SPUN LOGS *

Edwin E. Slosson

Science consists in learning from nature how to surpass nature.
The chemist in particular is never content till he can do something
that his teacher can't. In the field of fabrics he has made dyes
more brilliant than any to be found in the three kingdoms of
nature, animal, vegetable and mineral, and now he is inventing
new textiles to tint with them. He beat the indigo plant on its own
ground, and carried off the blue ribbon. He challenged a snail to a
race, the Mediterranean mollusk that produced the "royal purple"
of the ancients, and beat him, for now the chemist is making a
better dye out of coal tar and making it so cheap that anybody
can afford it.

Now the chemist is engaged in another competition. His rival
this time is a worm. He has challenged the champion spinner of
the world, one who has, for over four thousand years, held the
prize for the finest and most flossy fiber, the silkworm. The worm
chews up mulberry leaves and spins out through his mouth a silk
thread five hundred yards long. The chemist grinds up logs of
wood and spins out by means of his mechanical spinnerets a silky
thread as long as he likes, for the machines run day and night
and all the week long, throughout the year. And the thread the
chemist makes is more uniform in size and substance, for the
worm, although he was practising the spinning art thousands of
years before man appeared upon the earth, has never yet learned
how to produce a perfectly smooth and even filament.

Not long ago I had a chance to inspect a rayon plant, and it

* By permission of the author. Reprinted from *The Scientific Monthly*,
December, 1925. Dr. Slosson, late Director of Science Service, Washington,
D. C., delivered this address from Station WCAP, Washington, D. C., under
the auspices of the National Research Council and Science Service and the
direction of Mr. W. E. Tisdale, 1925.

was fascinating to watch the process. At one end of the factory spruce logs are floated in. At the other end skeins of glossy yarn are being shipped out. The wood pulp costs about five cents a pound and the synthetic silk sells for two dollars a pound, and more than that when you buy it in the form of neckties, shirts, sweaters and stockings.

And you buy it oftener than you think you do if you prefer to patronize worms rather than men. For nearly two thirds of what seems to you silk comes now-a-days from chemistry instead of the cocoon. But it is not the chemist's fault that he has to disguise himself as a worm in order to market his product. It is rather the fault of the people who have a prejudice for things that are old and familiar, and are unwilling to admit that their fellow-men can make anything as good as the plants, animals, or insects that have been longer in the business. The chemist would be proud to claim all his creations, but often he has to stand by while the merchant timidly introduces them to the public as "near" something or "imitation" something, or, what is worse, keeps silent and lets the buyer infer that he is getting the same old stuff instead of something new and often something better.

The dictionary is a heavy and clumsy volume and cannot keep up with the swift advance of science. That is why there is no common name yet for the thing that I am talking about, these synthetic fibers made from cellulose, although they have in the last ten years come into such common use. They are often called "artificial silk," or, what is worse, "imitation silk," although they are not the same as silk and should never pretend to be. Last year most of the manufacturers agreed to adopt, and introduce through advertising, a new name, "rayon," for all products of this sort, but some of the makers, those using the acetate process, refuse to accept this general term and stick to their own trade names, such as "celanese" and "lustron."

There are four different processes of making these synthetic fibers and very curiously they are all in actual use. There are now being built in the United States factories for each of the four rival processes.

They are easy to understand in a general way, though to run them so as to turn out a uniform and satisfactory thread is a delicate and difficult operation. They all use the same fundamental material, that is, the woody fiber that the chemist calls "cellulose," though some of them get it from timber and others from linters, the short bits of cotton that stick to the seeds after the long fiber has been picked off. This cellulose is the same stuff as paper is made of.

The first step is to get the cellulose into liquid form in order to squirt it out in a fine jet as the silk worm does. But you know it is not easy to dissolve wood, cotton, or paper. Water will not dissolve it, otherwise our floors would be washed away whenever they were scrubbed, or the trees whenever it rained, or our clothes whenever they are cleaned. But certain strong acids or alkalis will serve as solvents for cellulose.

The first of these solvents to be used was nitric acid, with which a French nobleman, Count Hilaire de Chardonnet, made an artificial silk in 1884. When nitric acid acts upon cotton it forms what is known as "nitro-cellulose" or gun-cotton, the basis of smokeless powder. This can be dissolved in a mixture of alcohol and ether, forming a thick gummy liquid that we know as "collodion" and use as new skin when our natural integument gets scratched off. After the spinning process the nitric acid is eliminated so that the threads are no longer explosive or more inflammable than the original cotton.

The second process of making synthetic silk gets the cellulose into solution by using an alkali instead of an acid, strong ammonia with copper dissolved in it.

The third process also makes use of an alkali, in this case caustic soda, with the addition of carbon bisulfide, a vile-smelling liquid that is used for killing gophers. This produces an orange-colored viscous liquid, and the product is known by the trade name of viscose. Four fifths of the synthetic silk is made by this method.

The fourth process employs an acid, concentrated acetic acid, familiar to us in dilute form as vinegar.

In whatever way the cellulose is dissolved the next step is to force the solution by pressure through glass tubes in the end of which are minute perforations, like fine pinholes, from ten to fifty of them. The liquid squirts out of these pinholes in thin streams which are coagulated into fine filaments by running into water containing something to neutralize and wash away the solvent. These filaments are then caught up by revolving wheels, twisted into a thread and dried in skeins. These are packed in ten-pound bundles containing one hundred and fifty thousand or three hundred thousand yards of yarn, according to the caliber. Each spinning machine in the great room is running off the thread at the rate of forty-five yards a minute.

The final product is brought back almost to its original state, for it is a form of cellulose, except where acetic acid is used which leaves it as cellulose acetate. Rayon is chemically much the same as cotton in composition, but has the sheen of silk and takes dyes even more brilliantly, which accounts largely for its popularity with this color-loving generation. By weaving artificial and natural fibers together it is possible to dye the cloth two colors, for one dye will fix on the rayon and the other on the silk, so bringing out a design invisible in the original white weave. Novel and beautiful velvet brocades are now made by this method.

None of the synthetic fibers is as strong or elastic as natural silk. Their strength is from half to two thirds of the natural when dry, and much less when wet. Rayon when wet takes up 40 per cent of water, and swells and weakens. The wet rayon is only a half or a quarter as strong as the dry, so these artificial fabrics should be handled tenderly while wet. The original strength returns on drying. The cellulose acetate does not weaken so much on wetting, because it does not absorb so much water. Whether this is an advantage or not depends on the advertiser. The viscose people claim that viscose underwear is the best because it absorbs the sweat and so keeps the skin dry and comfortable, summer and winter. The celanese people claim that celanese underwear is the best because it does not absorb sweat and so is chill-proof and comfortable, summer and winter. You pay your money and take your choice. In most fabrics it is found desirable to mix the rayon with wool, cotton, or real silk, and so get both strength and luster.

When this business first started a few years ago, the manufacturers were so delighted at their new-found power to rival silk in luster that they went too far. They turned out satin that was too silky and slick, too glossy and glary. Now they are tempering their ambition for such lustrous fabrics, perhaps in compliance with an improvement in popular taste, and they are now working for softer tones and textures, by using finer filaments, and more of them, in a single thread. Some of the filaments now spun are more delicate than the floss of a silk cocoon. These new forms of the synthetic fiber are softer to the touch and less garish to the eye than the crude products of a few years back.

Manufacturers at first thought it necessary to make their synthetic substitutes resemble silk in sound as well as to the sight. So they fussed about to find a way of giving the new fabrics the "scroop" of the old. The "scroop" is the sound referred to by Poe in his "Raven" as:

> The silken soft uncertain
> Rustling of each purple curtain.

In those days, when a lady had a silk petticoat she wanted everybody to know it, and since etiquette then required that petticoats, unlike children, should be heard and not seen, she had to rely upon the scroop to impress her proud possession upon the public. But after a process for putting the scroop into synthetic silk had been discovered the style changed and it is no longer considered necessary for a lady to rustle.

A new point in favor of the artificial over the natural product is the discovery that cellulose acetate is more transparent to the ultra-violet rays than wool or silk. Now these invisible ultra-violet rays are supposed to be responsible for the beneficial effects of sunshine in stimulating the blood to resist disease, so we may expect improvement in public health if the synthetic fabrics become common wear.

Although all the four present processes of making synthetic silk were first developed in Europe, the United States now leads the world in its production and consumption. In the field of science we Americans do not distinguish ourselves on the kick-off but we beat the world in keeping the ball going when once it is put in play. The world's output of these artificial cellulose products for the present year is estimated at about one hundred and eighty-five million pounds, and American manufacturers made nearly a third of the total. We may reasonably expect that next year the United States will turn out seventy-four million pounds, which will mean a 600 per cent increase in the last five years.

About half of the output of rayon goes now into knit goods, especially hosiery, which is usually combined with cotton, wool, or natural silk. For men's hose a mode of knitting called "plating" is commonly employed by which the inside surface of the sock is mercerized cotton and the outside is rayon, so getting the advantages of both kinds of thread.

In braid for dress trimmings the new material has almost entirely ousted natural silk.

Another use of these same cellulose synthetics, that is common but commonly unrecognized, is the thin, colorless, flexible transparent sheets, called "cellophane" or "visca," which wrap your candy or make a window in the envelope that brings you a check or bill.

This protean material seems to be a universal proxy. It can substitute for all sorts of substances. It is now appearing in the role of horsehair, Spanish lace, Smyrna rugs, Nottingham lace curtains, and furs of various kinds. Sometime it may be unnecessary to skin animals to get fur coats and collars, or to steal the silken blanket of the sleeping worm.

THE IDENTIFICATION UNIT *

Charles E. Kleinkauf

On May 23, 1928, four bandits descended upon the First National Bank of Lamar, Colorado, perpetrated a robbery of over $200,000, killed the president and the cashier of the bank, kidnapped two other employees, one of whom was later found murdered, fled across the Colorado border into western Kansas, where they proceeded to the home of Dr. Weininger, and compelled him to leave his home, to drive his car into the country, and to dress the wounds of one of their number who had been shot in the bank affray. After Dr. Weininger had finished his ministrations, he was murdered, his body thrown into a canyon, and his car pushed over after him. The body and car were found later. There were no clues found which would identify the murderers, except a bloody fingerprint impression on a window of Dr. Weininger's car. This was photographed and sent to the Identification Unit of the Division of Investigation here in Washington, where it was received in July, 1928. No similar prints were found in the files so it was handed to the technical employees with the request that the pattern, which was of a peculiar type, be clearly impressed on their minds for future reference.

Meanwhile, the outraged community of Lamar, Colorado, insisted upon retribution, and four suspects were apprehended in various parts of the country, returned to Lamar, identified as the bandits by numerous citizens and were held for trial.

After over a year had elapsed, one of the employees in the

* This speech was presented by Mr. Kleinkauf in a section of Public Speaking I, The George Washington University, in the fall of 1933.

Identification Unit here in Washington, while engaged in his regular work of verifying current fingerprint identifications, suddenly discovered a duplicate of the bloody fingerprint impression on a fingerprint card received from officials of Stockton, California. This card was that of an individual who had been arrested in Stockton and who, according to the records of the Identification Unit's files, was identical with one Jake Fleagle. Since Fleagle was not in the custody of the Stockton officers at the time, wires were dispatched to the Kansas and Colorado authorities stating that Fleagle was identical with the murderer whose fingerprint had been found on the window of the murdered Doctor's car. The Fleagle home was raided, as Fleagle was well known to the local authorities, and as a result the father and two brothers of Jake were arrested. Through these parties information was received which led to the apprehension of Ralph Fleagle, another brother, who when questioned finally broke down and confessed to his part in the crime at Lamar, and identified the three other bandits, one of whom was his brother Jake. The latter was killed while resisting arrest a few months later and the other three bandits were subsequently executed.

Their innocence in connection with this crime being established by the identification of the foregoing individuals, the charges of murder against the men originally arrested were dropped.

The foregoing case which I have just cited is only one of the many examples which I might use to illustrate the efficient and positive manner in which the Identification Unit of the Division of Investigation here in Washington, through its system of classifying, searching, and filing of criminal fingerprints, is directly responsible for causing the apprehension, monthly, of approximately three hundred fugitives from justice. In this case it served the double function of being both the means of causing the apprehension of fugitives and of establishing the innocence of four men who might have been unjustly forced to pay the penalty for the crime.

The question of crime and particularly the methods which are used in combating crime, are subjects which should be of vital importance to each one of us today, principally because of the manner in which crime has rapidly become an increasing menace to organized society during the past fifteen years.

Today, I shall first give you a brief history of the Identification

Unit of which I have just spoken, and then in a little more detail I shall explain just how this Unit functions as a clearing house for the entire United States, in serving as a depository for criminal fingerprints and for the exchange of information based on these fingerprints.

Fingerprinting was first introduced into the United States in 1903 from England, where it had been perfected by Sir E. R. Henry, former Commissioner of Police of New Scotland Yard in London. Its distinct advantages in identifying criminals were rapidly realized by law enforcement officials throughout this country, and these officials began the practice of exchanging fingerprints of individuals to see whether they were wanted elsewhere or had prior criminal records. In the larger cities and in several states, identification bureaus were established for this latter purpose, but it was found that these could not effectively meet the problem of dealing with the roving criminal. As a result, the need for a central agency to carry on this function for the entire United States soon became apparent, and in recognition of this need, on July 1, 1924, largely through the efforts of the International Association of Chiefs of Police, the Identification Unit of the Division of Investigation was established here in Washington for the purpose of providing, under federal supervision, a national fingerprint exchange, free of cost, to all law enforcement agencies desiring to avail themselves of its facilities.

In commenting upon the activities of the Division of Investigation in maintaining its fingerprint files, it is interesting to note that to begin its collection on July 1, 1924, it had only 810,188 fingerprint cards and was receiving a daily average of only 300 cards from 987 law enforcement officials. Of these 300 received daily, approximately 14 per cent were identified as those of individuals having a previous record on file. On September 30, 1933, there were 3,914,228 fingerprints on file, and a daily average of 2,200 cards were being received from 6,066 contributors. At the present time approximately 41 per cent of the cards received are identified as those of individuals who have been previously arrested.

I have here a fingerprint card of the type furnished, free of cost, to law enforcement officials throughout the country. When an individual is arrested, his fingerprints are placed on one of these cards, each finger of the right hand being placed in the space provided for it as shown here, and the corresponding fingers of the left hand placed in the space directly under that of the right.

On the card are also placed the name of the person, any known aliases, together with other pertinent information such as descriptive data, identifying marks, crime for which arrested, and any information which the official transmitting the card might have. The card is then mailed to the Identification Unit here in Washington. When the card is received here, it is first recorded under the contributor's name and then put through the various processes necessary to insure a positive identification or nonidentification. First it is sent to the Technical Section where, in the hands of a fingerprint expert, it is classified according to its own particular pattern.

The card is then routed to a cabinet containing master prints bearing a close classification to the print in question. A master

---

U. S. BUREAU OF INVESTIGATION, DEPARTMENT OF JUSTICE
WASHINGTON, D. C.

Record from _____ (Address) _____
On the above line please state whether Police Department, Sheriff's Office, or County Jail

Date of arrest _____

Charge _____

Disposition of case _____

Residence _____

Place of birth _____

PLEASE PASTE PHOTO HERE

Nationality _____

Criminal specialty _____

Age _____ Build _____

Height _____ Comp. _____ Hair _____

Weight _____ Eyes _____

Scars and marks _____

CRIMINAL HISTORY

NAME	NUMBER	CITY OR INSTITUTION	DATE	CHARGE	DISPOSITION OR SENTENCE

(Face of form)

print, by way of explanation, is the key print which tells the finger-print expert that the individual has been arrested before. For example, if several fingerprint cards have been received on an individual, each showing a different arrest, one of these cards, usually the one bearing the best fingerprint impressions, will be stamped as the MASTER PRINT, and given a number. The rest of the prints will be placed in a folder known as the jacket, the number given the master print placed on the outside, and this jacket is then filed in a separate room according to the number. The master print is filed in the master cabinet according to its classification. To return to our original fingerprint card. Let us suppose that the individual has been arrested before. In searching this card the fingerprint expert will find, in the master print cabi-

Name_____			Class_____	
Alias_____				
No._____ Color____ Sex____			Ref.____	
RIGHT HAND				
1. Thumb	2. Index Finger	3. Middle Finger	4. Ring Finger	5. Little Finger
LEFT HAND				
6. Thumb	7. Index Finger	8. Middle Finger	9. Ring Finger	10. Little Finger

Classified_____ Assembled_____	Note Amputations	Prisoner's Signature	
Searched_____ Verified_____			
Index Card_____ Answered_____			

| Four Fingers Taken Simultaneously | | | Four Fingers Taken Simultaneously |
| Left Hand | L.Thumb | R.Thumb | Right Hand |

(*Reverse of form*)

net, a master print bearing the classification given the card just received. He will draw out this master card and compare the fingerprint impressions with those on the new card to make sure they are identical. Assuring himself of this, he will place a charge out card in place of the master print, attach the latter to the new print, and send both to the jacket room. Here the jacket corresponding to the number on the master print will be drawn out, and in it, as explained before, will be found a complete record of the arrests and crimes committed by the individual who is under investigation.

The original print, together with the others, is then sent to the card index section where a brief of the cards received on an individual is kept on a small index card filed under the name of the individual and also under any aliases which he might have. Here our card is searched under the name appearing on it, and if our party has assumed a new alias, a new card is made out under the new name with the old aliases listed. The new name is similarly noted on the cards bearing the old names. Upon these index cards, under each name, is placed the fingerprint classification of the individual, thus insuring a double system of filing in identifying a criminal; under his fingerprint classification and under his name and aliases. When this last procedure has taken place, all the fingerprint cards of the individual are assembled and a letter is written to the law enforcement official who submitted the original fingerprints. This exchange of criminal information can be made of value only by doing it without any appreciable loss of time, and therefore a thirty-six-hour service is maintained at the Identification Unit; thirty-six hours after a fingerprint is received the answer is in the mails.

The great value of this exchange of criminal information in the Division is the location of fugitives from justice by the placing of what is known as wanted notices on file against a criminal's record. If an individual is wanted by a law-enforcement official in any part of the country, the official notifies the Identification Unit to place a wanted notice against the individual in the event he is arrested elsewhere. If a card is received on this person, then the information that he is wanted is discovered, and a wire is immediately sent to the official wanting the fugitive, giving the place and date of his arrest. The official can then communicate with the officer who has caused the last arrest and arrange for the detention of the criminal on his charge. Let us take for example John

Doe who has been arrested by the San Francisco police for murder. He escapes from the jail where he is confined and all trace of him is lost. The San Francisco police wire the Identification Unit here in Washington to the effect that their John Doe, whose fingerprints were forwarded at the time of his arrest, is wanted by them for escape on a charge of murder. Two months elapse and a fingerprint card is received from the Chicago, Illinois, police, who have arrested one Charles Smith as a vagrant and are holding him for investigation. When this print has been classified and searched in the manner just described, Charles Smith is found to be identical with John Doe who is the individual wanted by the San Francisco police for murder. Accordingly the latter are notified by wire, and another fugitive has been apprehended.

As indicated at the beginning of my talk, approximately 300 fugitives from justice are apprehended in this manner each month. The records of individuals which are compiled from these fingerprints are often of great aid to a prosecutor in prosecuting his case against a criminal, as the knowledge that a person is a habitual criminal is often of value to both court and jury.

The Identification Unit of the Division of Investigation with its collection of over 3,900,000 fingerprints is the largest of its kind in the world. Its importance, in serving as a clearing house for the exchange of criminal information based on fingerprints, is easily recognized by the large number of fugitives located through it each month. It is an effective weapon in combating crime in this country.

HOW THE HEART WORKS *

Benjamin F. Edwards II

Do you realize, as you are sitting here, that the heart of each of you is beating 70 times per minute, 4,200 times per hour, and over 100,000 times every day? And that, although each time it beats, only this much blood is squeezed out, [here, 65 cc. of red liquid is poured into a common drinking glass, to bring in the familiar] your heart pumps over 6,000 quarts of blood every day, and in 19 days, it would pump enough blood to fill this *whole* room.

* Mr. Edwards delivered this talk in a section of Public Speaking I, at The George Washington University, in the summer of 1940.

But what makes your heart beat? Why is it that it can beat year in and year out without tiring? What will speed it up, or slow it down? In the next five minutes I will try to answer these questions for you. In other words, I'm going to tell you how the heart works.

[Please note—in the following discussion each structure is pointed to as it is mentioned.]

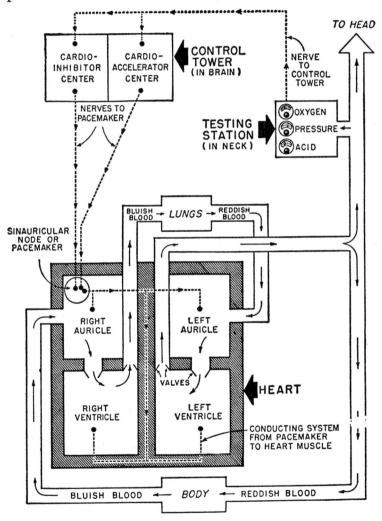

First, I would like to give you a brief description of the anatomy of the heart. *Here* is a picture of the heart as it really looks. As you can see, it is about the size of my fist. *Here* [pointing to chart] is the heart in diagram form. Think of this heart as being my heart. In other words, as I face you, the upper right hand corner of *this* heart corresponds to the upper right hand corner of *my* heart, the lower left hand corner of *this* heart, with the lower left hand corner of *my* heart, and so on.

Now—I want you to think of your heart as being a two-story, four-room house. The two upstairs rooms are known as "auricles." They receive the blood. The two downstairs rooms are known as "ventricles." They pump the blood. To reiterate then, the *auricles* are receiving stations, the *ventricles* are pumping stations.

But what makes the heart beat? I want you to compare this sinauricular node, or pacemaker of the heart, to a coxswain. Just as he sits in the back of a shell yelling "stroke, stroke," so does this pacemaker sit in the upper right-hand room, that is the right auricle, and yell "stroke" to the heart. This pacemaker does not actually yell, of course, but it sends out impulses over this conducting system which cause the heart muscle to contract every eight tenths of a second.

The impulse reaches the auricles first and they contract for one tenth of a second, and then rest for seven tenths of a second. Then the impulse reaches the ventricles, causing them to contract immediately after the auricles for three tenths of a second and then rest for five tenths of a second. Now you can see why the heart can beat indefinitely. Each cycle last eight tenths of a second, and out of this eight tenths, the auricles are resting seven tenths and the ventricles are resting five tenths.

By now you should be able to understand, in general, how the blood circulates. As you can see, the heart is really two different pumps, each consisting of an auricle and a ventricle. Well, the blood returns from the body, here, and enters the right auricle. This blood is bluish, since it has given up its oxygen to the body. From the right auricle it goes to the right ventricle [all the time pointing to the chart] and then out this way to the lungs. In the lungs it picks up oxygen, then goes back through the left auricle, left ventricle and back to the body. Get that now? Body, right heart, lungs, left heart, and back to the body.

But what governs the speed of the heart? A normal adult heart beats 70 times per minute, an athlete's heart 40 times per minute, and a child's 125 times per minute. This control tower in your brain is responsible for the speed of your heart. It consists of a cardioinhibitor and a cardioaccelerator center. The cardioinhibitor center sends impulses down this nerve to the coxswain or pacemaker and tells him to send out less impulses and thus make the heart go slower. In an opposite manner, the cardioaccelerator center sends impulses down this nerve and tells the pacemaker to speed up the heart.

However, although this control tower governs the speed of your heart, it in turn receives messages from this testing station which is located in the carotid artery in your neck. The carotid artery is the large blood vessel which carries blood to your head. In this testing station, or carotid sinus as we call it, are cells which are sensitive to changes in pressure, acidity, and oxygen content of your blood. Let me illustrate.

For instance, if the amount of oxygen in your blood tests too low, you will faint immediately, because your brain is not getting enough oxygen. This is prevented by the cells in the testing station which are sensitive to changes in the oxygen content of your blood. They send messages along this nerve, telling the cardioaccelerator center to work harder and the cardioinhibitor center to let up. The cardioaccelerator center then sends messages down this nerve, as I have explained. The heart goes faster, pumping more blood through the lungs where it, that is, the blood, picks up more oxygen, and the oxygen content of your blood is raised.

In a similar manner, pressure-sensitive cells in your testing station make the heart, when necessary, go faster, thus raising your blood pressure, or slower, thus lowering the blood pressure. Since too high blood pressure might result in a cerebral hemorrhage, or too low blood pressure might result in fainting, you can see that your testing station maintains an optimum pressure between these two extremes.

Again, in much the same manner, acid-sensitive cells cause your heart to beat faster when there is more acid in your blood from exercise.

Thus you can see that your heart is constantly under various influences attempting either to speed it up or slow it down. At one time, one of these influences may predominate, at another time some other influence may predominate. Also you should now be able to understand why your heart can beat day in and day out, since, as I have explained, the auricles rest seven eighths of each cycle and the ventricles rest five eights.

In conclusion, then, there are three things I would like you to remember. One, *auricles receive blood.* Two, *ventricles pump blood.* Three, blood goes from the body to the right side of the heart, to the lungs, to the left side, to the body again. *Body, right side, lungs, left side, body.* If you can't remember even these three points, *please* remember that the heart is *NOT* a one-chambered organ, and it does not look like the ones you see on valentines.

Informative—Impressive Speeches

THE GETTYSBURG ADDRESS
Abraham Lincoln

1. Fourscore and seven years ago, our fathers brought forth upon this continent a new nation, conceived in liberty, and dedicated to the proposition that all men are created equal. Now we are engaged in a great Civil War, testing whether that nation, or any nation so conceived and so dedicated, can long endure. We are met on a great battlefield of that war.

2. We have come to dedicate a portion of that field as a final resting place for those who here gave their lives that that nation might live. It is altogether fitting and proper that we should do this. But, in a larger sense, we cannot dedicate, we cannot consecrate, we cannot hallow this ground.

3. The brave men, living and dead, who struggled here, have consecrated it far above our poor power to add or detract. The world will little note nor long remember what we say here; but it can never forget what they did here. It is for us, the living, rather, to be dedicated here to the unfinished work which they who fought here have thus far so nobly advanced.

4. It is rather for us to be here dedicated to the great task remaining before us; that from these honored dead we take in-

creased devotion to that cause for which they gave the last full measure of devotion; that we here highly resolve that these dead shall not have died in vain; that this nation, under God, shall have a new birth of freedom; and that government of the people, by the people, and for the people, shall not perish from the earth.

THE EYES OF ALL PEOPLE
ARE UPON US *

John F. Kennedy

I have welcomed this opportunity to address this historic body and, through you, the people of Massachusetts to whom I am so deeply indebted for a lifetime of friendship and trust. For 14 years I have placed my confidence in the voters of this State— and they have generously responded by placing their confidence in me.

Now, on the Friday after next, I am to assume new and broader responsibilities. But I am not here to bid farewell to Massachusetts. For 43 years—whether I was in London, Washington, the South Pacific, or elsewhere—this has been my home; and God willing, wherever I serve, it will always remain my home.

It was here my grandparents were born—it is here I hope my grandchildren will be born.

I speak neither from false provincial pride nor artful political flattery. For no man about to enter high public office in this country can ever be unmindful of the contributions this State has made to our national greatness.

Its leaders have shaped our destiny since long before the great Republic was born. Its principles have guided our footsteps in times of crisis as well as calm. Its democratic institutions—including this historic body—have served as beacon lights for other nations as well as your sister States. For what Pericles said of the Athenians has long been true of this Commonwealth: "We do not imitate—but are a model to others."

And so it is that I carry with me from this State to that high and lonely office to which I now succeed more than fond mem-

* President-elect Kennedy delivered this address before the Massachusetts Legislature on January 9, 1961. *Congressional Record,* January 10, 1961, p. A169.

ories and fast friendships. The enduring qualities of Massachusetts—the common threads woven by the Pilgrim and the Puritan, the fisherman and the farmer, the Yankee and the immigrant—will not be and could not be forgotten in the Nation's Executive Mansion. They are an indelible part of my life, my convictions, my view of the past, my hopes for the future.

Allow me to illustrate: During the last 60 days, I have been engaged in the task of constructing an administration. It has been a long and deliberate process. Some have counseled greater speed. Others have counseled more expedient tests. But I have been guided by the standard John Winthrop set before his shipmates on the flagship *Arabella* 331 years ago, as they, too, faced the task of building a government on a new and perilous frontier.

"We must always consider," he said, "that we shall be as a city upon a hill—the eyes of all people are upon us."

Today, the eyes of all people are truly upon us—and our governments, in every branch, at every level, national, State, and local, must be as a city upon a hill—constructed and inhabited by men aware of their grave trust and their great responsibilities.

For we are setting out upon a voyage in 1961 no less hazardous than that undertaken by the *Arabella* in 1630. We are committing ourselves to tasks of statecraft no less awesome than that of governing the Massachusetts Bay Colony, beset as it then was by terror without and disorder within.

History will not judge our endeavors—and a government cannot be selected—merely on the basis of color or creed or even party affiliation. Neither will competence and loyalty and stature, while essential to the utmost, suffice in times such as these.

For of those to whom much is given, much is required. And when at some future date the high court of history sits in judgment on each of us—recording whether in our brief span of service we fulfilled our responsibilities to the state—our success or failure, in whatever office we hold, will be measured by the answers to four questions:

First, were we truly men of courage—with the courage to stand up to one's enemies—and the courage to stand up, when necessary, to one's associates—the courage to resist public pressure, as well as private greed?

Secondly, were we truly men of judgment—with perceptive judgment of the future as well as the past—of our own mistakes as well as the mistakes of others—with enough wisdom to know what we did not know and enough candor to admit it.

Third, were we truly men of integrity—men who never ran out on either the principles in which we believed or the men who believed in us—men whom neither financial gain nor political ambition could ever divert from the fulfillment of our sacred trust?

Finally, were we truly men of dedication—with an honor mortgaged to no single individual or group, and compromised of no private obligation or aim, but devoted solely to serving the public good and the national interest?

Courage—judgment—integrity—dedication—these are the historic qualities of the Bay colony and the Bay State—the qualities which this State has consistently sent to Beacon Hill here in Boston and to Capitol Hill back in Washington. And these are the qualities which, with God's help, this son of Massachusetts hopes will characterize our Government's conduct in the 4 stormy years that lie ahead.

Humbly I ask His help in this understanding—but aware that on earth His will is worked by men, I ask your help and your prayers, as I embark on this new and solemn journey.

ANNOUNCING THE ELECTION OF KENNEDY AND JOHNSON *

Richard M. Nixon

Mr. Speaker, since this is an unprecedented situation I would like to ask permission to impose upon the time of the Members of this Congress to make a statement which in itself is somewhat unprecedented.

I promise to be brief. I shall be guided by the 1-minute rule of the House rather than the unlimited time rule that prevails in the Senate.

This is the first time in 100 years that a candidate for the Presidency announced the result of an election in which he was

* Vice President Nixon, before a joint session of the two Houses of Congress declared the election of John F. Kennedy as President and Lyndon B. Johnson as Vice President of the United States. *Congressional Record*, January 6, 1961, p. 284.

defeated and announced the victory of his opponent. I do not think we could have a more striking and eloquent example of the stability of our constitutional system and of the proud tradition of the American people of developing, respecting, and honoring institutions of self-government.

In our campaigns, no matter how hard fought they may be, no matter how close the election may turn out to be, those who lose accept the verdict, and support those who win. And I would like to add that, having served now in Government for 14 years, a period which began in the House just 14 years ago, almost to the day, which continued with 2 years in the Senate and 8 years as Vice President, as I complete that 14-year period it is indeed a very great honor to me to extend to my colleagues in the House and Senate on both sides of the aisle who have been elected; to extend to John F. Kennedy and Lyndon Johnson, who have been elected President and Vice President of the United States, my heartfelt best wishes, as all of you work in a cause that is bigger than any man's ambition, greater than any party. It is the cause of freedom, of justice, and peace for all mankind.

It is in that spirit that I now declare that John F. Kennedy has been elected President of the United States, and Lyndon B. Johnson Vice President of the United States.

Members of the Congress, the purpose for which the joint session of the two Houses of Congress has been called pursuant to Senate Concurrent Resolution 1, having been accomplished, the Chair declares the joint session dissolved.

DEDICATION OF LOVEJOY MEMORIAL *

Adlai E. Stevenson

In May of 1827, Elijah Lovejoy left his native village in the State of Maine for his first journey to his future home in the Mississippi Valley. As he came by schooner into Boston harbor on the first leg of his long and arduous journey he saw a frigate which had been taken from the British in the War of 1812 by the gallantry of American arms. This chance encounter moved Lovejoy to write in his diary: "***As I gazed upon her and

* Mr. Stevenson gave this address November 9, 1952, at Alton, Illinois. The occasion was the formal dedication of a memorial placque in honor of Elijah P. Lovejoy, the martyred abolition editor.

thought of the glorious achievements of my countrymen my heart beat thick and proudly*** ."

The youth of 25 who wrote those words had perhaps not yet learned what was to be borne in so hardly upon the man of 35—that the glorious achievements of our countrymen are not all to be found in our military and naval annals; what he was yet to learn is that ordinary living affords many occasions for men to dare greatly, to live dangerously and even to die nobly.

A decade from the time Elijah Lovejoy set out in such exuberant spirits to live and work in the great new middle country, such an occasion came to him, to live dangerously, to die nobly.

And, as he met it—bravely, directly, unyieldingly—so today our hearts, in his phrase, "beat thick and proudly" as we meet to remember the first martyr in this country to the freedom of the press—the freedom not just to denounce heretics, but to pronounce heresies, the freedom to say lawful but unpopular things.

To many of his contemporaries it must have seemed that Lovejoy's case had ended in defeat. His own life was gone, his family stricken with grief, and destitute, his hearse and his memory reviled by those who wanted no talk of human freedom to disturb their complacency and the existing order of things.

Lovejoy embraced a great idea in an early perilous stage of that idea's development. And that is usually dangerous, particularly when the idea is a new idea, disturbing to existing institutions, habits and prejudices.

His idea was that the enslavement of black by white was wrong and should be ended. That was a very radical idea and much more blood was to flow, the lives of millions more to be wrecked before that idea was to prevail.

But the measure of Lovejoy's triumph is to be found in the fact that only a quarter of a century was required to establish it as the law of the land. And across this scene of Lovejoy's death there fell some 20 years later, the shadow of the tall, gaunt man who was to be the instrument to do this work. For not far from the plaque we dedicate today is the marker commemorating the last of the Lincoln–Douglas debates, held here in Alton, October, 1858.

Elijah Lovejoy, however, served a greater cause than that of the abolition of Negro slavery. And it was his devotion to this cause, I dare say, which we will long remember after the struggle over the abolition of slavery has all but been forgotten.

This greater cause, if you please, was the right—and the duty—of the individual to speak out for the truth; I make the reference to "duty" advisedly because that was the way Lovejoy thought of it. To his fellow citizens of Alton in meeting assembled to protest the turmoil provoked by his outspokenness, he said something like this:

"I am impelled to the cause I have taken because I fear God. As I shall answer to my God in the great day, I dare not abandon my sentiments or cease in all proper ways to propagate them.*** I can die at my post but I cannot desert it."

There are many and vigorous powerful statements of the right to be permitted to speak freely but I know of none more moving than this one and in these days of clamorous and jostling assertion of rights and privileges, it is sobering to be reminded by these words of duties as well as rights.

Lovejoy saw the problem in terms of what he felt obliged to say, not merely of what he might be entitled to say. The distinction is an important one; and only those who observe the one as well as claim the other serve fully the cause of truth.

Human character being what it is, heroes in the classic mould of Elijah Lovejoy are rare. Of such stuff were the martyrs made. Neither is it given to many to see the truth in human affairs with the clarity and the depth of Lovejoy's crusading convictions. But we can have confidence in the ultimate triumph of truth and in the certainty that our fellow men will seek it out and follow it if only they can hear and speak and sift the true and false in untrammeled peace.

Some of the residents of Alton did not have that confidence in 1837. Some of our fellow citizens of America do not have that confidence today.

The greatest and wisest, almost, of living Americans, speaking in the detachment and wisdom of his retirement from the bench, found words for his countrymen not long ago when he said: "I believe that that community is already in the process of dissolution where each man begins to eye his neighbor as a possible enemy, where nonconformity with the accepted creed, political as well as religious, is a mark of disaffection; where denunciation, without specification or backing, takes the place of evidence; where orthodoxy chokes freedom of dissent; where faith in the eventual supremacy of reason has become so timid that we dare not enter our convictions in the open lists to win or lose."

The American conviction could find no more accurate statement than this by Judge Learned Hand of New York.

It has been the American conviction from the beginning that men are only free when they respect each others' freedom.

It is said that religious creeds are written to mark the graves where heresies lie buried. Besides commemorating the birth and death of an editor who had to proclaim the truth at all costs, it seems to me that we are also dedicating a stone to mark the grave of a heresy.

It is a common heresy and its graves are to be found all over the earth. It is the heresy that says you can kill an idea by killing a man, defeat a principle by defeating a person; bury truth by burying its vehicle. Man may burn his brother at the stake but he cannot reduce truth to ashes; he may murder his fellowman with a shot in the back, but he does not murder justice; he may even slay armies of men, but as it is written, "Truth beareth off the victory."

It's fitting that we dedicate this memorial to Elijah Lovejoy here in Alton, as a constant reminder of our eternal struggle. For we fight not against flesh and blood, but we fight in the long run, against the spiritual enemies of man himself.

It is also the genius of American freedom that we admit our mistakes even as we confess our sins. So today we confess our sins even as we reaffirm our faith, that "Truth crushed to earth, will rise again," that a people under God, can have a new birth of freedom, and that every age needs men who will redeem the time by living with a vision of things that are to be.

I am proud, my friends, to have a part in the dedication of this reminder of the death place of a man who went all the way for what he believed.

THOMAS ALVA EDISON *

John E. Rankin

Mr. Speaker, I rise to pay my humble tribute to the memory of one of America's most illustrious sons. Yesterday was the

---

* *Vital Speeches,* April 1, 1940. Mr. Rankin, a member of the United States House of Representatives from Mississippi, delivered this address in the House Chamber, February 12, 1940.

ninety-third anniversary of the birth of Thomas Alva Edison, our country's greatest contribution to the world's list of scientific men.

He was the foremost inventive genius of the age and one of the leading benefactors of mankind. He was the greatest liberator the world has ever known. By the force of his matchless genius, aided by his tireless energy, he struck the shackles of drudgery from untold millions of human beings and lifted the world into the light of a new civilization, the like of which humanity had scarcely dreamed.

He stands in history among the leaders of the men of genius of all time—Homer, Galileo, Michelangelo, Rembrandt, Mozart, Cervantes, Shakespeare, Columbus, Jefferson, Newton, and Marconi. Towering amid that great galaxy rises the immortal figure of Edison, in glorified silhouette against the horizon of the ages, sending a glow of radiance down the centuries to come, to stir the hopes and fire the imaginations of toilers of the future who struggle for the betterment of mankind.

It is unnecessary to attempt to magnify his virtues, to minimize his vices, or to clothe him with qualities he did not have. All that is necessary to commend him to the minds and hearts of peoples of all climes is the simple story of this earnest, patient man, toiling through the silent hours of the night to make the world a better place in which to live.

He was the greatest public servant of his day; yet he held no political office, he founded no political party, he advanced no new political creeds. Therefore no array of illustrious speakers volunteers to sing his praise or use his name as a sounding board to further selfish ends.

He was one of the mightiest conquerors this world has ever seen; yet he waged no wars of human destruction, he fought no bloody battles, he stirred no fires of human hate nor pandered to the baser passions of the race. But he conquered the elements, as it were, and gave to humanity the greatest ascendancy over the forces of nature the world has ever known. He brought the dawn of a new civilization—the electric age.

He never intentionally hurt a human being. Therefore no memorial has been erected to him in his country's Capital, no monument dedicated to his name, no blazing epitaph upon these historic walls proclaims his services to the world.

I sometimes wonder if we really appreciate the services of men of genius. They scale the heights and blaze the way to those sublime achievements that mark the milestones in the progress of the race, while men of talent dig in, solidify, and hold the gains and enjoy the progress that genius makes.

Have you ever thought what would happen if we should lose all that men and women of genius have accomplished for the world? What this land would be like? It would be a different world—cold, pulseless, monotonous, and silent. Our transportation system would come to a standstill, the telephone and telegraph wires would become useless obstructions, the lights would go out, the radio would be silenced, and all the machinery of industry, as well as that of commerce would cease to move. As has been well and wisely said, if you take from the world all that genius has given, "all the niches would be empty, all the walls would become naked, meaning and connection would fall from words of poetry and fiction, music would go back to common air, and all the forms of subtle and enchanting art would lose proportion, to become the unmeaning waste and shattered spoil of thoughtless chance."

It would be useless to attempt to enumerate all the things that Edison did for mankind. His greatest contribution was the invention of the electric light,—the incandescent lamp. With that one act he did more to change the course of our civilization than has any other man who ever "lived in the tide of time." He not only lighted our halls, our homes, our streets, and our highways, but he gave us the spark that fires the gas that makes the motor machine possible.

He ushered in the electric age, and the motor age as well. He made possible the automobile, the X ray, the airplane, the submarine, the moving picture, and the radio. He gave us a new system of overland transportation, taught us to navigate the air, and enabled us to roam with safety on the bottom of the seas. He eliminated time and space and aided us to see through objects that were formerly supposed to exclude all light.

He made possible mass production through new industrial machinery, and gave us that great multiplicity of electrical appliances that add to the comforts and conveniences of every home and every business establishment. He made necessities luxuries, and luxuries necessities, and enabled us to electrify the farm homes of America and to lift from the shoulders of burdened humanity the great weight of drudgery under which farm men and women have struggled since the beginning of time.

He tapped a source of wealth richer than the diamond mines of Golconda, more valuable than all the oil fields and all the gold and diamond mines of the modern and ancient world—a wealth that is inexhaustible, and one that will last as long as rains fall and rivers flow to the sea.

His monument is in every home that turns an electric switch; his epitaph is written on every heart that beats in gratitude for the services he gave. He needs no pompous memorial to commemorate his life. He needs no monument save the eternal and indestructible substance of his own greatness to commend him to the consideration of all coming ages. His name will live and his fame will reach to the remotest times in which civilized man shall dwell upon the earth.

Someone has said that—

"They are the truly great who, as the centuries slowly pass, are found by each succeeding race near to the heart of human love."

Centuries may come and go, empires may flourish and pass away, republics may rise and fall, but the work of Edison will endure.

When the monuments to lesser men shall have perished with the lapse of time, when this Republic shall have run its course and taken its place among the dead nations of the past, when in the distant lapse of ages yet to come, errant wanderers from different lands shall stand before the crumbling columns of this Capitol and look down across the ruins of the District of Columbia, the name of Thomas A. Edison will remain, unscarred by the wreck of ages and undimmed by the floods of time.

AT HIS BROTHER'S GRAVE

Robert G. Ingersoll

MY FRIENDS: I am going to do that which the dead often promised he would do for me. The loved and loving brother, husband, father, friend died where manhood's morning almost touches noon, and while the shadows still were falling toward the west. He had not passed on life's highway the stone that marks the highest point, but being weary for the moment he laid down by the wayside, and, using a burden for a pillow, fell into that dreamless sleep that kisses down his eyelids still. While yet in love with life and raptured with the world, he passed to silence and pathetic dust. Yet, after all, it may be best, just in the happiest, sunniest hour of all the voyage, while eager winds are kissing every sail, to dash against the unseen rock, and in an instant hear the billows roar, a sunken ship. For whether in mid sea or among the breakers of the farther shore, a wreck must mark at last the end of each and all. And every life, no matter if its every hour is rich with love and every moment jeweled with a joy, will, to its close, become a tragedy, as sad, and deep, and dark as can be woven of the warp and woof of mystery and death. This brave and tender man in every storm of life was oak and rock, but in the sunshine he was love and flower. He was the friend of all heroic souls that climbed the heights and left all superstitions here below, while on his forehead fell the golden dawning of a grander day. He loved the beautiful, and was with color, form and music touched to tears. He sided with the weak, and with a willing hand gave alms; with loyal heart and with the purest hand he faithfully discharged all public trusts. He was a worshiper of liberty and a friend of the oppressed. A thousand times I have heard him quote the words: "For justice, all place a temple and all season summer." He believed that happiness was the only good, reason the only torch, justice the only worshiper, humanity the only religion and love the priest. He added to the sum of human joy, and were everyone for whom he did some loving service to bring a blossom to his grave he would sleep to-night beneath a wilderness of flowers. Life is a narrow vale between the cold and barren peaks of two eternities. We strive in vain to look beyond the heights. We cry aloud, and the only answer is the echo of a wailing cry. From the voiceless lips of the unreplying dead there comes no word; but in the night of death hope sees a star and listening love can hear the rustle of a wing. He who sleeps here, when dying, mistaking the approach of death for the return of health, whispered with his latest breath, "I am better now." Let us believe, in spite of doubts and dogmas and tears and fears, that these dear words are true of all the countless dead. And now, to you who have been chosen from among the many men he loved to do the last sad office for the dead, we give his sacred trust. Speech cannot contain our love. There was—there is—no gentler, stronger, manlier man.

ADDRESS TO CONGRESS *

John H. Glenn, Jr.

Mr. Speaker, Mr. President, Members of the Congress, I am only too aware of the tremendous honor that is being shown us at this joint meeting of the Congress today. When I think of past meetings that involved heads of state and equally notable persons, I can only say that I am most humble to know that you consider our efforts to be in the same class. [Applause.]

This has been a great experience for all of us present and for all Americans, of course, and I am certainly glad to see that pride in our country and its accomplishments is not a thing of the past. [Applause.]

I still get a hard-to-define feeling inside when the flag goes by—and I know that all of you do, too. Today as we rode up Pennsylvania Avenue from the White House and saw the tremendous outpouring of feeling on the part of so many thousands of our people I got this same feeling all over again. Let us hope that none of us ever loses it. [Applause.]

The flight of *Friendship 7* on February 20 involved much more than one man in the spacecraft in orbit. [Applause.] I would like to have my parents stand up, please. [Mr. and Mrs. John Glenn, Sr., stood and received the rising applause of the Members.]

My wife's mother and Dr. Castor. [Dr. and Mrs. H. W. Castor stood and received the rising applause of the Members.]

My son and daughter, David and Carolyn. [David and Carolyn Glenn rose and received the rising applause of the Members.]

* Congressional Record, February 26, 1962, p. 2653. Lieutenant Colonel Glenn, after making the first American orbital flight, was invited to address a joint meeting of the House and Senate. In the audience, in addition to the Congressmen, were members of the Supreme Court and the diplomatic corps. Also present were fellow astronauts Virgil L. Grissom, Alan B. Shepard, Jr., Donald K. Slayton, Malcolm S. Carpenter, and Walter M. Schirra. The other astronaut, Leroy G. Cooper, Jr., was in Australia. John W. McCormack, Speaker of the House of Representatives, introduced Col. Glenn as follows: "Members of the Congress, it is a privilege, and I deem it a high honor, to present to you a brave, a courageous American, a hero in World War II and in the Korean conflict, who recently in a most notable manner added glory and prestige to our country, the first U.S. astronaut to have achieved orbital flight, Lt. Col. John H. Glenn, Jr., U.S. Marine Corps." [Applause, the Members rising.]

And the real rock in my family, my wife Annie. [Mrs. John H. Glenn, Jr., rose and received the applause of the Members.]

There are many more people, of course, involved in our flight in *Friendship 7;* many more things involved, as well as people. There was the vision of Congress that established this national program of space exploration. Beyond that, many thousands of people were involved, civilian contractors and many subcontractors in many different fields; many elements—civilian, civil service and military, all blending their efforts toward a common goal.

To even attempt to give proper credit to all the individuals on this team effort would be impossible. But let me say that I have never seen a more sincere, dedicated, and hard-working group of people in my life. [Applause.]

From the original vision of the Congress to consummation of this orbital flight has been just over 3 years. This, in itself, states eloquently the case for the hard work and devotion of the entire Mercury team. This has not been just another job. It has been a dedicated labor such as I have not seen before. It has involved a cross cut of American endeavor with many different disciplines cooperating toward a common objective.

Friendship 7 is just a beginning, a successful experiment. It is another plateau in our step-by-step program of increasingly ambitious flights. The earlier flights of Alan Shepard and Gus Grissom were steppingstones toward *Friendship 7.* My flight in the *Friendship 7* spacecraft will, in turn, provide additional information for use in striving toward future flights that some of the other gentlemen you see here will take part in. [Applause.]

Scott Carpenter here, who was my backup on this flight; Walt Schirra, Deek Slayton, and one missing member, who is still on his way back from Australia, where he was on the tracking station, Gordon Cooper. A lot of direction is necessary for a project such as this, and the Director of Project Mercury since its inception has been Dr. Robert Gilruth, who certainly deserves a hand here. [Applause.]

I have been trying to introduce Walt Williams. I do not see him here. There he is up in the corner. [Applause.]

And the Associate Directory of Mercury, who was in the unenviable position of being Operational Director. He is a character, no matter how you look at him. He says hold the count-foul, and one thing and another.

With all the experience we have had so far, where does this leave us?

These are the building blocks upon which we shall build much more ambitious and more productive portions of the program.

As was to be expected, not everything worked perfectly on my flight. We may well need to make changes—and these will be tried out on subsequent 3-orbit flights, later this year, to be followed by 18-orbit, 24-hour missions.

Beyond that, we look forward to Project Gemini—a two-man orbital vehicle with greatly increased capability for advanced experiments. There will be additional rendezvous experiments in space, technical and scientific observations—then, Apollo orbital, circumlunar and finally, lunar landing flights.

What did we learn from the *Friendship 7* flight that will help us attain these objectives?

Some specific items have already been covered briefly in the news reports. And I think it is of more than passing interest to all of us that information attained from these flights is readily available to all nations of the world. [Applause.]

The launch itself was conducted openly and with the news media representatives from around the world in attendance. [Applause.] Complete information is released as it is evaluated and validated. This is certainly in sharp contrast with similar programs conducted elsewhere in the world and elevates the peaceful intent of our program. [Applause.]

Data from the *Friendship 7* flight is still being analyzed. Certainly, much more information will be added to our storehouse of knowledge.

But these things we know. The Mercury spacecraft and systems design concepts are sound and have now been verified during manned flight. We also proved that man can operate intelligently in space and can adapt rapidly to this new environment.

Zero G or weightlessness—at least for this period of time—appears to be no problem. As a matter of fact, lack of gravity is a rather fascinating thing.

Objects within the cockpit can be parked in midair. For example, at one time during the flight, I was using a hand held camera. Another system needed attention; so it seemed quite natural to let go of the camera, take care of the other chore in the spacecraft, then reach out, grasp the camera and go back about my business.

It is a real fascinating feeling, needless to say.

There seemed to be little sensation of speed although the craft was traveling at about 5 miles per second—a speed that I too find difficult to comprehend.

In addition to closely monitoring onboard systems, we were able to make numerous outside observations.

The view from that altitude defies description.

The horizon colors are brilliant and sunsets are spectacular. It is hard to beat a day in which you are permitted the luxury of seeing four sunsets.

I think after all of our talk of space, this morning coming up from Florida on the plane with President Kennedy, we had the opportunity to meet Mrs. Kennedy and Caroline before we took off. I think Caroline really cut us down to size and put us back in the proper position. She looked up, upon being introduced, and said, "Where is the monkey?" [Laughter.]

And I did not get a banana pellet on the whole ride.

Our efforts today and what we have done so far are but small building blocks in a huge pyramid to come.

But questions are sometimes raised regarding the immediate payoffs from our efforts. What benefits are we gaining from the money spent? The real benefits we probably cannot even detail. They are probably not even known to man today. But exploration and the pursuit of knowledge have always paid dividends in the long run—usually far greater than anything expected at the outset. [Applause.]

Experimenters with common, green mold, little dreamed what effect their discovery of penicillin would have.

The story has been told of Disraeli, Prime Minister of England at the time, visiting the laboratory of Faraday, one of the early experimenters with basic electrical principles. After viewing various demonstrations of electrical phenomena, Disraeli asked, "But of what possible use is it?" Faraday replied, "Mister Prime Minister, what good is a baby?"

That is the stage of development in our program today—in its infancy. And it indicates a much broader potential impact, of course, than even the discovery of electricity did. We are just probing the surface of the greatest advancements in man's knowledge of his surroundings that has ever been made, I feel.

There are benefits to science across the board. Any major effort such as this results in research by so many different specialties that it is hard to even envision the benefits that will accrue in many fields.

Knowledge begets knowledge. The more I see, the more impressed I am—not with how much we know—but with how tremendous the areas are that are as yet unexplored.

Exploration, knowledge, and achievement are good only insofar as we apply them to our future actions. Progress never stops. We are now on the verge of a new era, I feel.

Today, I know that I seem to be standing alone on this great platform—just as I seemed to be alone in the cockpit of the *Friendship 7* spacecraft. But I am not. There were with me then—and with me now—thousands of Americans and many hundreds of citizens of many countries around the world who contributed to this truly international undertaking voluntarily and in a spirit of cooperation and understanding.

On behalf of all those people, I would like to express my and their heartfelt thanks for the honors you have bestowed upon us here today.

We are all proud to have been privileged to be part of this effort, to represent our country as we have. As our knowledge of the universe in which we live increases, may God grant us the wisdom and guidance to use it wisely.

Thank you, gentlemen. [Applause, the Members rising.]

DUTY, HONOR, COUNTRY *

Douglas MacArthur

General Westmoreland, General Groves, distinguished guests, and gentlemen of the corps: As I was leaving the hotel this morning, a doorman asked me, "Where are you bound for, General?" and when I replied, "West Point," he remarked, "Beautiful place, have you ever been there before?"

* Congressional Record, May 31, 1962, pp. A4008-09. General of the Army Douglas MacArthur accepted the Sylvanus Thayer award for service to his nation at ceremonies in Washington Hall, the cadet mess hall, at the Military Academy at West Point, May 12, 1962. Speaking without text or notes, the 82-year-old General bade farewell to the cadet corps and gave it a code of conduct.

No human being could fail to be deeply moved by such a tribute as this [Thayer Award]. Coming from a profession I have served so long, and a people I have loved so well, it fills me with an emotion I cannot express. But this award is not intended primarily to honor a personality, but to symbolize a great moral code—the code of conduct and chivalry of those who guard this beloved land of culture and ancient descent. That is the meaning of this medallion. For all eyes and for all time, it is an expression of the ethics of the American soldier. That I should be integrated in this way with so noble an ideal arouses a sense of pride and yet of humility which will be with me always.

Duty—honor—country: Those three hallowed words reverently dictate what you ought to be, what you can be, what you will be. They are your rallying points: to build courage when courage seems to fail; to regain faith when there seems to be little cause for faith; to create hope when hope becomes forlorn. Unhappily, I possess neither that eloquence of diction, that poetry of imagination, nor that brilliance of metaphor to tell you all that they mean. The unbelievers will say they are but words, but a slogan, but a flamboyant phrase. Every pedant, every demagog, every cynic, every hypocrite, every troublemaker, and, I am sorry to say, some others of an entirely different character, will try to downgrade them even to the extent of mockery and ridicule. But these are some of the things they do. They build your basic character, they mold you for your future roles as the custodians of the Nation's defense, they make you strong enough to know when you are weak, and brave enough to face yourself when you are afraid. They teach you to be proud and unbending in honest failure, but humble and gentle in success; not to substitute words for actions, nor to seek the path of comfort, but to face the stress and spur of difficulty and challenge; to learn to stand up in the storm but to have compassion on those who fail; to master yourself before you seek to master others; to have a heart that is clean, a goal that is high; to learn to laugh yet never forget how to weep; to reach into the future yet never neglect the past; to be serious yet never to take yourself too seriously; to be modest so that you will remember the simplicity of true greatness, the open mind of true wisdom, the meekness of true strength. They give you a temper of the will, a quality of the imagination, a vigor of the emotions, a freshness of the deep springs of life, a temperamental predominance of courage over timidity, an appetite for adventure over love of ease. They create in your heart the sense of wonder, the unfailing hope of what next, and the joy and inspiration of life. They teach you in this way to be an officer and a gentleman.

And what sort of soldiers are those you are to lead? Are they reliable, are they brave, are they capable of victory? Their story is known to all of you; it is the story of the American man-at-arms. My estimate of him was formed on the battlefield many, many years ago, and has never changed. I regarded him then as I regard him now—as one of the world's noblest figures, not only as one of the finest military characters but also as one of the most stainless. His name and fame are the birthright of every American citizen. In his youth and strength, his love and loyalty he gave— all that mortality can give. He needs no eulogy from me or from any other man. He has written his own history and written it in red on his enemy's breast. But when I think of his patience under adversity, of his courage under fire, and of his modesty in victory, I am filled with an emotion of admiration I cannot put into words. He belongs to history as furnishing one of the greatest examples of successful patriotism; he belongs to posterity as the instructor of future generations in the principles of liberty and freedom; he belongs to the present, to us, by his virtues and by his achievements. In 20 campaigns, on a hundred battlefields, around a thousand campfires, I have witnessed that enduring fortitude, that patriotic self-abnegation, and that invincible determination which have carved his statue in the hearts of his people. From one end of the world to the other he has drained deep the chalice of courage.

As I listened to those songs of the glee club, in memory's eye I could see those staggering columns of the First World War, bending under soggy packs, on many a weary march from dripping dusk to drizzling dawn, slogging ankle deep through the mire of shell-shocked roads, to form grimly for the attack, blue lipped, covered with sludge and mud, chilled by the wind and rain; driving home to their objective, and, for many, to the judgement seat of God. I do not know the dignity of their birth but I do know the glory of their death. They died unquestioning, uncomplaining, with faith in their hearts, and on their lips the hope that we would go on to victory. Always for them—duty—honor—country; always their blood and sweat and tears as we sought the way and the light and the truth.

And 20 years after, on the other side of the globe, again the filth of murky foxholes, the stench of ghostly trenches, the slime of dripping dugouts; those boiling suns of relentless heat, those torrential rains of devastating storms; the loneliness and utter desolation of jungle trails, the bitterness of long separation from those they loved and cherished, the deadly pestilence of tropical disease, the horror of stricken areas of war; their resolute and determined defense, their swift and sure attack, their indomitable purpose, their complete and decisive victory—always victory. Always through the bloody haze of their last reverberating shot, the vision of gaunt, ghastly men reverently following your password of duty—honor—country.

The code which those words perpetuate embraces the highest moral laws and will stand the test of any ethics or philosophies ever promulgated for the uplift of mankind. Its requirements are for the things that are right, and its restraints are from the things that are wrong. The soldier, above all other men, is required to practice the greatest act of religious training—sacrifice. In battle and in the face of danger and death, he discloses those divine attributes which his Maker gave when he created man in His own image. No physical courage and no brute instinct can take the place of the divine help which alone can sustain him. However horrible the incidents of war may be, the soldier who is called upon to offer and to give his life for his country, is the noblest development of mankind.

You now face a new world—a world of change. The thrust into outer space of the satellite, spheres and missiles marked the beginning of another epoch in the long story of mankind—the chapter of the space age. In the 5 or more billions of years the scientists tell us it has taken to form the earth, in the 3 or more million years of development of the human race, there has never been a greater, a more abrupt or staggering evolution. We deal now not with things of this world alone, but with the illimitable distances and as yet unfathomed mysteries of the universe. We are reaching out for a new and boundless frontier. We speak in strange terms: of harnessing the cosmic energy; of making winds and tides work for us; of creating unheard synthetic materials to supplement or even replace our old standard basics; of purifying sea water for our drink; of mining ocean floors for new fields of wealth and food; of disease preventatives to expand life into the hundreds of years; of controlling the weather for a more equitable distribution of heat and cold, or rain and shine; of spaceships to the moon; of the primary target in war, no longer limited to the armed forces of an enemy, but instead to include his civil populations; of ultimate conflict between a united human race and the sinister forces of some other planetary galaxy; of such dreams and fantasies as to make life the most exciting of all time.

And through all this welter of change and development, your mission remains fixed, determined, inviolable—it is to win our wars. Everything else in your professional career is but corollary to this vital dedication. All other public purposes, all other public projects, all other public needs, great or small, will find others for their accomplishment; but you are the ones who are trained to fight: yours is the profession of arms—the will to win, the sure knowledge that in war there is no substitute for victory; that if you lose, the Nation will be destroyed; that the very obsession of your public service must be duty—honor—country. Others will debate the controversial issues, national and international, which divide men's minds; but serene, calm, aloof, you stand as the Nation's war-guardian, as its lifeguard from the raging tides of international conflict, as its gladiator in the arena of battle. For a century and a half you have defended, guarded, and protected its hallowed traditions of liberty and freedom, of right and justice. Let civilian voices argue the merits or demerits of our processes of government; whether our strength is being sapped by deficit financing, indulged in too long, by Federal paternalism grown too mighty, by power groups grown too arrogant, by politics grown too corrupt, by crime grown too rampant, by morals grown too low, by taxes grown too high, by extremists grown too violent; whether our personal liberties are as thorough and complete as they should be. These great national problems are not for your professional participation or military solution. Your guidepost stands out like a tenfold beacon in the night— duty—honor—country.

You are the leaven which binds together the entire fabric of our national system of defense. From your ranks come the great captains who hold the Nation's destiny in their hands the moment the war tocsin sounds. The long gray line has never failed us. Were you to do so, a million ghosts in olive drab, in brown khaki, in blue and gray, would rise from their white crosses thundering those magic words—duty—honor—country.

This does not mean that you are war-mongers. On the contrary, the soldier, above all other people, prays for peace, for he must suffer and bear the deepest wounds and scars of war. But always in our ears ring the ominous words of Plato, that wisest of all philosophers, "Only the dead have seen the end of war."

The shadows are lengthening for me. The twilight is here. My days of old have vanished tone and tint; they have gone glimmering through the dreams of things that were. Their memory is one of wondrous beauty, watered by tears, and coaxed and caressed by the smiles of yesterday. I listen vainly for the witching melody of faint bugles blowing reveille, of far drums beating the long roll. In my dreams I hear again the crash of guns, the rattle of musketry, the strange, mournful mutter of the battle-field.

But in the evening of my memory, always I come back to West Point. Always there echoes and reechoes duty—honor—country.

Today marks my final rollcall with you, but I want you to know that when I cross the river my last conscious thoughts will be of the corps, and the corps, and the corps.

I bid you farewell.

Persuasive Speeches

THE WAR ADDRESS *

Franklin D. Roosevelt

1. Yesterday, December 7, 1941—a date which will live in infamy—the United States of America was suddenly and deliberately attacked by naval and air forces of the Empire of Japan.

The United States was at peace with that nation, and, at the solicitation of Japan, was still in conversation with its Government and its Emperor looking toward the maintenance of peace in the Pacific.

* December 8, 1941. Delivered to a joint session of Congress.

2. Indeed, one hour after Japanese air squadrons had commenced bombing Oahu, the Japanese Ambassador to the United States and his colleague delivered to the Secretary of State a formal reply to a recent American message. While this reply stated that it seemed useless to continue the existing diplomatic negotiations, it contained no threat or hint of war or armed attack.

3. It will be recorded that the distance of Hawaii from Japan makes it obvious that the attack was deliberately planned many days or even weeks ago. During the intervening time, the Japanese government has deliberately sought to deceive the United States by false statements and expressions of hope for continued peace.

The attack yesterday on the Hawaiian Islands has caused severe damage to American military and naval forces. Very many American lives have been lost. In addition, American ships have been reported torpedoed on the high seas between San Francisco and Honolulu.

4. Yesterday the Japanese Government also launched an attack against Malaya.

Last night Japanese forces attacked Hong Kong.

Last night Japanese forces attacked Guam.

Last night Japanese forces attacked the Philippine Islands.

Last night the Japanese attacked Wake Island.

Last night the Japanese attacked Midway Island.

Japan has, therefore, undertaken a surprise offensive extending throughout the Pacific area. The facts of yesterday speak for themselves. The people of the United States have already formed their opinions and well understand the implications to the very life and safety of our nation.

5. As Commander in Chief of the Army and Navy I have directed that all measures be taken for our defense.

Always will we remember the character of the onslaught against us. No matter how long it may take us to overcome this premeditated invasion, the American people in their righteous might will win through to absolute victory.

6. I believe I interpret the will of the Congress and of the people when I assert that we will not only defend ourselves to the uttermost but will make very certain that this form of treachery shall never endanger us again.

Hostilities exist. There is no blinking at the fact that our people, our territory, and our interests are in grave danger.

With confidence in our armed forces—with the unbounding

determination of our people—we will gain the inevitable triumph —so help us God.

I ask that the Congress declare that since the unprovoked and dastardly attack by Japan on Sunday, December 7, a state of war has existed between the United States and the Japanese Empire.

THE NEW SOUTH *

Henry W. Grady

"There was a South of slavery and secession—that South is dead. There is a South of union and freedom—that South, thank God, is living, breathing, growing every hour." These words, delivered from the immortal lips of Benjamin H. Hill, at Tammany Hall, in 1866, true then and truer now, I shall make my text tonight.

Mr. President and Gentlemen: Let me express to you my appreciation of the kindness by which I am permitted to address you. I make this abrupt acknowledgement advisedly, for I feel that if, when I raise my provincial voice in this ancient and august presence, I could find courage for no more than the opening sentence, it would be well if in that sentence I had met in a rough sense my obligation as a guest, and had perished, so to speak, with courtesy on my lips and grace in my heart. Permitted, through your kindness, to catch my second wind, let me say that I appreciate the significance of being the first Southerner to speak at this board, which bears the substance, if it surpasses the semblance, of original New England hospitality—and honors the sentiment that in turn honors you, but in which my personality is lost, and the compliment to my people made plain.

I bespeak the utmost stretch of your courtesy tonight. I am not troubled about those from whom I come. You remember the man whose wife sent him to a neighbor with a pitcher of milk, and who, tripping on the top step, fell with such casual interruptions as the landings afforded into the basement, and, while pick-

* J. C. Harris, *Henry W. Grady—His Writings and Speeches*, 1893, pp. 83 ff. This famous persuasive speech was delivered December 21, 1886, before the New England Society of New York. It brought Grady national fame as an orator.

ing himself up, had the pleasure of hearing his wife call out: "John, did you break the pitcher?"

"No, I didn't," said John, "but I'll be dinged if I don't."

So, while those who call me from behind may inspire me with energy, if not with courage, I ask an indulgent hearing from you. I beg that you will bring your full faith in American fairness and frankness to judgment upon what I shall say. There was an old preacher once who told some boys of the Bible lesson he was going to read in the morning. The boys, finding the place, glued together the connecting pages. The next morning he read on the bottom of one page, "When Noah was one hundred and twenty years old he took unto himself a wife, who was"—then turning the page—"140 cubits long—40 cubits wide, built of gopher wood —and covered with pitch inside and out." He was naturally puzzled at this. He read it again, verified it, and then said. "My friends, this is the first time I ever met this in the Bible, but I accept this as an evidence of the assertion that we are fearfully and wonderfully made." If I could get you to hold such faith tonight I could proceed cheerfully to the task I otherwise approach with a sense of consecration.

Pardon me one word, Mr. President, spoken for the sole purpose of getting into the volumes that go out annually freighted with the rich eloquence of your speakers—the fact that the Cavalier as well as the Puritan was on the continent in its early days, and that he was "up and able to be about." I have read your books carefully and I find no mention of that fact, which seems to me an important one for preserving a sort of historical equilibrium if for nothing else.

Let me remind you that the Virginia Cavalier first challenged France on the continent—that Cavalier John Smith gave New England its very name, and was so pleased with the job that he has been handing his own name around ever since—and that while Miles Standish was cutting off men's ears for courting a girl without her parents' consent, and forbade men to kiss their wives on Sunday, the Cavalier was courting everything in sight, and that the Almighty had vouchsafed great increase to the Cavalier colonies, the huts in the wilderness being as full as the nests in the woods.

But having incorporated the Cavalier as a fact in your charming little books, I shall let him work out his own salvation, as he has always done, with engaging gallantry, and we will hold no controversy as to his merits. Why should we? Neither Puritan nor Cavalier long survived as such. The virtues and good traditions of both happily still live for the inspiration of their sons and the saving of the old fashion. But both Puritan and Cavalier were lost in the storm of the first Revolution, and the American citizen, supplanting both and stronger than either, took possession of the republic bought by their common blood and fashioned to wisdom, and charged himself with teaching men government and establishing the voice of the people as the voice of God.

My friends, Dr. Talmadge has told you that the typical American has yet to come. Let me tell you that he has already come. Great types, like valuable plants, are slow to flower and fruit. But from the union of these colonists, Puritans and Cavaliers, from the straightening of their purposes and the crossing of their blood, slow perfecting through a century, came he who stands as the first typical American, the first who comprehended within himself all the strength and gentleness, all the majesty and grace of this republic—Abraham Lincoln. He was the sum of Puritan and Cavalier, for in his ardent nature were fused the virtues of both, and in the depths of his great soul the faults of both were lost. He was greater than Puritan, greater than Cavalier, in that he was American, and that in his honest form were first gathered the vast and thrilling forces of his ideal government—charging it with such tremendous meaning and elevating it above human suffering that martyrdom, though infamously aimed, came as a fitting crown to a life consecrated from the cradle to human liberty. Let us, each cherishing the traditions and honoring his forefathers, build with reverent hands to the type of this simple but sublime life, in which all types are honored, and in our common glory as Americans there will be plenty and to spare for your forefathers and for mine.

Dr. Talmadge has drawn for you, with a master's hand, the picture of your returning armies. He has told you how, in the pomp and circumstance of war, they came back to you, marching with proud and victorious tread, reading their glory in a nation's eyes! Will you bear with me while I tell you of another army that sought its home at the close of the late war—an army that marched home in defeat and not in victory—in pathos and not in splendor, but in glory that equaled yours, and to hearts as loving as ever welcomed heroes home! Let me picture to you the footsore Confederate soldier, as buttoning up in his faded gray jacket the parole which was to bear testimony to his children of his fidelity and faith, he turned his face southward from Appomattox in April, 1865. Think of him as ragged, half-starved, heavy-hearted, enfeebled by want and wounds; having fought to exhaustion, he surrenders his gun, wrings the hands of his comrades in silence, and lifting his tear-stained and pallid face for the last time to the graves that dot the old Virginia hills, pulls his gray cap over his brow and begins the slow and painful journey. What does he find—let me ask you who went to your homes eager to find, in the welcome you had justly earned, full payment for four years' sacrifice—what does he find when, having followed the battle-stained cross against overwhelming odds, dreading death not half so much as surrender, he reaches the home he left so prosperous and beautiful? He finds his house in ruins, his farm devastated, his slaves free, his stock killed, his barns empty, his trade destroyed, his money worthless, his social system, feudal in its magnificence, swept away; his people without law or legal status; his comrades slain, and the burdens of others heavy on his shoulders. Crushed by defeat, his very traditions are gone. Without money, credit, employment, material, or training; and beside all this, confronted with the gravest problem that ever met human intelligence—the establishing of a status for the vast body of his liberated slaves.

What does he do—this hero in gray with a heart of gold? Does he sit down in sullenness and despair? Not for a day. Surely God, who had stripped him of his prosperity, inspired him in his adversity. As ruin was never before so overwhelming, never was restoration swifter. The soldier stepped from the trenches into the furrow; horses that had charged Federal guns marched before the plow, and fields that ran red with human blood in April were green with the harvest in June; women reared in luxury cut up their dresses and made breeches for their husbands, and, with a patience and heroism that fit women always as a garment, gave their hands to work. There was little bitterness in all this. Cheerfulness and frankness prevailed. "Bill Arp" struck the key-note when he said: "Well, I killed as many of them as they did of me, and now I'm going to work." Or the soldier returning home after defeat and roasting some corn on the roadside, who made the remark to his comrades: "You may leave the South if you want to, but I am going to Sandersville, kiss my wife and raise a crop, and if the Yankees fool with me any more, I'll whip 'em again." I want to say to General Sherman, who is considered an able man in our parts, though some people think he is a kind of careless man about fire, that from the ashes he left us in 1864 we have raised a brave and beautiful city; that somehow or other we have caught the sunshine in the bricks and mortar of our homes, and have builded therein not one ignoble prejudice or memory.

But what is the sum of our work? We have found out that in the summing up the free negro counts more than he did as a slave. We have planted the school house on the hilltop and made it free to white and black. We have sowed towns and cities in the place of theories, and put business above politics. We have challenged your spinners in Massachusetts and your ironmakers in Pennsylvania. We have learned that the four hundred million dollars annually received from our cotton crop will make us rich when the supplies that make it are home raised. We have reduced the commercial rate of interest from 24 to 6 per cent, and are floating 4 per cent bonds. We have learned that one northern immigrant is worth fifty foreigners; and have smoothed the path to southward, wiped out the place where Mason's and Dixon's line used to be, and hung out the latchstring to you and yours. We have reached the point that marks perfect harmony in every household, when the husband confesses that the pies which his wife cooks are as good as those his mother used to bake; and we admit that the sun shines as brightly and the moon as softly as it did before the war. We have established thrift in city and country. We have fallen in love with work. We have restored comfort to homes from which culture and elegance never departed. We have let economy take root and spread among us as rank as the crab-grass which sprung from Sherman's cavalry camps, until we are ready to lay odds on the Georgia Yankee as he manufactures relics of the battlefield in a one-story shanty and squeezes pure olive oil out of his cotton seed, against any down-easter that ever swapped wooden nutmegs for flannel sausage in the valleys of Vermont. Above all, we know that we have achieved in these "piping times of peace" a fuller independence for the South than that which our fathers sought to win in the forum by their eloquence or compel in the field by their swords.

It is a rare privilege, sir, to have had a part, however humble, in this work. Never was nobler duty confided to human hands than the uplifting and upbuilding of the prostrate and bleeding South—misguided, perhaps, but beautiful in her suffering, and honest, brave, and generous always. In the record of her social, industrial, and political illustration we await with confidence the verdict of the world.

But what of the negro? Have we solved the problem he presents or progressed in honor and equity toward solution? Let the record speak to the point. No section shows a more prosperous laboring population than the negroes of the South, none in fuller sympathy with the employing and land-owning class. He shares our school fund, has the fullest protection of our laws and the friendship of our people. Self-interest, as well as honor, demand that he should have this. Our future, our very existence, depend upon our working out this problem in full and exact justice. We understand that when Lincoln signed the emancipation proclamation, your victory was assured, for he then committed you to the cause of human liberty, against which the arms of man cannot prevail—while those of our statesmen who trusted to make slavery the cornerstone of the Confederacy doomed us to defeat as far as they could, committing us to a cause that reason could not defend or the sword maintain in sight of advancing civilization.

Had Mr. Toombs said, which he did not say, "that he would call the roll of his slaves at the foot of Bunker Hill," he would have been foolish, for he might have known that whenever slavery becomes entangled in war it must perish, and that the chattel in human flesh ended forever in New England when your fathers—not to be blamed for parting with what didn't pay—sold their slaves to our fathers—not to be praised for knowing a paying thing when they saw it. The relations of the southern people with the negro are close and cordial. We remember with what fidelity for four years he guarded our defenseless women and children, whose husbands and fathers were fighting against his freedom. To his eternal credit be it said that whenever he struck a blow for his own liberty he fought in open battle, and when at last he raised his black and humble hands that the shackles might be struck off, those hands were innocent of wrong against his helpless charges, and worthy to be taken in loving grasp by every man who honors loyalty and devotion. Ruffians have maltreated him, rascals have misled him, philanthropists established a bank for him, but the South, with the North, protests against injustice to this simple and sincere people. To liberty and enfranchisement is as far as law can carry the negro. The rest must be left to conscience and common sense. It might be left to those among whom his lot is cast, with whom he is indissolubly connected, and whose prosperity depends upon their possessing his intelligent sympathy and confidence. Faith has been kept with him, in spite of calumnious assertions to the contrary by those who assume to speak for us or by frank opponents. Faith will be kept with him in the future, if the South holds her reason and integrity.

But have we kept faith with you? In the fullest sense, yes. When Lee surrendered—I don't say when Johnston surrendered, because I understand he still alludes to the time when he met General Sherman last as the time when he determined to abandon any further prosecution of the struggle—when Lee surrendered, I say, and Johnston quit, the South became, and has since been, loyal to this Union. We fought hard enough to know that we were whipped, and in perfect frankness accept as final the arbitrament of the sword to which we had appealed. The South found her jewel in the toad's head of defeat. The shackles that had held her in narrow limitations fell forever when the shackles of the negro slave were broken. Under the old regime the negroes were slaves to the South; the South was a slave to the system. The old plantation, with its simple police regulations and feudal habit, was the only type possible under slavery. Thus was gathered in the hands of a splendid and chivalric oligarchy the substance that should have been diffused among the people, as the rich blood, under certain artificial conditions, is gathered at the heart, filling that with affluent rapture but leaving the body chill and colorless.

The old South rested everything on slavery and agriculture, unconscious that these could neither give nor maintain healthy growth. The new South presents a perfect democracy, the oligarchs leading in the popular movement—a social system compact and closely knitted, less splendid on the surface, but stronger at the core—a hundred farms for every plantation, fifty homes for every palace—and a diversified industry that meets the complex need of this complex age.

The new South is enamored of her new work. Her soul is stirred with the breath of a new life. The light of a grander day is falling fair on her face. She is thrilling with the consciousness of growing power and prosperity. As she stands upright, full-statured and equal among the peoples of the earth, breathing the keen air and looking out upon the expanded horizon, she understands that her emancipation came because through the inscrutable wisdom of God her honest purpose was crossed, and her brave armies were beaten.

This is said in no spirit of time-serving or apology. The South has nothing for which to apologize. She believes that the late struggle between the states was war and not rebellion; revolution and not conspiracy, and that her convictions were as honest as yours. I should be unjust to the dauntless spirit of the South and to my own convictions if I did not make this plain in this presence. The South has nothing to take back. In my native town of Athens is a monument that crowns its central hill—a plain, white shaft. Deep cut into its shining side is a name dear to me above the names of men—that of a brave and simple man who died in brave and simple faith. Not for all the glories of New England, from Plymouth Rock all the way, would I exchange the heritage he left me in his soldier's death. To the foot of that shaft I shall send my children's children to reverence him who ennobled their name with his heroic blood. But, sir, speaking from the shadow of that memory which I honor as I do nothing else on earth, I say that the cause in which he suffered and for which he gave his life was adjudged by higher and fuller wisdom than his or mine, and I am glad that the omniscient God held the balance of battle in His almighty hand and that human slavery was swept forever from American soil, the American Union was saved from the wreck of war.

This message, Mr. President, comes to you from consecrated ground. Every foot of soil about the city in which I live is sacred as a battleground of the republic. Every hill that invests it is hallowed to you by the blood of your brothers who died for your victory, and doubly hallowed to us by the blood of those who died hopeless, but undaunted, in defeat—sacred soil to all of us—rich with memories that make us purer and stronger and better—silent but staunch witnesses in its red desolation of the matchless valor of American hearts and the deathless glory of American arms— speaking an eloquent witness in its white peace and prosperity to the indissoluble union of American States and the imperishable brotherhood of the American people.

Now, what answer has New England to this message? Will she permit the prejudice of war to remain in the hearts of the conquerors, when it has died in the hearts of the conquered? Will she transmit this prejudice to the next generation, that in their hearts which never felt the generous ardor of conflict it may perpetuate itself? Will she withhold, save in strained courtesy, the hand which straight from his soldier's heart Grant offered to Lee at Appomattox? Will she make the vision of a restored and happy people, which gathered above the couch of your dying captain, filling his heart with grace; touching his lips with praise, and glorifying his path to the grave—will she make this vision on which the last sigh of his expiring soul breathed a benediction, a cheat and delusion? If she does, the South, never abject in asking for comradeship, must accept with dignity its refusal; but if she does not refuse to accept in frankness and sincerity this message of good will and friendship, then will the prophecy of Webster, delivered in this very society forty years ago amid tremendous applause, become true, be verified in its fullest sense, when he said: "Standing hand to hand and clasping hands, we should remain united as we have been for sixty years, citizens of the same country, members of the same government, united, all united now and united forever." There have been difficulties, contentions, and controversies, but I tell you that in my judgment,

> Those opposed eyes,
> Which like the meteors of a troubled heaven,
> All of one nature, of one substance bred,
> Did lately meet in th' intestine shock,
> Shall now, in mutual well beseeming ranks,
> March all one way.

VIVE LA FRANCE! *

Winston Churchill

Frenchmen! For more than thirty years, in peace and war, I marched with you and I am marching still along the same road.

Tonight I speak to you at your firesides wherever you may be, or whatever your fortunes are. I repeat the prayer around the louis d'or—Dieu protège la France, God protect France.

Here at home in England, under the fire of the Boche, we do not forget the ties and links that unite us to France, and we are persevering steadfastly and in good heart in the cause of Euro-

* *Vital Speeches*, November 1, 1940. The Right Honorable Winston Churchill, Prime Minister of Great Britain, delivered this radio address from London, October 19, 1940.

pean freedom and fair dealing for the common people of all countries for which, with you, we draw the sword.

When good people get into trouble because they are attacked and heavily smitten by the vile and wicked, they must be very careful not to get at loggerheads with one another. The common enemy is always trying to bring this about, and, of course, in bad luck a lot of things happen which play into the enemy's hands. We must just make the best of things as they come along.

Here in London, which Herr Hitler says he will reduce to ashes and which his airplanes are now bombarding, our people are bearing up unflinchingly. Our air force has more than held its own. We are waiting for the long-promised invasion—so are the fishes.

But, of course, this brush is only the beginning. Now in 1940, in spite of occasional losses, we have, as ever, the command of the seas. In 1941 we shall have the command of the air. Remember what that means.

Herr Hitler, with his tanks and other mechanical weapons and also by fifth-column intrigue with traitors, has managed to subjugate for the time being most of the finest races in Europe, and his little Italian accomplice is trotting along hopefully and hungrily, but rather wearily and very timidly, at his side. They both wish to carve up France and her empire as if it were a fowl—to one a leg, to another a wing, or perhaps part of the breast.

Not only the French Empire will be devoured by these two ugly customers, but Alsace-Lorraine will go once again under the German yoke and Nice, Savoy, and Corsica, Napoleon's Corsica, will be torn from the fair realm of France.

But Herr Hitler is not thinking only of stealing other people's territories, of flinging gobbets of them to his little confederate. I tell you truly what you must believe when I say this evil man, this monstrous abortion of hatred and deceit, is resolved on nothing less than the complete wiping out of the French nation and the disintegration of its whole life and future.

By all kinds of sly and savage means he is plotting and working to quench forever the fountain of characteristic French culture and French inspiration to the world. All Europe, if he has his way, will be reduced to one uniform Bocheland, to be exploited, pillaged, and bullied by his Nazi gangsters.

You will excuse my speaking frankly, because this is not a time to mince words. It is not defeat that France will now be made to suffer at German hands, but the doom of complete obliteration—army, navy, air force, religion, laws, language, culture, institutions, literature, history, tradition—all are to be effaced by the brute strength of a triumphant army and the scientific, low cunning of a ruthless police force.

Frenchmen! Rearm your spirits before it is too late. Remember how Napoleon said before one of his battles—these same Prussians who are so boastful today were three to one at Jena and six to one at Montmirail—"Never will I believe that the soul of France is dead; never will I believe that her place among the greatest nations of the world has been lost forever."

All these schemes and crimes of Herr Hitler are bringing upon him and upon all who belong to his system a retribution which many of us will live to see. The story is not yet finished, but it will not be so long. We are on his track and so are our friends across the Atlantic Ocean and your friends across the Atlantic Ocean. If he cannot destroy us we will surely destroy him and all his gang and all their works.

Therefore, have hope and faith, for all will come right.

Now, what is it we British ask of you in this present hard and bitter time? What we ask at this moment in our struggle to win the victory which we will share with you is that if you cannot help us, at least you will not hinder us.

Presently you will be able to weight the arm that strikes for you and you ought to do so. But even now we trust that Frenchmen, wherever they may be, will feel their hearts warm and the proud blood tingle in their veins when we have some success in the air or on the sea, or presently, for that will come, upon the land.

Remember, we shall never stop, never weary and never give in, and that our whole people and empire have vowed themselves to the task of cleansing Europe from the Nazi pestilence and saving the world from the new Dark Ages. Do not imagine, as the German-controlled wireless tells you, that we English seek to take your ships and colonies. We seek to beat the life and soul out of Hitler and Hitlerism—that alone, that all the time, that to the end.

We do not covet anything from any nation, except their respect.

Those Frenchmen who are in the French Empire and those who are in so-called unoccupied France may see their way from time to time to useful action. I will not go into details. Hostile ears are listening.

As for those to whom English hearts go out in full because they see them under sharp discipline, oppression and spying of the Hun—as to those Frenchmen in the occupied regions, to them I say, when they think of the future let them remember the words which [Leon] Gambetta, that great Frenchman, uttered after 1870 about the future of France and what was to come: "Think of it always. Speak of it never."

Good night, then. Sleep to gather strength for the morning, for the morning will come. Brightly will it shine on the brave and true; kindly upon all who suffer for the cause; glorious upon the tombs of heroes—thus will shine the dawn.

Vive la France! Long live, also, the forward march of the common people in all the lands toward their just and true inheritance and toward the broader and fuller age.

HEAVEN WON'T WAIT *

Frederick E. Christian

Luke 6:24 "You can not serve God and mammon [self]."

Young people know more about the kind of music that exudes from a juke-box than any oldsters and especially more than a proper preacher. But every now and then a piece is turned out that, by its tune, its title or its text, sings its way into the mind and heart of the general public. It gathers up into its lilt or into its lines an attitude of the hour or a whole philosophy of life. It is hummed by people as they go about their work, it is sung between their foot falls, because it tells the story of what they are thinking as individuals or that people about them are feeling in the deep places of their lives.

One whose life spans a few years recalls the songs of his youth. Who knows in this day of "revivals" when one of these may become the hit of the day? Here was a song we sang between the two great World Wars. It said something about "building a sweet little nest somewhere in the West and letting the rest of the world go by." This was more than a love song of the moment. It was a

---

* Baccalaureate address, by permission of the author.

philosophy of life held by many then and possessing many more now. They were saying "Let's build our little nest off here in the West and let the rest of the world go by."

Some time later we were singing about "Pennies from Heaven." That was during the depression when many of us didn't have two pennies to rub together. We didn't see where another penny might come from. We wanted "pennies from heaven."

At the close of World War II, we sang of a hapless young man shut outside the door of a comfortable home after a prolonged binge. He had lost the key. So that generation began to chant everywhere "Open the door for Richard." We were looking for a new and satisfying life.

The jitterbug, jive and rock n' roll of the current decade all express the abandon, the aimlessness or the irresponsibility that many feel toward life and its more serious problems. Each generation sings and dances what it senses and feels about life.

One such song, grown old by popular standards, might well even now enjoy a "revival." It expresses so aptly the philosophy of life that so many hold. It said "Heaven Can Wait." You may have said it yourself. "After all, I'm only young once. There's plenty of time later for serious thoughts and responsible action. I'm out for a good time. 'Heaven Can Wait.'"

This mood is ageless. Robert Herrick in the seventeenth century put it into the music of these swinging lines,

> Gather ye rose buds while ye may,
> Old time is fast a-flying.
> And this same flower that smiles today
> Tomorrow will be dying.

Epicurus many centuries earlier had said, too, "Eat, drink and be merry for tomorrow you die." "Heaven Can Wait."

But can Heaven wait? Is it possible to put off serious thoughts and solemn responsibilities and eventually to stumble upon satisfying and abiding joys? Can one find happiness in the deep places of one's heart by just drifting along, gathering rose buds while one may? Can Heaven wait?

To ask this question is to answer it. Heaven can't wait. There are decisions which you must make now. There are choices you can not avoid. Now is the time, not later, during which the whole fashion and fabric of your future are being determined. By these day-by-day choices, these fleeting companionships, these fast

growing habits that fasten themselves upon you like hands of
steel, you are deciding the big issues of life. Heaven won't wait.
Life's greatest permanent choices are made now.

An unknown poet puts the thought aptly into these abrupt
lines,

> Sow a thought, reap an act,
> Sow an act, reap a habit,
> Sow a habit, reap a character,
> Sow a character, reap a destiny.

Heaven won't wait. It is as if you were to take one matchstick
between your fingers and were to add to it another and yet another until there were fifty such sticks. Though you have hands
like iron, you can not break the bundle. Take one stick at a time
and you can break it, but not the bundle. It is of such stuff that
life's greatest permanent choices are made. You are making them
now.

The way you make these momentary, day by day choices will
largely be decided by what you put first in life, by your dominant
mood.

Today people put all kinds of things first. One runs his eye
over the advertising screen of the T.V. What does he see? The
advertising man appeals to those emotions and desires that are
apt to get a ready response. Here is the appeal to physical beauty.
"Use this cream or that lotion and you'll keep that sweet sixteen
complexion from now until the day of your death." Here is the
appeal to cleverness. We all like to do the clever thing or say the
smart word—to roll clever clichés off our tongues. Would you like
to amaze your friends? Take our short and breezy lessons in piano
or in Spanish! Your friends will be staggered after six weeks. Or
here is the appeal to comfort. Perhaps you are nervous, irritable
or restless. Could it be you need a new compact car—or that one
of the members of your household is a bulb-snatcher? And then
there is that vast volume of advertising that appeals to the physical appetites. "Are you smoking more and enjoying it less?" Smoke
this cigarette or that. You may get smoke in your eyes, but you'll
clear your throat. Or, drink this kind of liquor or that kind of
potion. Give yourself and your friends the best. They and you
deserve it. These are the things—yes, the things, how our lives
get cluttered up with them—the things for which multitudes live

today. And one or the other of these things stands first for many in life.

Was it not a professor at Duke University who reminded us some time back that there is more money spent in America on cosmetics than on all religion—Jewish, Roman Catholic and Protestant put together? That is to say that we are more interested in the outward appearance of our women than we are in their inward spiritual character. What do you put first, girls—outward glamor or inward charm and beauty? Boys, what do you want above all else in your girls? A girl may be very alluring under dim lights with lots of the kind of charm that comes from boxes on her face. But be sure to take a good look at her next morning. Most girls can look pretty good, with a little help, under twenty. But the question is, "How will she look after fifty?" If a girl is beautiful under twenty, it is not to her credit. But, if she's beautiful after fifty, it is to her credit, for such beauty comes from the inside and not from without.

What do you put first? What is your dominant mood? The Master Teacher once said, "You can not serve God and Self." You can not find these permanent and abiding joys in live and live now for the immediate selfish ends and desires and whims that strike your momentary fancy. You must take one or the other. Choose now.

See, if you will, how true this is. Think of your mission in life —what you are going to do with your life. You will not have lived very long before people about you will have discovered whether you are driving somewhere or are drifting nowhere. "You can not serve God and Self." You should have a definite mission in life. Discover it. Don't just drift into it.

Fortunately for those who would put God first there are helps in discovering that mission. God has a plan for your life and mine and we can discover it. That is the real romance of living. It is the knowledge that every experience that comes may be like a finger pointing out God's way. Discover that way!

Here are some guideposts. Put down on a piece of paper, sometime, all the things you like to do and that you do the best. Then, on another piece, put down the things you don't do well or don't really enjoy doing. You will soon discover the direction your life should take. You may be good at dealing in numbers, but poor at handling ideas. You will soon learn whether you should enter one of the skills or one of the professions.

Find out what you can do and what you can do the best. You may be a good musician but a better speaker. Don't spoil a good lawyer or preacher to make an average musician. You may be good at painting, but better at purchasing. Don't spoil a good businessman to make a poor artist. Find out what you can do and what you can do the best.

Then, with that, discover that to do which will give this inner self the clearest expression. For you who would walk God's way, that means only one thing. Find that by which you may serve the most people.

> The rose that adorns itself
> Adorns it too the garden.

So Goethe once put this thought. This is our job in life, isn't it, if we would serve God and not Self? It is not simply to adorn and enhance our own lives. It is to minister to others. "You can not serve God and Self."

Then remember this if you would find your true mission. Pay heed to some of the great causes of life and give yourself to one of them. Whittier once put it this way, "Choose early in life some great unpopular cause and give yourself to it. When it triumphs, you shall know the greatest joy that comes to anyone. You too shall triumph."

This is not to say that all unpopular causes are good. But good causes are frequently unpopular and call for a daring response. In a recent trip around the world, it was my privilege to observe first hand what several years ago the late Wendell Willkie saw so clearly in the Christian missionaries he met. He said, "These people have in other days been ridiculed or overlooked. Today, they are the hope of that new world that shall one day arise. They are the first world citizens." Could it be that the current Peace Corps effort is a belated recognition of that?

We are, of course, not saying that all of us need to go to the ends of the earth to find our mission in life; yet a fair share of us from this privileged land should consider it. But what we are saying is that all of us who would serve God must be willing to take up a cause and to stand by it, even if unpopular and in disfavor—and when it triumphs, we shall know one of life's greatest joys. "Choose you whom you will serve, you can not serve God and Self."

Another point in life at which you must determine now to

serve God or you will serve yourself is in your choice of a mate for life. This is one of life's greatest permanent choices and whether you realize it or not, many of you are making that choice now.

Read the biographies of some great people. Walk into the lives of a lot of every day folks as a minister or a doctor must do and you'll discover this: There are a lot of great and good people who have become great and good because of the kind of person they have married. And there are a lot of great and good people who have been made average or less than average because of the kind of person they have married. But there are few who become great or good in spite of the kind of person they marry.

Once again, the one who would serve God is fortunate. For God plants in the hearts and minds of those who serve Him an ideal, a picture as it were, of that ideal mate. Robert Browning spoke of his ideal in this way,

> Would I could adopt your will,
> See with your eyes, keep my heart
> Beating to yours.

Most of us, especially when we are young, don't look for that kind of a person. That is not to say that we don't have our moments of "heart trouble." But as a usual thing, we look for other qualities of attraction. We want momentary glitter and glamour. We look for the person who dresses well or who dances smoothly. We want some one to show us a good time. And we forget almost altogether the fact that our choices *now* may determine our choices permanently, and we drift into marriage.

Some actually deceive themselves into thinking that they can marry and later change the habits of their partners to suit them. This is an illusion into which girls readily fall. If you can't reform a man before you marry him, be sure that you probably won't be able to reform him after you marry him. Your powers of persuasion, if anything, will not increase, but decrease after the wedding. Move now in that circle of friends out of which you could find the kind of person with whom you could happily share life. Find that person who shares the same ideals—the same hopes—the same dreams. "Be not unevenly yoked together" said a wise man long ago. And that means that the best rule to follow is to find a person who shares your faith and conviction about life.

Robert Browning obviously found such a one as the one of

whom he had dreamed. Of their meeting, Elizabeth Barrett Browning later wrote,

> The face of all the world is changed, I think,
> Since first I heard the footsteps of Thy soul.

Theirs was a "marriage made in Heaven" because they did not keep Heaven waiting. You don't snatch such a marriage out of thin air. You have to build for it *now*. It is woven out of the fabric of your daily companionships—your hourly friendships, "You can not serve God and Self."

Your master choice in life, however, that you are making *now*, is your choice of a Master. The text puts the choice frankly "You can not serve God and Self." In other words, you are either mastered by God or you are under the tyranny of yourself; and the unhappiest people in the world are those who are under the tyranny of themselves, their own passions, and their own pleasures.

There are, of course, some people who for a while are mastered by something bigger than they are. Under its magic spell they cast their all upon an altar of sacrifice. It happens often in war-time. It happens frequently when men give themselves to their business or profession with utter abandon. But the danger is that the spell may one day be broken and they'll begin again to live for Self, utterly for Self.

Some of us remember the story of "Sergeant York" which has become one of the legends of World War I. From this story a "movie" was once made. When the scout from the motion picture industry went out to seek for surviving members of Sergeant York's valiant company, they discovered after some weeks ten men. Seven were just ordinary citizens to whom the $250 offered for the privilege of impersonating them on the screen was a nice windfall. The remaining three, however, are of special interest to us here. One was a hopeless drunkard; a second was living in a hobo jungle and the third was a hermit who barred himself behind the door when the movie scout came near his home.

Some twenty years earlier these men were heroes. They were caught up in an over-mastering loyalty that made them daring and courageous. But something happened. True, times had been hard. War takes its toll. Depressions eat like acids into the souls of men. But the real trouble was that they had lost their over-mastering loyalty. Self, at length, came once more to the throne of their lives. And Self always does, unless God is there first by choice.

A friend and upper-classman at Princeton University, one day visited the study of the late Dr. Henry Van Dyke. On the wall he saw a portrait of Alfred Lord Tennyson inscribed with affectionate greetings to Dr. Van Dyke. He observed its presence and Dr. Van Dyke said, "Yes, take it down and read what is on the back. There, first, read the lines from Locksley Hall, which are my favorite lines from Tennyson."

> Cursed be the social wants that sin against the strength of youth
> Cursed be the social lies that warp us from the living truth.

"I asked Lord Tennyson to write those lines for me," said Van Dyke, then, as excitedly as a little boy, as he wrote the others, he said, "These, I think, are the best I have ever written."

> Love took up the harp of life, and smote on all the chords with might
> Smote on the chord of self, that trembling, passed in music out of sight.

That's it precisely. For God is Love, and when He strikes upon the harp of your life, all the discords that bring unhappiness and all the dissonances that produce despair and defeat, tremble and pass in music out of sight.

Choose you whom you will serve—now—in every choice—in every companionship—in every moment. "You can not serve God and Self." Heaven won't wait!

ADDRESS TO THE HARVARD CLUB *

Paul C. Reinert, S.J.

Tonight I would like to talk about an affinity between our two universities that is critically important—an affinity born out of a deep concern for the future of higher education in our country, a subject that relates to us, too, as fellow citizens of this community, who are concerned about the future of higher education

* Father Reinert, president of Saint Louis University, gave this address before the Harvard Club of St. Louis, Missouri, March 8, 1962.

in Metropolitan St. Louis. Any university worthy of the name has three major obligations: to teach, to do research, and to serve the community in which it is situated. Today in each of these essential functions, your university and mine face some new and some difficult problems of which you as university graduates should be vividly aware. First—in regard to the obligation to teach, the public concept of the American college or university has changed considerably since Harvard or St. Louis University was founded. But we needn't go that far back. This concept of the American college or university has changed remarkably within the last quarter of a century. Under the pressures of an expanding population and technology, it is changing rapidly today. The old honored phrase that education is a matter of Mark Hopkins on one end of the log and the student the other is looked upon by some as a ridiculous cliché.

It seems that we are more concerned today with the question: How many can we accommodate on the log, and how quickly can we get them off of it? In the interest of coping with the large number of young men and women seeking a spot on the log we have resorted to large classes, closed circuit television, and other mass production techniques.

To satisfy our computers, our universities have reduced courses to a number, and students to a hole in an IBM card. Some faculty members even at Harvard actually complain about the presence of students in an institution which has as one of its principal purposes the transmission to the coming generation of the wisdom of the ages. Nor is this loss of concern for the person confined to big institutions. I have visited relatively small colleges where students complain of being treated as a number instead of as a person. They are stung by the impersonality of a fixed gaze from the professor whose lecture they have just heard. They wonder about the wisdom of status-seeking college presidents who authorize thousands for monumental structures and only hundreds for library books; thousands for facilities for a few athletes, and and little or nothing for the faceless thousands of students who are the fans in the stands; millions for brick and mortar, but relatively little for warm-hearted men and women who will listen and understand. They look askance at faculty and administrative officers so completely preoccupied with securing the monetary rewards of their discipline and their profession that they have forgotten the opportunities to inspire the youth of America that led them into educational work in the first place.

I don't mean to minimize the tremendous problems that all of our colleges and universities share today—the burgeoning number of high school graduates, compounded with the ever-increasing percentage of those students who want to go to college, the responsibility of our colleges and universities to accept every qualified student who applies. The tremendous numbers require us to get rid of the ledgers and the fountain pens, and to put the names of our students on IBM cards and run them through computers. But we needn't treat our students simply as holes in an IBM card, and I'm afraid that this is a tendency that is becoming more and more pronounced in educational circles today. The solution lies with the attitude of the teacher and educator. And that attitude, in turn, rests with our convictions about the respect and concern we have for the dignity of the student as a person, and his rights as a human being.

There is no incompatibility between a genuine and uncompromising dedication to scholarship, for students as well as faculty, and a simultaneous conviction that an education which we expect to be humanizing and liberalizing in its effects should also be human and liberal in its process. If we are going to treat students as machines, we are going to produce machines. If we treat them as intelligent young men and women with a capacity for knowledge and creativity, we will educate the intelligent and productive citizens that the future of our country demands.

Learning will always be a struggle—a struggle shared by teacher and student. It can't be fed through a computer. It takes human initiative and energy. The responsibility lies with all leaders in education to create among administrative officers, faculty and staff not a sentimental attitude towards students, but a recognition of the dignity and importance of the young man or woman who has been placed in their charge, and a dedicated desire to draw out of that individual the capabilities that are latent within him.

It is also my conviction that too much of our educational system has become truncated and isolated. For example—in our determination to completely separate church and state, we have separated our schools from God, and thereby, shut off any opportunity for the moral education of young people. In a sincere effort to rigidly uphold our American freedoms, as protected by the Constitution, we have, in fact, been guilty of misreading the Constitution. Our American heritage is based upon a belief in God, yet we have ostracized Him from our classrooms. And, by so doing, we have precluded the teaching of moral standards. I am aware, of course, of the philosophic and religious differences in America, yet I am more painfully aware of the failure of American education to make a positive contribution to our nation's moral standards and to our fight against Communism. Your president, Dr. Pusey, has expressed this same concern. Look at his repeated proposals for the recognition of theology as an important source for the totality of truth and for its restoration to a respected place in the curriculum of the American university.

Now let us turn to problems complicating the second function of every university—research. What we are doing to teach young men and women directly relates, of course, to what we are doing in research. Or, at least it should. Traditionally, our research programs have been media for expanding the knowledge and teaching ability of our faculty and for offering greater educational opportunities for our students. Today, I am afraid, a partition has been built between the laboratory and the classroom. On the one side of the curtain, the faculty member pursues his own special interests in the laboratory. On the other side sits the student.

The federal government, which last year allotted the tremendous sum of 879 million dollars to campus research, three times as much as it did five years ago—recognizes the problem: that its grants, along with those of other agencies, allow less and less time for the nation's best professors to exercise their responsibilities in the classroom. An official of the Department of Health, Education and Welfare pinpointed the problem when he said: "The fact that Federal funds are for research, while the universities must also fulfill other functions such as teaching, gives rise to such restrictive effects as the universities have felt. The federal money tends to emphasize the research functions and consequently makes it more difficult for the universities to sustain a balance between teaching and research. . . . Encroachment of research upon space for undergraduate teaching causes problems. The general status of and financial rewards for research tend to make concentration upon undergraduate teaching relatively less attractive."

I would be the last, of course, to underrate the value of university research, and what it has done for the advancement of human knowledge and the benefit of the human race. What concerns me is a growing tendency to make research the primary pursuit of our universities and to isolate it from what is really our main function—the education of young men and women. Again, the solution lies in the attitude of the administration and faculty.

Finally, in addition to teaching and research, the university performs a third function that has been accelerated—namely, meeting the needs of the community and the nation, the area of community service. This function is generally a byproduct of the first two, but it is almost as broad in the amount of activity that goes on, both on and off the campus. Health services account for a significant percentage of these incidental benefits, as do special educational programs. To mention a few that were held on our campus—in the last year or so, there were special programs for high school teachers, traffic judges, stock brokers, attorneys, orthodontists, advertising men, and so on. Then, of course, there is the whole area of non-credit adult education programs.

In sponsoring these activities, the university is recognizing an obligation it has, as the outstanding corporate citizen, to harness all of its resources for the welfare of the community. Faculty members are no longer secluded behind ivy-covered walls, but, more and more, are serving on civic committees, speaking before local organizations, lending their knowledge to whatever need exists in the community.

The university not only recognizes an obligation to perform these services, but does so willingly and enthusiastically, as an institution that has been founded for the sake of service.

At the same time, however, our colleges and universities must exercise great caution that this involvement with causes outside the university walls does not impair or obstruct the university's traditional freedom. While continuing to serve business and the professions, the university must remain clear of any special interest groups that would hinder the university in its pursuit of truth and free inquiry. If the university allows such groups to dictate what is to be taught in its classrooms, the real function of the university gradually will erode, leaving it without purpose or direction. The university can avoid this problem, I believe, by exercising more control over the types of programs it offers, by leading instead of following, by recognizing certain needs in the community and planning special programs to meet them. Above all, the university must avoid selling its services, in other words, sponsoring special programs for the sake of monetary profit. This is dangerous ground, and can only lead to the erosion I've described.

By and large, our colleges and universities, I believe, have accepted the challenges that have been placed before them by America's physical, cultural, and scientific growth. In turn, private philanthropy and corporate interests have pledged their support to our colleges and universities towards strengthening them for the job ahead.

They will perform this job in the best tradition of American higher education, that began with the early days of Harvard, if, as I have said, we rededicate ourselves to three basic ideas: the priority of teaching, based on recognition of the personal dignity of the individual student; the recognition of research as an aid to the teaching program; and the preservation of the intellectual integrity of the individual college or university.

In so doing, we will continue to strengthen our educational system, and thereby strengthen our country, girding it for today's bitter struggle between the free world and the slave world, the free mind and the slave mind, producing intelligent, morally responsible citizens of whom we can all be justly proud.

THE COOPER INSTITUTE ADDRESS *

Abraham Lincoln

MR. PRESIDENT AND FELLOW-CITIZENS OF NEW YORK: The facts with which I shall deal this evening are mainly old and familiar; nor is there anything new in the general use I shall make of them. If there shall be any novelty, it will be in the mode of presenting the facts, and the inferences and observations following that presentation. In his speech last autumn at Columbus, Ohio, as reported in the *New York Times,* Senator Douglas said:—

* Lincoln gave this famous speech in Cooper Institute, New York City, February 27, 1860. The audience was composed mainly of Eastern Republicans.

Our fathers, when they framed the government under which we live, understood this question just as well, and even better, than we do now.

I fully endorse this, and I adopt it as a text for this discourse. I so adopt it because it furnishes a precise and an agreed starting-point for a discussion between Republicans and that wing of the Democracy headed by Senator Douglas. It simply leaves the inquiry: What was the understanding those fathers had of the question mentioned?

What is the frame of government under which we live? The answer must be, "The Constitution of the United States." That Constitution consists of the original, framed in 1787, and under which the present government first went into operation, and twelve subsequently framed amendments, the first ten of which were framed in 1789.

Who were our fathers that framed the Constitution? I suppose the "thirty-nine" who signed the original instrument may be fairly called our fathers who framed that part of the present government. It is almost exactly true to say they framed it, and it is altogether true to say they fairly represented the opinion and sentiment of the whole nation at that time. Their names, being familiar to nearly all, and accessible to quite all, need not now be repeated.

I take these "thirty-nine," for the present, as being "our fathers who framed the government under which we live." What is the question which, according to the text, those fathers understood "just as well, and even better, than we do now?"

It is this: Does the proper division of local from Federal authority, or anything in the Constitution, forbid our Federal Government to control as to slavery in our Federal Territories?

Upon this, Senator Douglas holds the affirmative, and Republicans the negative. This affirmation and denial form an issue; and this issue—this question—is precisely what the text declares our fathers understood "better than we." Let us now inquire whether the "thirty-nine," or any of them, ever acted upon this question; and if they did, how they acted upon it—how they expressed that better understanding. In 1784, three years before the Constitution, the United States then owning the Northwestern Territory, and no other, the Congress of the Confederation had before them the question of prohibiting slavery in that Territory, and four of the "thirty-nine" who afterward framed the Constitution were in that Congress, and voted on that question. Of these, Roger Sherman, Thomas Mifflin, and Hugh Williamson voted for the prohibition, thus showing that, in their understanding, no line dividing local from Federal authority, nor anything else, properly forbade the Federal Government to control as to slavery in Federal territory. The other of the four, James Mc-Henry, voted against the prohibition, showing that for some cause he thought it improper to vote for it.

In 1787, still before the Constitution, but while the convention was in session framing it, and while the Northwestern Territory still was the only Territory owned by the United States, the same question of prohibiting slavery in the Territory again came before the Congress of the Confederation; and two more of the "thirty-nine" who afterward signed the Constitution were in that Congress, and voted on the question. They were William Blount and William Few; and they both voted for the prohibition—thus showing that in their understanding no line dividing local from Federal authority, nor anything else, properly forbade the Federal Government to control as to slavery in Federal territory. This time the prohibition became a law, being part of what is now well known as the Ordinance of '87.

The question of Federal control of slavery in the Territories seems not to have been directly before the convention which framed the original Constitution; and hence it is not recorded that the "thirty-nine," or any of them, while engaged on that instrument, expressed any opinion on that precise question.

In 1789, by the first Congress which sat under the Constitution, an act was passed to enforce the Ordinance of '87, including the prohibition of slavery in the Northwestern Territory. The bill for this act was reported by one of the "thirty-nine"—Thomas Fitzsimmons, then a member of the House of Representatives from Pennsylvania. It went through all its stages without a word of opposition, and finally passed both branches without ayes and nays, which is equivalent to a unanimous passage. In this Congress there were sixteen of the thirty-nine fathers who framed the original Constitution. They were John Langdon, Nicholas Gilman, Wm. S. Johnson, Roger Sherman, Robert Morris, Thomas Fitzsimmons, Abraham Baldwin, William Few, Rufus King, William Patterson, George Clymer, Richard Bassett, George Read, Pierce Butler, Daniel Carroll, and James Madison.

This shows that, in their understanding, no line dividing local from Federal authority, nor anything in the Constitution, properly forbade Congress to prohibit slavery in the Federal territory; else both their fidelity to correct principle, and their oath to support the Constitution, would have constrained them to oppose the prohibition.

Again, George Washington, another of the "thirty-nine," was then President of the United States, and as such approved and signed the bill, thus completing its validity as a law, and thus showing that, in his understanding, no line dividing local from Federal authority, nor anything in the Constitution, forbade the Federal Government to control as to slavery in Federal territory.

No great while after the adoption of the original Constitution, North Carolina ceded to the Federal Government the country now constituting the State of Tennessee; and a few years later Georgia ceded that which now constitutes the States of Mississippi and Alabama. In both deeds of cession it was made a condition by the ceding States that the Federal Government should not prohibit slavery in the ceded country. Besides this, slavery was then actually in the ceded country. Under these circumstances, Congress, on taking charge of these countries, did not absolutely prohibit slavery within them. But they did interfere with it— take control of it—even there, to a certain extent. In 1798 Congress organized the Territory of Mississippi. In the act of organization they prohibited the bringing of slaves into the Territory from any place without the United States, by fine, and giving freedom to slaves so brought. This act passed both branches of Congress without yeas and nays. In that Congress were three of the "thirty-nine" who framed the original Constitution. They were John Langdon, George Read, and Abraham Baldwin. They all probably voted for it. Certainly they would have placed their opposition to it upon record if, in their understanding, any line dividing local from Federal authority, or anything in the Constitution, properly forbade the Federal Government to control as to slavery in Federal Territory.

In 1803, the Federal Government purchased the Louisiana country. Our former territorial acquisitions came from certain of our own States; but this Louisiana country was acquired from a foreign nation. In 1804, Congress gave a territorial organization to that part of it which now constitutes the State of Louisiana. New Orleans, lying within that part, was an old and comparatively large city. There were other considerable towns and settlements, and slavery was extensively and thoroughly intermingled with the people. Congress did not, in the Territorial Act, prohibit slavery; but they did interfere with it—take control of it—in a more marked and extensive way than they did in the case of Mississippi. The substance of the provision therein made in relation to slaves was:

1st. That no slave should be imported into the Territory from foreign parts.

2d. That no slave should be carried into it who had been imported into the United States since the first day of May, 1798.

3d. That no slave should be carried into it, except by the owner, and for his own use as a settler; the penalty in all cases being a fine upon the violator of the law, and freedom to the slave.

This act also was passed without ayes or nays. In the Congress which passed it there were two of the "thirty-nine." They were Abraham Baldwin and Jonathan Dayton. As stated in the case of Mississippi, it is probable they both voted for it. They would not have allowed it to pass without recording their opposition to it if, in their understanding, it violated either the line properly dividing local from Federal authority, or any provision of the Constitution.

In 1819-20 came and passed the Missouri question. Many votes were taken, by yeas and nays, in both branches of Congress, upon the various phases of the general question. Two of the "thirty-nine"—Rufus King and Charles Pinckney—were members of that Congress. Mr. King steadily voted for slavery prohibition and against all compromises, while Mr. Pinckney as steadily voted against slavery prohibition and against all compromises. By this, Mr. King showed that, in his understanding, no line dividing local from Federal authority, nor anything in the Constitution, was violated by Congress prohibiting slavery in Federal territory; while Mr. Pinckney, by his votes, showed that, in his understanding, there was some sufficient reason for opposing such prohibition in that case.

The cases I have mentioned are the only acts of the "thirty-nine," or of any of them, upon the direct issue, which I have been able to discover.

To enumerate the persons who thus acted as being four in 1784, two in 1787, seventeen in 1789, three in 1798, two in 1804, and two in 1819-20, there would be thirty of them. But this would be counting John Langdon, Roger Sherman, William Few, Rufus King, and George Read each twice, and Abraham Baldwin three times. The true number of those of the "thirty-nine" whom I have shown to have acted upon the question which, by the text, they understood better than we, is twenty-three, leaving sixteen not shown to have acted upon it in any way.

Here, then, we have twenty-three out of our thirty-nine fathers "who framed the government under which we live," who have, upon their official responsibility and their corporal oath, acting upon the very question which the text affirms they "understood just as well, and even better, than we do now"; and twenty-one of them—a clear majority of the whole "thirty-nine"—so acting upon it as to make them guilty of gross political impropriety and wilful perjury if, in their understanding, any proper division between local and Federal authority, or anything in the Constitution they had made themselves, and sworn to support, forbade the Federal Government to control as to slavery in the Federal Territories. Thus the twenty-one acted; and, as actions speak louder than words, so actions under such responsibility speak still louder.

Two of the twenty-three voted against Congressional prohibition of slavery in the Federal Territories, in the instances in which they acted upon the question. But for what reasons they so voted is not known. They may have done so because they thought a proper division of local from Federal authority, or some provision or principle of the Constitution, stood in the way; or they may, without any such question, have voted against the prohibition on what appeared to them to be sufficient grounds of expediency. No one who has sworn to support the Constitution can conscientiously vote for what he understands to be an unconstitutional measure, however expedient he may think it; but one may and ought to vote against a measure which he deems constitutional if, at the same time, he deems it inexpedient. It, therefore, would be unsafe to set down even the two who voted against the prohibition as having done so because, in their understanding, any proper division of local from Federal authority, or anything in the Constitution, forbade the Federal Government to control as to slavery in Federal territory.

The remaining sixteen of the "thirty-nine," so far as I have discovered, have left no record of their understanding upon the direct question of Federal control of slavery in the Federal

Territories. But there is much reason to believe that their understanding upon that question would not have appeared different from that of their twenty-three compeers, had it been manifested at all.

For the purpose of adhering rigidly to the text, I have purposely omitted whatever understanding may have been manifested by any person, however distinguished, other than the thirty-nine fathers who framed the original Constitution; and, for the same reason, I have also omitted whatever understanding may have been manifested by any of the "thirty-nine" even on any other phase of the general question of slavery. If we should look into their acts and declarations on those other phases, as the foreign slave-trade, and the morality and policy of slavery generally, it would appear to us that on the direct question of Federal control of slavery in Federal Territories, the sixteen, if they had acted at all, would probably have acted just as the twenty-three did. Among that sixteen were several of the most noted anti-slavery men of those times—Dr. Franklin, Alexander Hamilton, and Gouverneur Morris—while there was not one now known to have been otherwise, unless it may be John Rutledge, of South Carolina.

The sum of the whole is that of our thirty-nine fathers who framed the original Constitution, twenty-one—a clear majority of the whole—certainly understood that no proper division of local from Federal authority, nor any part of the Constitution, forbade the Federal Government to control slavery in the Federal Territories; while all the rest had probably the same understanding. Such, unquestionably, was the understanding of our fathers who framed the original Constitution; and the text affirms that they understood the question "better than we."

But, so far, I have been considering the understanding of the question manifested by the framers of the original Constitution. In and by the original instrument, a mode was provided for amending it; and, as I have already stated, the present frame of "the government under which we live" consists of that original, and twelve amendatory articles framed and adopted since. Those who now insist that Federal control of slavery in Federal Territories violates the Constitution, point us to the provisions which they suppose it thus violates; and, as I understand, they all fix upon provisions in these amendatory articles, and not in the original instrument. The Supreme Court, in the Dred Scott case, plant themselves upon the fifth amendment, which provides that no person shall be deprived of "life, liberty, or property without due process of law"; while Senator Douglas and his peculiar adherents plant themselves upon the tenth amendment, providing that "the powers not delegated to the United States by the Constitution" "are reserved to the States respectively, or to the people."

Now it so happens that these amendments were framed by the first Congress which sat under the Constitution—the identical Congress which passed the act, already mentioned, enforcing the prohibition of slavery in the Northwestern Territory. Not only was it the same Congress, but they were the identical, same individual men who, at the same session, and at the same time within the session, had under consideration, and in progress toward maturity, these constitutional amendments, and this act prohibiting slavery in all the territory the nation then owned. The constitutional amendments were introduced before, and passed after the act enforcing the Ordinance of '87; so that, during the whole pendency of the act to enforce the Ordinance, the constitutional amendments were also pending.

The seventy-six members of that Congress, including sixteen of the framers of the original Constitution, as before stated, were preëminently our fathers who framed that part of "the governmen under which we live," which is now claimed as forbidding the Federal Government to control slavery in the Federal Territories.

Is it not a little presumptuous in anyone at this day to affirm that the two things which that Congress deliberately framed, and carried to maturity at the same time, are absolutely inconsistent with each other? And does not such affirmation become impudently absurd when coupled with the other affirmation, from the same mouth, that those who did the two things alleged to be inconsistent, understood whether they really were inconsistent better than we—better than he who affirms that they are inconsistent?

It is surely safe to assume that the thirty-nine framers of the original Constitution, and the seventy-six members of the Congress which framed the amendments thereto, taken together, do certainly include those who may be fairly called "our fathers who framed the government under which we live." And so assuming, I defy any man to show that any one of them ever, in his whole life, declared that, in his understanding, any proper division of local from Federal authority, or any part of the Constitution, forbade the Federal Government to control as to slavery in the Federal Territories. I go a step further. I defy anyone to show that any living man in the world ever did, prior to the beginning of the present century (and I might almost say prior to the beginning of the last half of the present century), declare that, in his understanding, any proper division of local from Federal authority, or any part of the Constitution, forbade the Federal Government to control as to slavery in the Federal Territories. To those who now so declare I give not only "our fathers who framed the government under which we live," but with them all other living men within the century in which it was framed, among whom to search, and they shall not be able to find the evidence of a single man agreeing with them.

Now, and here, let me guard a little against being misunderstood. I do not mean to say we are bound to follow implicitly in whatever our fathers did. To do so would be to discard all the lights of current experience—to reject all progress, all improvement. What I do say is that if we would supplant the opinions and policy of our fathers in any case, we should do so upon evidence so conclusive, and argument so clear, that even their great authority, fairly considered and weighed, cannot stand; and most surely not in a case whereof we ourselves declare they understood the question better than we.

If any man at this day sincerely believes that a proper division of local from Federal authority, or any part of the Constitution, forbids the Federal Government to control as to slavery in the Federal Territories, he is right to say so, and to enforce his position by all truthful evidence and fair argument which he can. But he has no right to mislead others, who have less access to history, and less leisure to study it, into the false belief that "our fathers who framed the government under which we live" were of the same opinion—thus substituting falsehood and deception for truthful evidence and fair argument. If any man at this day sincerely believes "our fathers who framed the government under which we live" used and applied principles, in other cases, which ought to have led them to understand that a proper division of local from Federal authority, or some part of the Constitution, forbids the Federal Government to control as to slavery in the Federal Territories, he is right to say so. But he should, at the same time, brave the responsibility of declaring that, in his opinion, he understands their principles better than they did themselves; and especially should he not shirk that responsibility by asserting that they "understood the question just as well, and even better, than we do now."

But enough! Let all who believe that "our fathers who framed the government under which we live understood this question just as well, and even better, than we do now," speak as they spoke, and act as they acted upon it. This is all Republicans ask— all Republicans desire—in relation to slavery. As those fathers marked it, so let it be again marked, as an evil not to be extended, but to be tolerated and protected only because of and so far as its actual presence amongst us makes that toleration and protection a necessity. Let all the guaranties those fathers gave it be not grudgingly, but fully and fairly maintained. For this Republicans contend, and with this, so far as I know or believe, they will be content.

And now, if they would listen—as I suppose they will not—I would address a few words to the Southern people.

I would say to them: You consider yourselves a reasonable and a just people; and I consider that in the general qualities of reason and justice you are not inferior to any other people. Still, when you speak of us Republicans, you do so only to denounce us as reptiles, or, at the best, as no better than outlaws. You will grant a hearing to pirates or murderers, but nothing like it to "Black Republicans." In all your contentions with one another, each of you deems an unconditional condemnation of "Black Republicanism," as the first thing to be attended to. Indeed, such condemnation of us seems to be an indispensable prerequisite— license, so to speak—among you to be admitted or permitted to speak at all. Now can you or not be prevailed upon to pause and to consider whether this is quite just to us, or even to yourselves? Bring forward your charges and specifications, and then be patient long enough to hear us deny or justify.

You say we are sectional. We deny it. That makes an issue; and the burden of proof is upon you. You produce your proof; and what is it? Why, that our party has no existence in your section—gets no votes in your section. The fact is substantially true; but does it prove the issue? If it does, then in case we should, without change of principle, begin to get votes in your section, we should thereby cease to be sectional. You cannot escape this conclusion; and yet, are you willing to abide by it? If you are, you will probably soon find that we have ceased to be sectional, for we shall get votes in your section this very year. You will then begin to discover, as the truth plainly is, that your proof does not touch the issue. The fact that we get no votes in your section is a fact of your making, and not of ours. And if there be fault in that fact, that fault is primarily yours, and remains so until you show that we repel you by some wrong principle or practice. If we do repel you by any wrong principle or practice, the fault is ours; but this brings you to where you ought to have started—to a discussion of the right or wrong of our principle. If our principle, put in practice, would wrong your section for the benefit of ours, or for any other object, then our principle, and we with it, are sectional, and are justly opposed and denounced as such. Meet us, then, on the question of whether our principle, put in practice, would wrong your section; and so meet us as if it were possible that something may be said on your side. Do you accept the challenge? No! Then you really believe that the principle which "our fathers who framed the government under which we live" thought so clearly right as to adopt it, and indorse it again and again, upon their official oaths, is in fact so clearly wrong as to demand your condemnation without a moment's consideration.

Some of you delight to flaunt in our faces the warning against sectional parties given by Washington in his Farewell Address. Less than eight years before Washington gave that warning, he had, as President of the United States, approved and signed an act of Congress enforcing the prohibition of slavery in the North-western Territory, which act embodied the policy of the government upon that subject up to and at the very moment he penned that warning; and about one year after he penned it, he wrote Lafayette that he considered that prohibition a wise measure, expressing in the same connection his hope that we should at some time have a confederacy of free States.

Bearing this in mind, and seeing that sectionalism has since arisen upon this same subject, is that warning a weapon in your hands against us, or in our hands against you? Could Washington himself speak, would he cast the blame of that sectionalism upon us, who sustain his policy, or upon you, who repudiate it? We respect that warning of Washington, and we commend it

to you, together with his example pointing to the right application of it.

But you say you are conservative—eminently conservative—
while we are revolutionary, destructive, or something of the
sort. What is conservatism? Is it not adherence to the old and
tried, against the new and untried? We stick to, contend for,
the identical old policy on the point in controversy which was
adopted by "our fathers who framed the government under which
we live"; while you with one accord reject, and scout, and spit
upon that old policy, and insist upon substituting something
new. True, you disagree among yourselves as to what that substitute shall be. You are divided on new propositions and plans,
but you are unanimous in rejecting and denouncing the old
policy of the fathers. Some of you are for reviving the foreign
slave-trade; some for a Congressional slave code for the Territories; some for Congress forbidding the Territories to prohibit
slavery within their limits; some for maintaining slavery in the
Territories though the judiciary; some for the "gur-reat pur-
rinciple" that "if one man would enslave another, no third man
should object," fantastically called "popular sovereignty," but
never a man among you is in favor of Federal prohibition of
slavery in Federal Territories, according to the practice of "our
fathers who framed the government under which we live." Not
one of all your various plans can show a precedent or an advocate
in the century within which our government originated. Consider,
then, whether your claim of conservatism for yourselves, and
your charge of destructiveness against us, are based on the most
clear and stable foundations.

And again, you say we have made the slavery question more
prominent than it formerly was. We deny it. We admit that it
is more prominent, but we deny that we made it so. It was not
we, but you, who discarded the old policy of the fathers. We
resisted, and still resist, your innovation; and thence comes the
greater prominence of the question. Would you have that question reduced to its former proportions? Go back to that old policy.
What has been will be again, under the same conditions. If you
would have the peace of the old times, re-adopt the precepts and
policy of the old times.

You charge that we stir up insurrections among your slaves.
We deny it; and what is your proof? Harper's Ferry! John Brown!!

John Brown was no Republican; and you have failed to implicate a single Republican in his Harper's Ferry enterprise. If any member of our party is guilty in that matter, you know it or you do not know it. If you do know it, you are inexcusable for not designating the man and proving the fact. If you do not know it, you are inexcusable for asserting it, and especially for persisting in the assertion after you have tried and failed to make the proof. You need not be told that persisting in a charge which one does not know to be true is simply malicious slander.

Some of you admit that no Republican designedly aided or encouraged the Harper's Ferry affair, but still insist that our doctrines and declarations necessarily lead to such results. We do not believe it. We know we hold no doctrine, and make no declaration which were not held to and made by "our fathers who framed the government under which we live." You never dealt fairly by us in relation to this affair. When it occurred, some important State elections were near at hand, and you were in evident glee with the belief that, by charging the blame upon us, you could get an advantage of us in those elections. The elections came, and your expectations were not quite fulfiled. Every Republican man knew that, as to himself at least, your charge was a slander, and he was not much inclined by it to cast his vote in your favor. Republican doctrines and declarations are accompanied with a continual protest against any interference whatever with your slaves, or with you about your slaves. Surely this does not encourage them to revolt. True, we do, in common with "our fathers who framed the government under which we live," declare our belief that slavery is wrong; but the slaves do not hear us declare even this. For anything we say or do, the slaves would scarcely know there is a Republican party. I believe they would not, in fact, generally know it but for your misrepresentations of us in their hearing. In your political contests among yourselves each faction charges the other with sympathy with Black Republicanism; and then, to give point to the charge, defines Black Republicanism to simply be insurrection, blood, and thunder among the slaves.

Slave insurrections are no more common now than they were before the Republican party was organized. What induced the Southampton insurrection, twenty-eight years ago, in which at least three times as many lives were lost as at Harper's Ferry? You can scarcely stretch your very elastic fancy to the conclusion that Southampton was "got up by Black Republicanism." In the present state of things in the United States, I do not think a general, or even a very extensive, slave insurrection is possible. The indispensable concert of action cannot be attained. The slaves have no means of rapid communication; nor can incendiary freemen, black or white, supply it. The explosive materials are everywhere in parcels; but there neither are, nor can be supplied, the indispensable connecting trains.

Much is said by Southern people about the affection of slaves for their masters and mistresses; and a part of it, at least, is true. A plot for an uprising could scarcely be devised and communicated to twenty individuals before some one of them, to save the life of a favorite master or mistress, would divulge it. This is the rule; and the slave revolution in Hayti was not an exception to it, but a case occurring under peculiar circumstances. The Gunpowder Plot of British history, though not connected with slaves, was more in point. In that case, only about twenty were admitted to the secret; and yet one of them, in his anxiety to save a friend, betrayed the plot to that friend, and, by consequence, averted the calamity. Occasional poisonings from the kitchen, and open or stealthy assassinations in the field, and local revolts extending to a score or so, will continue to occur as the natural results of slavery; but no general insurrection of slaves, as I think, can happen in this country for a long time. Whoever much fears, or much hopes for, such an event will be alike disappointed.

In the language of Mr. Jefferson, uttered many years ago, "It is still in our power to direct the process of emancipation and deportation peaceably, and in such slow degrees as that the evil will wear off insensibly; and their places be, *pari passu*, filled up by free white laborers. If, on the contrary, it is left to force itself on, human nature must shudder at the prospect held up."

Mr. Jefferson did not mean to say, nor do I, that the power of emancipation is in the Federal Government. He spoke of Virginia; and, as to the power of emancipation, I speak of the slaveholding States only. The Federal Government, however, as we insist, has the power of restraining the extension of the institution—the power to insure that a slave insurrection shall never occur on any American soil which is now free from slavery.

John Brown's effort was peculiar. It was not a slave insurrection. It was an attempt by white men to get up a revolt among slaves, in which the slaves refused to participate. In fact, it was so absurd that the slaves, with all their ignorance, saw plainly enough it could not succeed. That affair, in its philosophy, corresponds with the many attempts, related in history, at the assassination of kings and emperors. An enthusiast broods over the oppression of a people till he fancies himself commissioned by Heaven to liberate them. He ventures the attempt, which ends in little else than his own execution. Orsini's attempt on Louis Napoleon, and John Brown's attempt at Harper's Ferry, were, in their philosophy, precisely the same. The eagerness to cast blame on old England in the one case, and on New England in the other, does not disprove the sameness of the two things.

And how much would it avail you, if you could, by the use of John Brown, Helper's book, and the like, break up the Republican organization? Human action can be modified to some extent, but human nature cannot be changed. There is a judgment and a feeling against slavery in this nation, which casts at least a million and a half of votes. You cannot destroy that judgment and feeling—that sentiment—by breaking up the political organization which rallies around it. You can scarcely scatter and disperse an army which has been formed into order in the face of your heaviest fire; but if you could, how much would you gain by forcing the sentiment which created it out of the peaceful channel of the ballot-box into some other channel? What would that other channel probably be? Would the number of John Browns be lessened or enlarged by the operation?

But you will break up the Union rather than submit to a denial of your constitutional rights.

That has a somewhat reckless sound; but it would be palliated, if not fully justified, were we proposing, by the mere force of numbers, to deprive you of some right plainly written down in the Constitution. But we are proposing no such thing.

When you make these declarations, you have a specific and well-understood allusion to an assumed constitutional right of yours to take slaves into the Federal Territories, and to hold them there as property. But no such right is specially written in the Constitution. That instrument is literally silent about any such right. We, on the contrary, deny that such a right has any existence in the Constitution, even by implication.

Your purpose, then, plainly stated, is that you will destroy the government, unless you be allowed to construe and force the Constitution as you please, on all points in dispute between you and us. You will rule or ruin in all events.

This, plainly stated, is your language. Perhaps you will say the Supreme Court has decided the disputed constitutional question in your favor. Not quite so. But, waiving the lawyer's distinction between dictum and decision, the court has decided the question for you in a sort of way. The court has substantially said, it is your constitutional right to take slaves into the Federal Territories, and to hold them there as property. When I say the decision was made in a sort of way, I mean it was made in a divided court, by a bare majority of the judges, and they not quite agreeing with one another in the reasons for making it; that it is so made as that its avowed supporters disagree with one another about its meaning, and that it was mainly based upon a mistaken statement of fact—the statement in the opinion that "the right of property in a slave is distinctly and expressly affirmed in the Constitution."

An inspection of the Constitution will show that the right of property in a slave is not "distinctly and expressly affirmed" in it. Bear in mind, the judges do not pledge their judicial opinion that such right is impliedly affirmed in the Constitution; but they pledge their veracity that it is "distinctly and expressly" affirmed there—"distinctly," that is, not mingled with anything else—"expressly," that is, in words meaning just that, without the aid of any inference, and susceptible of no other meaning.

If they had only pledged their judicial opinion that such right is affirmed in the instrument by implication, it would be open to others to show that neither the word "slave" nor "slavery" is to be found in the Constitution, nor the word "property" even, in any connection with language alluding to the thing slave or slavery; and that wherever in that instrument the slave is alluded to, he is called a "person"; and wherever his master's legal right in relation to him is alluded to, it is spoken of as "service or labor which may be due"—as a debt payable in service or labor. Also it would be open to show, by contemporaneous history, that this mode of alluding to slaves and slavery, instead of speaking of them, was employed on purpose to exclude from the Constitution the idea that there could be property in man.

To show all this is easy and certain.

When this obvious mistake of the judges shall be brought to their notice, is it not reasonable to expect that they will withdraw the mistaken statement, and reconsider the conclusion based upon it?

And then it is to be remembered that "our fathers who framed the government under which we live"—the men who made the Constitution—decided this same constitutional question in our favor long ago; decided it without division among themselves when making the decision; without division among themselves about the meaning of it after it was made, and, so far as any evidence is left, without basing it upon any mistaken statement of facts.

Under all these circumstances, do you really feel yourselves justified to break up this government unless such a court decision as yours is shall be at once submitted to as a conclusive and final rule of political action? But you will not abide the election of a Republican president! In that supposed event, you say, you will destroy the Union; and then, you say, the great crime of having destroyed it will be upon us! That is cool. A highwayman holds a pistol to my ear, and mutters through his teeth, "Stand and deliver, or I shall kill you, and then you will be a murderer!"

To be sure, what the robber demanded of me—my money—was my own; and I had a clear right to keep it; but it was no more my own than my vote is my own; and the threat of death to me, to extort my money, and the threat of destruction to the Union, to extort my vote, can scarcely be distinguished in principle.

A few words now to Republicans. It is exceedingly desirable that all parts of this great Confederacy shall be at peace, and in harmony one with another. Let us Republicans do our part to have it so. Even though much provoked, let us do nothing through passion and ill temper. Even though the Southern people will not so much as listen to us, let us calmly consider their demands, and yield to them if, in our deliberate view of our duty, we possibly can. Judging by all they say and do, and by the subject and nature of their controversy with us, let us determine, if we can, what will satisfy them.

Will they be satisfied if the Territories be unconditionally surrendered to them? We know they will not. In all their present complaints against us, the Territories are scarcely mentioned. Invasions and insurrections are the rage now. Will it satisfy them if, in the future, we have nothing to do with invasions and insurrections? We know it will not. We so know, because we know we never had anything to do with invasions and insurrections; and yet this total abstaining does not exempt us from the charge and the denunciation.

The question recurs, What will satisfy them? Simply this: we must not only let them alone, but we must somehow convince them that we do let them alone. This, we know by experience, is no easy task. We have been so trying to convince them from the very beginning of our organization, but with no success. In all our platforms and speeches we have constantly protested our purpose to let them alone; but this has had no tendency to convince them. Alike unavailing to convince them is the fact that they have never detected a man of us in any attempt to disturb them.

These natural and apparently adequate means all failing, what will convince them? This, and this only: cease to call slavery wrong, and join them in calling it right. And this must be done thoroughly—done in acts as well as in words. Silence will not be tolerated—we must place ourselves avowedly with them. Senator Douglas's new sedition law must be enacted and enforced, suppressing all declarations that slavery is wrong, whether made in politics, in presses, in pulpits, or in private. We must arrest and return their fugitive slaves with greedy pleasure. We must pull down our free State constitutions. The whole atmosphere must be disinfected from all taint of opposition to slavery, before they will cease to believe that all their troubles proceed from us.

I am quite aware they do not state their case precisely in this way. Most of them would probably say to us, "Let us alone; do nothing to us, and say what you please about slavery." But we do let them alone—have never disturbed them—so that, after all, it is what we say which dissatisfies them. They will continue to accuse us of doing, until we cease saying.

I am also aware they have not as yet in terms demanded the overthrow of our free-State constitutions. Yet those constitutions declare the wrong of slavery with more solemn emphasis than do all other sayings against it; and when all these other sayings shall have been silenced, the overthrow of these constitutions will be demanded, and nothing be left to resist the demand. It is nothing to the contrary that they do not demand the whole of this just now. Demanding what they do, and for the reason they do, they can voluntarily stop nowhere short of this consummation. Holding, as they do, that slavery is morally right and socially elevating, they cannot cease to demand a full national recognition of it as a legal right and a social blessing.

Nor can we justifiably withhold this on any ground save our conviction that slavery is wrong. If slavery is right, all words, acts, laws, and constitutions against it are themselves wrong, and should be silenced and swept away. If it is right, we cannot justly object to its nationality—its universality; if it is wrong, they cannot justly insist upon its extension—its enlargement. All they ask we could readily grant, if we thought slavery right; all we ask they could as readily grant, if they thought it wrong. Their thinking it right and our thinking it wrong is the precise fact upon which depends the whole controversy. Thinking it right, as they do, they are not to blame for desiring its full recognition as being right; but thinking it wrong, as we do, can we yield to them? Can we cast our votes with their view, and against our own? In view of our moral, social, and political responsibilities, can we do this?

Wrong as we think slavery is, we can yet afford to let it alone where it is, because that much is due to the necessity arising from its actual presence in the nation; but can we, while our votes will prevent it, allow it to spread into the national Territories, and to overrun us here in these free States? If our sense of duty forbids this, then let us stand by our duty fearlessly and effectively. Let us be diverted by none of those sophistical contrivances wherewith we are so industriously plied and belabored—contrivances such as groping for some middle ground between the right and the wrong: vain as the search for a man who should be neither a living man nor a dead man; such as a policy of "don't care" on a question about which all true men do care; such as Union appeals beseeching true Union men to yield to Disunionists, reversing the divine rule, and calling, not the sinners, but the righteous to repentance; such as invocations to Washington, imploring men to unsay what Washington said and undo what Washington did.

Neither let us be slandered from our duty by false accusations against us, nor frightened from it by menaces of destruction to the government, nor of dungeons to ourselves. Let us have faith that right makes might, and in that faith let us to the end dare to do our duty as we understand it.

Entertaining Speeches

Excerpt from

ACRES OF DIAMONDS *

Russell H. Conwell

1. Ladies and Gentlemen: The title of this lecture originated away back in 1869. I was going down the Tigris River, and we had hired a guide from Baghdad to show us down to the Arabian gulf. . . . He told me that there once lived near the shore of the River Indus, toward which we were then travelling, an ancient Persian by the name of Al Hafed. He said that Al Hafed owned a farm, with orchards, grain fields, and gardens, that he had money at interest, had a beautiful wife and lovely children, and was a contented and happy man. Contented because he was wealthy, and wealthy because he was contented.

2. One day there visited this old Persian farmer one of those ancient Buddhist priests, one of the wise men of the East, who sat down by Al Hafed's fireside and told the old farmer "how this world was made." He told him that the world was once a great bank of fog, and the Almighty thrust his finger into this bank of fog, and began slowly to move his finger around, and then in-

* From *The Delivery of a Speech*, by R. K. Immel, 1921. George Wahr, Ann Arbor, publisher. This excerpt is the opening story in the famous popular lecture.

creased the speed of his finger until he whirled this bank of fog into a solid bank of fire; and as it went rolling through the Universe, burning its way through other banks of fog, it condensed the moisture until it fell in floods of rain on the heated surface of the world, and cooled the outward crust. Then the internal fires, bursting the cooling crust, threw up the mountains and the hills and the valleys of this wonderful world of ours.

3. "And," said the old priest, "if this internal melted mass burst forth and cooled very quickly it became granite; if it cooled more slowly it became copper; if it cooled less quickly, silver; less quickly, gold; and after gold, diamonds were made." Said the old priest, "A diamond is a congealed drop of sunlight." That statement is literally true.

The old priest told Al Hafed if he had a diamond the size of his thumb he could purchase a dozen farms like his. "And," said the priest, "if you had a handful of diamonds you could purchase the county, and if you had a mine of diamonds you could purchase kingdoms and place your children on thrones through the influence of your great wealth."

Al Hafed heard all about the diamonds that night and went to bed a poor man. He wanted a whole mine of diamonds.

4. Early in the morning he sought the priest and awoke him. Al Hafed said, "Will you tell me where I can find diamonds?" . . . "Well," said the priest, "if you want diamonds, all you have to do is go and find them, and then you will have them." "But," said Al Hafed, "I don't know where to go." "If you will find a river that runs over white sands between high mountains, in those white sands you will always find diamonds," said the priest. . . . "Well," said Al Hafed, "I will go." So he sold his farm, collected his money that was at interest, left his family in charge of a neighbor, and away he went in search of diamonds.

5. And he began his search, very properly, to my mind, at the Mountains of the Moon. Afterwards he came around into Palestine, and then wandered into Europe. At last, when his money was all gone, and he was in rags, poverty, and wretchedness, he stood at the shore in Barcelona in Spain, when a great tidal wave swept through the Pillars of Hercules. And the poor, starving, afflicted stranger could not resist the temptation to cast himself into that incoming tide, and he sank beneath its foaming crest, never to rise again in his life.

6. The man who purchased Al Hafed's farm led his camel out into the garden to drink, and as the animal put his nose in the shallow waters of the garden brook, Al Hafed's successor noted a curious flash of light from the white sands of the stream. Reaching in, he pulled out a large black stone containing a strange eye of light. He took it into the house as a curious pebble and putting it on the mantel that covered the central fire went his way and forgot all about it. But not long after, that same old priest came to visit Al Hafed's successor. The moment he opened the door he noticed the flash of light.

7. He rushed to the mantel, and said: "Here is a diamond! Here is a diamond! Has Al Hafed returned?"

"Oh, no, Al Hafed has not returned, and we have not heard from him since he went away, and that is not a diamond. It is nothing but a stone we found out in our garden."

"But," said the priest, "I know a diamond when I see it, and I tell you that is a diamond." Then together they rushed out into the garden. They stirred up the white sands with their fingers, and there came up other, more beautiful, more valuable gems than the first.

"Thus," said the guide, "and friends, it is historically true, were discovered the diamond mines of Golconda, the most valuable diamond mines in the history of the ancient world."

8. The guide then tossed his Turkish red cap into the air . . . and said to me: "Had Al Hafed remained at home and dug in his own cellar, or underneath his own wheat field, instead of wretchedness, poverty, starvation, and death in a strange land, he would have had acres of diamonds."

ACRES OF DIAMONDS! For every acre of the old farm, yes, every shovelful afterwards revealed the gems that have since decorated the crowns of monarchs.

. . . I then perceived why the guide reserved this story for his particular friends. It was that mean old Arab's way of going around the point . . . and saying indirectly, that in his private opinion there was a certain young man travelling down the Tigris River who might better be at home in America.

WHERE WE COME FROM *
Booth Tarkington

Mr. Toastmaster and Gentlemen: I feel that the least I can do to show my appreciation of your kindness in allowing me to be here tonight would be to have prepared you in some manner for the kind of speech I am going to make. A long time ago I was a candidate for the Indiana Legislature, and the campaign managers told me that I would have to make speeches. I did; that is, I made two. [Laughter.] Those speeches attracted the attention of William Jennings Bryan in his own newspaper. You may feel that I am speaking too much of my own achievements, but I cannot refrain from reminding you that *The Commoner* referred to me and my orations, devoting several paragraphs which led up to an important place among the editorials. It said: "Mr. Tarkington made two speeches during the recent campaign. On the first occasion he is reported to have suffered so from stage fright that he was unable to utter a syllable. From what we have read of his second effort we think it is a pity he didn't have it both times." [Laughter.] Unless it be considered too wide a digression, I might best state that in spite of my oratory I succeeded in being elected, but I hope, however, your committee didn't invite me to address you tonight from the same motive that brought me the solid vote of the farmers in Marion County. Friends of mine

* By permission of the author. The third annual banquet of the Indiana Society of Chicago was held at the Congress Hotel the evening of January 28, 1908. The master of ceremonies, Mr. John T. McCutcheon, the well-known cartoonist, introduced Mr. Tarkington as follows: Gentlemen: It is a great pleasure to introduce a man you have all heard about. He has written many great things. If I were to refer to him as "The Gentleman from Indiana" you would suspect to whom I was referring. If I were to say that he's "The Man from Home," I might also reveal the identity of the next speaker, all of which would be bad tactics in a toastmaster. I must say that we have with us tonight one whom we all delight to honor; one whose name is a household word; one whose work has reflected much glory on your state and given much gratification to his fellow statesmen. Perhaps you may have an inkling of his identity. Down at Purdue University in the early nineties we all predicted that he would be a great man if he only tried, but we feared that he would not try. He has fooled us and succeeded. Gentlemen, it gives me great pleasure to introduce Mr. Booth Tarkington, who will respond to the toast, Where We Come From.

were out on election day who asked a group of farmers whom they were for. "We're all for Tarkington out here," they said. "We want him to get in." This puzzled my friends a little, because they couldn't think of anything I had done to arouse any particular enthusiasm among the farmers. So one of my friends asked them why they were so strong for me. "Why," they said, "we want to see what the darned fool will do." [Laughter.]

"From" is not the important word in my speech, as it is in that sentence, "the wise men came from the east." Of course they did. We emphasize where we come from because no matter where we go we're always from Indiana. We don't quit being from Indiana. Hoosiers we remain. I never knew but one man who did quit. He went abroad when he was about eighteen or twenty, and he stayed too long. In time he gave up being from Indiana altogether and become a British subject. Why, I almost hesitate to speak of the horrible punishment that overtook him. "Vengeance is mine," saith the Lord, and in time He smote. This young man had tried to look like an Englishman for so long, he had talked like one for so long, that at last you couldn't tell him from one; and if that isn't a horrible punishment I don't know what it is! [Laughter.]

Pride of birthplace is a conspicuous quality. Of course for some places there is no pride at all. I don't know that anybody ever selected Southern Patagonia to be born in, deliberately, nor Timbuctoo. If anybody did select one of these places he probably didn't brag of his birthplace in after years. Possibly we might add London to this list. No Londoner ever showed any particular excitement about being born in London. If two Londoners, strangers to each other, met by accident in the middle of the Sahara, it probably wouldn't develop at all where they were born. They were born some place, but, if it were to develop where, it would excite the same enthusiasm in them as a Beethoven sonata would in a ham. [Laughter.] But it seems to me that Hoosiers would have found each other out and have elected a President of the United States from Indiana within ten minutes after they arrived, even if they got no farther from home than the lobby of a hotel near Columbus, Ohio. The fact is, none of us has ever quite got over being from Indiana. It seems as if we were not sure we deserved it. And wherever we go the fact that we are from Indiana seems to have something of the pleasantness of good news. So we mention it. [Laughter.] Not that we brag. We leave that to our friends in the suburbs, our good neighbors and friends in the bordering states.

When I was in college one of my club-mates was a Kentuckian. You know the style of his patriotism. It is only necessary for me to mention that he was from Louisville. You know that the first thing he worships is Louisville, then Kentucky, then the Deity, then the United States as a whole, concluding with Indiana. [Laughter.] One day we were discussing the populations of our different great cities, and the Kentuckian carelessly remarked that the population of Louisville was two hundred and fifty thousand, whereupon a gentleman from New Jersey drew forth the table of the census, which gave the official figures for Louisville at one hundred and seventy-five thousand, a difference merely of seventy-five thousand from the Kentuckian's statement. The company looked to see him show some signs of confusion, but he didn't even blush. On the contrary, he coolly explained that just before the reports of that census were to be closed in Washington the census taker for the largest ward in Louisville was hurrying to catch the last mail that would get to Washington in time, when he fell down a well and was drowned, and unfortunately the books showing just seventy-five thousand names were under his arm at the time, and it took so long to fish them out and get them properly blotted that the reports closed without them. [Laughter.] He said the circumstances were familiar to every Kentuckian, and I haven't a doubt that you couldn't have found a citizen in the length and breadth of Louisville who wouldn't have corroborated his statement.

Our neighbors do seem to stretch the facts a little sometimes; but I don't see that we can altogether blame them. So often they seem to feel it's an absolute necessity. And it's not altogether owing to our superior virtues that we don't stretch the facts about Indiana. It's because you can't. You can't lie about Indiana. It's all true. Anything of any kind that any Hoosier ever said about Indiana is true. For instance, George Ade, when in Rome two years ago, told a Cardinal that Indiana was one of the thirteen original states. [Laughter.] Isn't that true? Of course it is. Indiana is not only one of the thirteen original states; it's the most original state there is. [Laughter.]

There was a time, as we all know, when the great life purpose of our eastern cousins seemed to be to make fun of Indiana. I've known an Indiana convention in an eastern hotel to be spoken of as exhibiting a cosmopolitan people who looked like a group photograph of a Christian Endeavor Society in the prehistoric or Hayes and Wheeler age. [Laughter.] The easterners express surprise that we do not regard the term "Hoosier" as a taunt. A taunt, when we know it refers to the people of Indiana! Of course we don't claim there aren't some pretty poor specimens amongst us here and there. You find them in Indiana just as you find bad people in a church, and for the same reason—they come here to get better. [Laughter.]

We know that our Indiana is a young state, old only in honor and in the affections of her sons, and in the pride of their heritage that they are from Indiana. In the words of the Honorable H. P. Sherman of Decatur: "Well we know the grand old state of Indiana will go crashing down the ages with her head up and her tail over the dashboard!" [Laughter.] However mixed the metaphor, every man of us holds to this same sentiment, and I thank you for the honor and privilege of being with you tonight. [Applause.]

HONORS TO THE MAYOR *

Chauncey M. Depew

Mr. President: When you were describing the gentleman upon whom you were about to call, I thought until the last clause of your last sentence, that you were referring to the judiciary of the State. There are many points of resemblance between the New York Central Railroad and the State Judiciary, in that in the administration of the affairs of the commonwealth they both deal out equal justice to all. [Laughter and applause.]

I have been a member of the Lotos Club for many years, but this is the most extraordinary gathering which I have ever attended. [Laughter.] Judge Davis and myself have during the

* The New York Tribune, January 13, 1879. On the evening of January 11, 1879, a dinner, in honor of the incoming and outgoing mayors of New York, attended by many well known public men, was given by the Lotos Club. Several of the diners had been active contestants for the same offices. However, only the humorous features of politics were touched upon. The new mayor and his defeated competitor sat together. Speeches were made by Mayor Cooper, ex-Mayor Ely, Chauncey M. Depew, and a number of other well-known men.

evening been looking at a work of art which for more than ten years has adorned the walls of the Lotos Club, and that is this lion with a toothache that hangs on an adjoining wall. [Great laughter.] The question in our minds is, where is the lamb? And the only location we can decide upon for it is that the lamb must be inside. [Renewed laughter.] Well, gentlemen, that is a very suitable picture.

I find here on one side of this table the Grand Sachem of Tammany and immediately opposite a gentleman who wanted to be Grand Sachem. [Laughter.] I find here the gentleman who ran for mayor and was elected, and the gentleman who contested for that honor with him and was defeated. I find here Tammany and Anti-Tammany, Administration Republicans and Anti-Administration Republicans, and every representative of public spirit and public opinion except Liberal Republican. [Laughter.] I think there are gathered around this festive board more integrity [laughter], more devotion to the public service, more capacity for the public good, more distinguished men in and out of office [laughter] and more abominable politics than were ever gathered anywhere else. [Great laughter.] Mr. Reid represents bullion, Mr. Croly silver, and together they seek to restore a standard by which each can receive in his own metal all that he can possibly lay his hands on. [Great laughter.]

It is a peculiarity of the Lotos Club that it welcomes the incoming and bids farewell to the outgoing mayor. There have been chief magistrates of this city who have endeavored to ignore this courtesy, but their administrations in every instance have proved lamentable failures. [Laughter.]

When a mayor is elected, he reads the messages of his predecessors for the purpose of forming his own, until he is threatened with water on the brain. [Laughter.] He reads the report of the comptroller for the purpose of ascertaining the financial condition of the city, until his friends call on Doctor MacDonald to watch over him to keep him out of the asylum to which he is rapidly making his way. [Laughter.] Then it is found necessary to brace him up with some intellectual stimulants and hopeful atmosphere which is only to be found within the periphery of the Lotos Club. [Laughter.]

I had occasion once to criticize Mayor Cooper's precedessor on the ground that his "bread basket" resembled the municipal treasury: the more he put into it the less good it seemed to do.

[Laughter.] I believe in this era of reform; we have reached a reform in that respect. [Renewed laughter.]

It is expected by every good citizen in this metropolis that its Mayor shall have the fluency of Henry Clay, the solidity of Daniel Webster, the firmness of Andrew Jackson, and the digestion of an ostrich, [great laughter] to which fulfillment of all the duties the Lotos Club welcomes Mr. Cooper. [Laughter.]

I have often noticed this peculiarity about mayors, and I know a good many of them—not so many however as Mayor Ely, whose mature recollection runs back about forty mayors—I have observed that they think a great deal more of themselves during the first month of their office than they do in the last. [Laughter.] The only exception that I ever met to this rule was in the case of the late lamented Mayor Havemeyer. In the closing days of his administration, I was in his office one day. He led me to the window and pointed to the moving crowds on Broadway. Said he, "Depew, look there. There go business men, capitalists, men of influence and property. There they are hurrying on to provide for themselves, their families and the future and paying no attention to political affairs. Not one of them looks over to this office, because they know that the old Dutchman is here, protecting their lives and property against the thieves of Tammany Hall and the gamblers of the Republican Party." [Renewed laughter.]

Now I am probably more competent to speak in this mixed assembly than any person here. I served the Republicans for many years, and ran for Lieutenant Governor on the Liberal Democratic ticket. [Laughter.] While running for Lieutenant Governor, I remember that once I was speaking at Potsdam. There were six Democrats in the town. I was told that there was one man in the town who had read The Day Book all through the war and believed in it still, and that if I could secure him I could get the solid vote. During my speech, that man was present. When I got through he came to me and said, "If what our paper has been saying about you for the last ten years is true, you are probably the d—st rascal agoing [laughter] but if you will exercise your peculiar talents as well for the Democratic Party as you have for the Republicans, I will vote for you with my whole heart." [Great laughter.] That is about the only town in the state in which I got the solid vote. [Renewed laughter.]

Now, the Lotos Club welcomes Mayor Cooper upon his entrance upon his important duties with that enthusiasm and encouragement that only a body comprising the intellect and influence of this Club can possibly bestow. [Laughter.] We welcome him, and bid him good cheer, in common with all our fellow citizens. [Applause.] It is a common thing to criticize, but it has almost uniformly been the habit of all parties in the City of New York to put forward as candidate for its Chief Magistrate for the suffrages of citizens, men, men on either side, who, if elected, would be eminently worthy of the dignity and honor to which they aspire. The late contest was between men of high intelligence and solid citizenship. Both candidates were gentlemen of worth, character, virtue, and independence.

The citizens of New York have accorded the honor to the gentleman who is our guest tonight. It is a worthy honor, worthily bestowed, and I have no doubt that the office will be worthily administered. [Long-continued applause.]

MY EXPERIENCES AS A TEACHER *

Mary Ellen Ludlum

Many of you will some day be teachers. Some of you are preparing to be teachers and others of you probably will be teachers. You will probably be English teachers. Most people are at some time English teachers. It makes no difference to a school board whether or not you have majored in English, history, mathematics, or astronomy; they think you can teach English. In view of this I think it only fair to let you know what you are up against by telling you some of my experiences as teacher.

One of the important prerequisites of a teacher is that she have a philosophy. My philosophy before I started to teach was a very progressive one, "Spare the Rod and Spoil the Child," but after seeing the size of my Freshmen boys I decided it would have to be changed to "Mind over Matter."

In addition to a philosophy you should always have a good definition of education. One I like is, "Education is the inculcation of the incomprehensible into the uninterested by the incompetent." Most teachers, however, prefer the one that says, "Edu-

* By permission of the author. Mrs. Ludlum presented this speech in a public speaking class, Ohio State University, May, 1949.

cation is that, by means of which one hopes to make more money, unless he becomes an educator."

As a teacher, there are several things you should always remember. The first of these is never throw away an English composition; they will later serve as material for speeches such as this. For instance I remember the theme one boy wrote on George Washington's life which he started by saying "George Washington married Martha Custis and in due time became the father of his country." I will never forget one composition on ants which went something like this: "Ants is of two kinds, insects and female uncles. Aunts live in the ground, the sugar bowl, and with their married sisters."

The second point you should remember is that when you ask a student to define a word or to use a word in a sentence you should be ready for anything. One day I asked a student to define "home," and he replied: "Home is where everyone waits to get the car to go out." In asking a boy to define "nonsense" I got this reply: "If an elephant hung over the edge of a cliff supported only by his tail wrapped around a daisy—that would be nonsense."

Another time I was explaining that the suffix "ous" means "full of." For instance "joyous" means "full of joy" and "glorious" means "full of glory." Then I asked if anyone could think of an example. Some little fellow in the back row raised his hand and when called upon said "pious." The superintendent was visiting my room once, and I wanted to make an especially good impression, so I decided to ask a simple question which all could answer. I asked my little geniuses to use the word "beans" in a sentence. One boy said, "My father plants beans." Another said, "My mother cooks beans." Just then one student who seldom raised his hand volunteered, "We are all human beans."

Another point the new teacher should remember is that when she asks a question she should be prepared for anything. I remember that my class had just read a Jack London story about a man who was lost in the very cold climate of the North. In the discussion of this story which followed I asked "Why was the dog better able to get along in the extreme cold than the man?" The quick reply was "Because the dog had hair all over, and the man only had hair on his chin."

Finally, a teacher should remember never to expect her students to learn. I learned this early in my career. One of my students continually said "I have went." After patiently correcting his themes with red pencil and telling him to say "I have gone" for several weeks, I finally lost my temper. I made him stay after school and write on the board one hundred times "I have gone." I was called to the principal's office, and when I returned the young man had finished. "I have gone" was written neatly one hundred times and down below it my pupil had added, "I finished and have went home."

After all maybe we can't blame our students too much. Sometimes parents are just as much of a problem. Like a good speech teacher, I explained to my class the use of the diaphragm in breathing and how important proper use of it was for speech. The next day I received this angry reply from the mother of one of my students. "It's always something. Now my Johnny needs a diafram! Maybe rich kids can have diaframs, but I have to support an invalid husband and five kids. I can't afford no extras."

So, remember my experiences and profit by them when you become teachers. However, before you accept a teaching job be sure you are thoroughly prepared. Such preparation should include at least sixteen years of college with emphasis in such fields as physical culture and jujitsu. In addition to this the prospective teacher needs certain physical and personality requirements. He or she should be at least forty years of age, six feet two inches in height and weigh approximately two hundred pounds. And most important, he should have a sense of humor of the type developed by having a practical joker for a roommate for four years.

LANDLADIES *

Shirley Brigance

My speech this afternoon is really one concerning one of the extracurricular subjects that is required by most graduate students. Most of you think, I suppose, that a graduate student is concerned mainly with reading books, magazines, periodicals, attending class lectures, and, if you are employed by one of the departments, teaching a class or two. However, this is only a part of the work that is required, for a major part of education concerns a course in practical experience—that in learning how to

* By permission of the author. Miss Brigance delivered this speech in a public speaking class, Ohio State University, May, 1949.

deal with landladies. Although I have had six years' experience in this field, four as an undergraduate and two as a graduate, I feel that I am still more or less of an amateur at this business. I should hesitate to call the various landladies I have known, "professionals," but the fact remains that they have had a good deal of experience in renting rooms and are usually able to wangle something extra out of me—usually, money. From my experience with them, however, I think that they might be classified into four major types. The first three are of the common garden variety—they can be found nearly everywhere and grow on you like weeds, while the fourth type is somewhat of a rarity. You are lucky, indeed, if you can find one of these.

The first type I should like to mention I call the Economical Type. You will find in the room a list of regulations which include: Room rent, thirty dollars per month; hot plate, five dollars per month extra; iron, a dollar a month extra; radio, a dollar a month extra; an electric fan, two dollars a month extra; laundry privileges, a dollar a week extra. Now these are the ones that are listed in the room. Naturally, there are other regulations that are mentioned regularly—usually every time she sees you. Little things, such as: "Never use over two inches of bath water for a bath—and don't take a bath oftener than necessary. It wastes water." It goes without saying, of course, that overnight visitors are strongly discouraged or forbidden entirely—the girl might want to take a bath. This is the type of landlady that I always think of whenever I hear the expression, "To hell with the expense, give the bird another seed!"

The second type that I have found is the Anti-Noise Type. At a place of this sort, it always seems necessary to tiptoe around your room at all times. You are asked not to brush your teeth or wash your hands after 9:00 P.M. because the running water makes too much noise, and disturbs the rest of the household. And, of course, it goes without saying that coming in as late as 11:00 P.M. is looked on with horror. One place where I stayed, the landlady was quite fussy about noise. She was a spinster who always insisted on calling a car a "machine." She always maintained that she was very nervous and that she was exhausted whenever she had company of an evening. Considering her rate of speech, and her verbosity, it wasn't surprising—one needed an edgewise to get a word in with.

And then there is the Prudish Type. This type has two subtypes or varieties—the Old Maid variety and the Religious Fanatic. Under the first variety, the Old Maid kind, we have the ones who insist that you always turn your boy friends' pictures to the wall at night when you're undressing, and tell you never to wear a red dress because it's suggestive. One house I lived in had five locks on the front door. One of them, a Yale lock, was locked at all times so that it was necessary to carry a key to get in, even in the middle of the day. At night, the other four were put on. First there was the Yale lock, then a little bolt that kept the Yale lock from being unlocked with a key, then a bolt below that, a chain above, and a lock on the screen door. It would have taken a better man than Houdini to have gotten into that place. Then the Religious Fanatic. One room I looked at had a funeral wreath hanging above the bed. The landlady there informed me that it was in memory of her husband who had died in that very bed twenty years before, and that it had hung there ever since. Needless to say I did not rent that room. One place I lived in, the landlady was very insistent that all of us go to church every Sunday. If, for some reason, one of us did not go, she popped into the room, woke us up, and said a prayer for the salvation of our souls before she went off to church. She was especially fond of the couple who lived on the third floor because they were regular church goers. What she didn't know, however, was that they used to bring home grain alcohol with the formaldehyde still in it, and get "looped" every Sunday night.

The last type I shall mention is a rare type—the Ideal Type. She is the kind who gives you kitchen privileges, so that you can cook any time of the day or night that you feel like, and living room privileges where you can have your friends in and feel as if it were your own home. She is even the kind who, when she stays up late, talking to you and your date, is so interesting that you both enjoy it. But, as I said, these are very rare.

Most of the time, however, wherever you are living, you feel that maybe the grass is greener on the other side. One day you take the fatal plunge and tell the landlady you're going to move. Then she gets upset. She tells you that you've taken the room for the entire year—which you haven't done at all—and starts yelling, her voice rising in pitch and volume as she starts threatening you with all kinds of things. Finally, after being beaten down verbally —and you are in constant fear of being beaten physically—you tell her you'll pay the extra month's rent. Then, scraping together the remains of your dignity, you walk out—looking forward with hope, eagerness, and anticipation, only to have to go through the whole nasty mess all over again.

A HUSBAND'S GIFT TO HIS WIFE *
Dorothy Smith

At other times I have mentioned several things to you about my children, but this time my husband is the victim. The idea for this entertaining speech came to me through the Christmas present which I received from him a few days ago; but before I tell what it was let me go back to other Christmases.

Shortly after we were married we celebrated our first Christmas and he gave me a lovely large coffee percolator. Though I didn't then and do not now care for coffee, I thought very little about it for as long as he liked coffee it had to be made every morning and we might as well have a good percolator to make it in. The next Christmas brought me a very beautiful toaster from him, although I have never cared for toast at all—I have always preferred plain bread and butter. And year after year there were other gifts often reminding me of Joe and Vi of the "funnies"—you know how Joe is always buying something for Vi which will benefit him.

About six weeks ago, my husband made a business trip and while he was away he was invited to a friend's house where the hostess served chicken and waffles. Upon his return, he kept talking about this wonderful treat, but I was only about half interested, as, while I am very fond of chicken, I care very little for waffles. Suddenly the idea popped into my head that he was thinking of getting me a waffle iron for Christmas. So I immediately set out to head him off! I thought that something more personal would be lovely, so I began to stress my need for new dresses. I had heard of other men who had bought their wives dresses for Christmas, and I didn't understand why my husband shouldn't.

Christmas morning finally came and when I peered under the tree for my package, I was somewhat surprised at the shape of it.

* Mrs. Smith gave this speech in a section of Public Speaking 1, at The George Washington University in January, 1934.

I had never bought a dress that came in a package like that. But I didn't give up hope; I opened the package and there was my waffle iron, a very beautiful one but nevertheless a waffle iron. Well, there have been worse husbands! I knew one who bought his wife a washing machine for her birthday, because he didn't like the way his shirts were done at the laundry. However, I showed no disappointment whatsoever by word or sign. I realized that the way to a man's heart was to feed the brute. And if he liked coffee and waffles I certainly would see that he had coffee and waffles!

After thinking it over, I realized that he never could have bought a dress to satisfy me anyway. He would have bought a yellow one, although I never wear anything but blues and greens, and he wouldn't have known whether I wear a size fourteen or forty. He might have judged the size like the woman did, whom I saw buying a pair of sport trousers for her husband last summer. When the clerk asked, "What size?" she replied, "I don't know what size he wears but he is just this big around." Whereupon, she put her arms in front of her in the position of just barely being able to reach around him.

So, I believe, after all, that I'd rather have the waffle iron and make him waffles than to have had a dress which I would have had to tuck away in a trunk and find excuses the rest of my life for not wearing. And I imagine that keeping him well fed on waffles will mean keeping him good natured and generous, which will make it possible for me to get what I want in other ways.

Part Four

ASSIGNMENTS FOR
SPEAKING PRACTICE

Introduction

Part Four is offered to assist the student in his actual preparation of classroom speeches.

The assignments described have been used in the universities in which the authors have taught. They are arranged here in approximately the order used, although not all of them are used in any one class. Recently, for example, the speech of self-introduction and the speech on "A Speech that Impressed Me" have been used during the first two weeks of the course in St. Louis University, and the "personal experience" talk has been omitted. The days devoted to special practice in delivery (numbered 5–6–7–8 here) are spaced at about three-week intervals in the semester.

Because of variations which exist in the number and frequency of class meetings, we have not suggested specific time limits for any of the practice talks. Our feeling in general is that frequent practice with short talks is most desirable.

The student is offered here, first, some directions for his procedure in preparing all talks; second, a composite chart of speech composition; third, directions for reference to chapters in Parts One and Two; and fourth, directions for the preparation of each kind of practice speech.

General Procedure

1. Do not wait until a day or two before your speaking assignment to prepare. Select your topic immediately upon announcement of the assignment. Early preparation is essential.

2. Once you have chosen a topic, do not change it at a later date. The advantage of a number of days to think about the subject matter of your speech would be lost in the event of a last-minute change.

3. Devote parts of several days to reflection on your topic—determine your Specific Purpose, consider what the Principal Ideas should be, and think of possible Speech Details. This preliminary thinking is vital to good speech preparation—and it can't be done if you neglect an early start.

4. After your preliminary analysis, make a tentative outline. Then do whatever reading or interviewing may be needed to complete your preparation. Make a final outline.

5. The final outline should be completed in time to give you several days for rehearsal.

6. Rehearse the speech *from ideas,* not word-for-word. Rehearse it aloud, and talk as if in the actual presence of an audience. Direct your speech to a roommate, or to an empty chair —but do it aloud.

7. Notes will not be taken to the platform: learn to fix the outline of your speech in mind and to get along without artificial aids.

8. Do not write out a speech. Avoid memorizing. State your Purpose, Principal Ideals, and Details, using the best words that you can to express them. You will gain in confidence, fluency, and the ability to remember points if you follow this method.

Note: The type of preparation suggested above will

  a. make it easier for you to make good talks.
  b. give you the opportunity of getting the most out of the course and of making your speeches "do you justice."
  c. avoid nervous tension caused by last-minute preparation.
  d. avoid the necessity of saying "I couldn't find the material last night so I'm not prepared" (that's evidence only that you started preparation far too late).
  e. insure your preparedness even if, at the last moment, you have a rush of other work.
  f. enable you, in case you must be absent on the day of your speaking engagement, to arrange with the instructor to speak ahead of time, and thus maintain your standing in the course.

PRINCIPLES OF SPEECH COMPOSITION (SUMMARY)

PARTS OF SPEECHES	INFORMATIVE (Matters of Fact)
SPECIFIC PURPOSE—	Exact understanding or appreciation desired.
ELEMENTS OF INTEREST—	*Familiar,* specific, striking, vital, varied.
PRINCIPAL IDEAS—	Must define: answer questions *how, in what way, to what extent.* Statements of fact.
SPEECH DETAILS—	Comparisons, examples, reiteration, statistics, testimony. Matters of fact.
INTRODUCTION—	To arouse interest. Consider partition for clarity in exposition. Any of the special forms, especially in impressive talks.
CONCLUSION—	In exposition main function is summary. Consider special forms in impressive talks.
EXAMPLES OF TYPE	EXAMPLES OF TYPE

PUBLIC SPEECHES—	Classroom lecture
	Explanation, Description, Narration
	Oral reports (usually)
	Speeches of:
	  Eulogy (usually)
	  Dedication
	  Commemoration
	  Acceptance
	  Presentation
	  Introduction
	  Acknowledgment
	  Sermons (sometimes)

CONVERSATION—	Explanations, instructions, informal reports, ordering goods, giving specifications, narrating, describing, etc.

Notes: (1) Elements of interest and speech details are listed under each speech type in *approximate* order of importance for that type.

PRINCIPLES OF SPEECH COMPOSITION (SUMMARY)

PERSUASIVE (Matters of Opinion)	ENTERTAINING (Fact and Opinion)
Exact conviction or action desired.	Exact trait of subject to be made amusing.
Vital, familiar, specific, striking, varied.	*Striking (the novel),* familiar, specific, vital, varied.
Must give *reasons why* and make motive appeal. Statements of opinion.	Must stress the novel and familiar. Principle of incongruity. Consider mock-serious treatment.
Examples, testimony, statistics, comparisons, reiteration. On matters of opinion.	*Comparisons, examples,* reiteration, testimony, statistics. Novel, familiar, or incongruous.
To arouse interest. Partition optional. Consider use of one of the special forms.	To arouse interest, amusement. Consider use of the special forms.
Functions summary or appeal, or both. Consider use of one of the special forms.	Rarely demands formal summary. Brief, good-humored close essential. May be a serious tribute.
EXAMPLES OF TYPE	EXAMPLES OF TYPE
Legal arguments Political arguments Debates Informal discussions Group conferences Sales and promotional talks Inspirational speeches Campaign speeches—political, civic, etc. Sermons (usually) Good-will speeches (but informative in rhetorical pattern, usually)	After-dinner speeches (usually) Popular lectures (usually) Travel talks (usually) Monologues, etc.
Sales interview, application for position, discussions of policy, offer of employment, seeking privilege or favor, etc.	Social conversation, where the end is merely delight or enjoyment.

(2) All suggestions made in this chart should be considered *general* in their application, and reference to the appropriate chapters for more specific discussion is urged.

Some Specific Directions

1. USE OF THE TEXTBOOK

Read Chapters 1–5 as early as possible. Here the basics of oral communication, whether in conversation or in platform speaking, are set forth.

Chapters 6–11 inclusive contain specific directions on speech preparation and outlining and on each of the principal kinds of speeches, with suggestions on topics and materials. They also present, in the latter parts of Chapters 7–10 inclusive, techniques that can help you develop greater proficiency: techniques that go beyond the basics and that can add greatly to your skills. Read these chapters, especially 7–10 inclusive, before you prepare the kinds of talks treated in them.

Part Three presents valuable examples of skilled speechmaking to illustrate what you have learned in the text. Famous speeches of all the different kinds are presented there. We believe it valuable to analyze these from the point of view of their structure, their use of elements of interestingness, and their style. Whether they are specifically assigned or not, read them thoughtfully. This can give "depth" to your speaking efforts.

2. SPEECH OF SELF-INTRODUCTION

This short, informal talk is your first opportunity to communicate effectively to your classmates. Make your talk informal and friendly. Try to make a good impression on your hearers. Here are some of the things you might tell about briefly: Name, home town, high school attended and your interests here, your college aims, your travel or work experiences, your hobbies, your hoped-for life work, AND what you hope to accomplish in your Speech course.

Since you are the world's greatest authority on the subject of yourself, you can be confident that this talk will give you no trouble!

By the way, make a list of your classmates' names: get acquainted!

3. A "PERSONAL EXPERIENCE" SPEECH

This is a speaking assignment which does not require research. Select an incident from your own experience which you believe will be of interest to the class. It may be an outgrowth of your war experience, your participation in athletics, a job you have held, a vacation trip, or any other stimulating experience. Give sufficient details as to place, time, and date to identify essential characters and to permit listeners to recreate your experience in their own imaginations. Make them relive the experience with you. Plan the speech so that it builds up to a climax—a high point of interest—and conclude shortly thereafter. The list of endings from Aesop's fables which follows is to be used in providing a general statement or central idea which your experience serves to illustrate.

Each of the following statements is the last sentence of one of Aesop's fables.

> The race is not always to the swift.
> It is very foolish to be greedy.
> Do not believe everything that you hear.
> Pride goes before a fall.
> A small gain is worth a large promise.
> Might makes right.
> Learn from the misfortunes of others.
> Friends in fine weather only are not worth much.
> A kindness is never wasted.
> The man who talks for both sides is not to be trusted by either.
> If you try to please all, you please none.
> Self help is the best help.

Ability proves itself by deeds.

The true leader proves himself by his qualities.

Misfortune is the test of true friendship.

Whatever you do, do with all your might.

Common sense is always worth more than cunning.

Set your sails with the wind.

There is nothing worth so much as liberty.

A possession is worth no more than the use we make of it.

Wicked deeds will not stay hid.

Do not count your chickens before they are hatched.

Take warning from the misfortunes of others.

An act of kindness is well repaid.

Be content with your lot.

Honesty is the best policy.

In unity is strength.

Act in haste and repent at leisure.

Greediness leads to misfortune.

Industry is of itself a treasure.

The useful is of much more importance and value than the ornamental.

Do not trust alone to outward appearances

Look before you leap.

Be sure of your pedigree before you boast of it.

The laws of nature are unchangeable.

Do not grudge others what you cannot enjoy yourself.

A fine coat is not always an indication of an attractive mind.

Do not try to do impossible things.

The strong are apt to settle questions to their own advantage.

Do not let your hopes carry you away from reality.

Greatness has its penalties.

Take what you can get when you can get it.

Borrowed feathers do not make fine birds.

One falsehood leads to another.

Stick to your trade.

Do not try to ape your betters.

Preparedness for war is the best guarantee of peace.

The deceitful have no friends.

Those who have all the toil do not always get the profit.

SPEECH OUTLINE—PERSONAL EXPERIENCE SPEECH

Aesop's statement ....

....

An experience of mine which illustrates this point: ....

....

....

....

....

Concluding statement ....

....

4. REPORTS ON SPEECHES

You are to talk on "A Speech That Impressed Me." This may be further explained as a report on any speech, radio or television talk, sermon, public address, interview, or conference that moved, interested, or influenced you greatly. You have a short time in which to tell the class who the speaker was, what it was about his talk that impressed you, and to conclude.

The purpose of the assignment is to bring before the class the views of a number of persons on *what good speaking is.* As a member of an audience, you heard an effective talk: what was it about what was said, the manner of speaking, or the choice of words and illustrations, that moved you? Tell it simply; tell it conversationally; use illustrations from the talk to convey to the audience the merits of the speaker you admire.

When all the reports have been made, *the class will sum up* and thus arrive at some notion of what qualities or characteristics contribute to effectiveness in oral communication. So take notes on the reports made by others; build for yourself a conception of good speaking.

Suggestions

1. As soon as this assignment is made, decide upon what speaker and speech you will report. Do this *now.* It is important

in preparing any talk that you determine your subject early and give yourself the opportunity to turn it over in your mind.

2. After deciding upon what speech (talk, interview, sermon, etc.) to report, decide for yourself what it was about this speech that impressed you—*some one thing* or perhaps *two*. It may have been the ideas expressed: the originality, novelty, strength, or forcefulness of the speaker's ideas; it may have been the speaker's words and illustrations that gave the speech an inspirational and unforgettable quality; or it may have been the manner in which it was spoken—the communicativeness, enthusiasm, or expressiveness of voice and manner. Take *one* or *two* qualities or characteristics of his speaking, then, as the topics for your report.

3. Having selected the topic or topics upon which you are to build your report, try to recall more details of the speech that illustrate the characteristics you have chosen. Use examples, quotations from the speech, description of how it was said or of how you felt. Make it *vivid* to the audience.

4. Organize your report as follows:

a. Make your opening statement tell who-when-where-what. Don't ramble, come to the point, so your audience will know what your topic is.

Example: "On December 8, 1941, Franklin D. Roosevelt spoke to Congress on the declaration of war with Japan. I have never forgotten the *persuasiveness* of that great speech."

Here the student told *when, who, where,* and *what,* and he designated clearly the quality or characteristic of the speech that impressed him.

b. Develop your point by description, quotation, examples, and comparisons, within the time limit, to emphasize the characteristics of the speech that impressed you.

c. Conclude briefly with a summary sentence, again stressing the point that you have been developing.

Example: "When Roosevelt finished, the whole nation, and I was one of its citizens, was persuaded to go to war, with faith in 'the ultimate triumph' that he predicted."

5. No special outline form is required. Prepare in any way you choose, but don't try to memorize your talk word for word—*it won't work!* Learn it by ideas: rehearse it aloud, practice it silently, and finally check it against your time limit.

6. When called on for your report, just come forward and talk informally. Concentrate on your purpose, which is to make the class *understand* and *feel* the reason why this speech impressed you when you heard it. Do *not* use notes.

7. Take notes liberally on the ideas brought out by other speakers.

8. At the end of this project, make a chart showing the principal characteristics of good speaking as brought out in all these reports. Suggested headings: The Speaker Himself; How He Organized His Material; How He Presented His Material.

PREPARATION BLANK FOR REPORT ON A SPEECH

1. Name of speaker upon whom I choose to report
   ....

2. When, on what subject, and under what circumstances did he speak?
   ....

3. What one or two qualities or characteristics of his talking affected or impressed me the most? ....

4. What can I relate about the speech that brings out these qualities? ....
   ....

5. To what might I *compare* this speaker's outstanding qualities or characteristic? ....

6. Are there brief quotations I could use from this speech to illustrate my point? (Write them down) ....
   ....

SPEECH OUTLINE

1. Introductory remarks: (Who-what-where-when) ....
   Name the characteristics you will emphasize ....

2. Main body of report:
   Description ....
   Examples ....
   Comparisons ....
   Quotations ....

3. Conclusion: (A sentence summing up and re-emphasizing the characteristics upon which you reported) ....
   ....

5-6-7-8. ASSIGNMENTS ON DELIVERY

At intervals during the course, practice sessions in Oral Presentation may be scheduled. This reflects the vital importance of effective delivery, the way in which the speaker expresses his ideas through the use of voice and body, and the spirit and intent behind his speaking.

These sessions, properly understood and carried out, will help you to become a more effective speaker.

Although we will use short excerpts from the speeches of others, these are not programs in "declamation" or "elocution." On the contrary they call for the most direct, forceful, colorful delivery that you can give them. Your task is (1) to understand fully the meaning of the excerpt assigned to you; (2) to speak it with a high degree of communicativeness and energy; (3) to bring out the shades of meaning and feeling contained in it.

Different elements of effective presentation will be emphasized at each practice session.

On the *Gettysburg Address,* the "fundamental qualities" of delivery will be emphasized. Sense of communication, sincerity, and animation are the fundamentals. Read about them; practice them. Text in Part 3.

On *Acres of Diamonds,* the action of the whole body in speech, as well as the fundamentals, will be stressed. Text in Part 3.

On the Roosevelt *War Speech,* the use of the voice for expressive speaking will be stressed. Text in Part 3.

Special assignments to help you overcome any particular problems may be made by your teacher.

An Important Comment

Often students of speaking will say, "I'm not *naturally* communicative; it's not *natural* for me to be active physically and to gesture while speaking; it's not *natural* for me to breathe deeply and enunciate clearly," etc.

Substitute the word *habitual* for *natural* and you will come nearer the actual truth!

One of the problems faced by every group in speaking is that of overcoming habitual inhibitions or fears, forced upon individuals originally by parents or teachers or by their unfamiliarity with platform speaking.

Ninety per cent of all persons who study speaking need to use greater physical activity, for instance. The task in class, then, is to "break through" and do some of the desirable things, and especially, even to overdo physical and vocal activity. Remember this if you feel that it isn't "natural" to do some of these things. Here is the place to overcome past restraints and to become an effective, forceful speaker.

"Act enthusiastic and you'll be enthusiastic" is another doctrine that we need to practice in speaking. And it is psychologically sound. "Act forceful and you'll be forceful" is another.

There is no better way to overcome timidity than to go into vigorous physical and vocal action . . . the very causes of timidity are found in physical restraint and repression. Above all, focus on highly communicative, sincere, and animated presentation. You'll find that confidence and effectiveness increase.

INVENTORY SHEET ON DELIVERY

A check-mark indicates O.K.; and X or XX, good. An O indicates room for improvement.

Use this inventory sheet to meet and solve your problems in delivery. It is a nondetailed, nontechnical analysis of your speaking. The goals are ones that any person can attain.

I. FUNDAMENTAL QUALITIES OF DELIVERY (Communication, Animation, and Sincerity)

1. Does speaker show the WILL to communicate? .... 1.
2. Does he *look* at his hearers, individually? .... 2.
3. Does he *lean* toward his hearers? .... 3.
4. Does he show enthusiasm? .... 4.
5. Does he speak as if thoroughly interested and convinced himself? .... 5.
6. Does he check on audience attentiveness and do something about it? .... 6.
7. Does he "get his message over"? .... 7.
8. Is he sufficiently prepared? .... 8.

II. PHYSICAL ELEMENTS OF DELIVERY

    9. Does speaker have sufficient general animation and bodily activity? .... 9.

  10. Does he have facial expressivenes? ....10.

  11. Does he use hand and head gestures? ....11.

  12. Is he poised and balanced physically? ....12.

  13. Does he emphasize major points with vigorous action? ....13.

  14. Does he "keep his audience awake"? ....14.

III. VOCAL ELEMENTS OF DELIVERY

  15. Breathing adequate; volume sufficient? ....15.

  16. Rate too fast .... too slow .... O.K.? ....16.

  17. Enunciation clear .... pronunciation ....17.

  18. Does he use enough vocal force to emphasize key points? ....18.

  19. Is he vocally expressive? ....19.

  20. Free from "word-whiskers." (ers and ums) ....20.

Major Suggestion ....

....

....

All these gains, and many more, can be found in these assignments. They can have a profound effect for the better upon your personality. Don't fail to capitalize on this fact!

9. INFORMATIVE SPEECHES OF EXPLANATION AND DEMONSTRATION

Refer to Chapter 6 for ideas on preparation and outlining, and if necessary to Chapter 11 for help on topics and materials. Follow Chapter 7 as it relates to your type of speech. You are to explain to the class some machine, invention, device, process, theory, article or organization: *to inform,* not to persuade. You may give instructions or make a report rather than use simple explanation.

To facilitate communication, it is suggested that you prepare *an exhibit* or other visual aid for use in this speech. This is discussed in Chapter 7, which tells you how to prepare this particular sort of talk. A full outline is suggested. However, do not take outline or notes to the platform. Doing so inhibits effective delivery.

10. INFORMATIVE-IMPRESSIVE SPEECHES

The latter part of Chapter 7 is your guide for the specific preparation of this talk. Select a topic that lends itself to development for its importance, its beauty, its complexity, its influence, or other characteristic as explained in Chapter 7. Try to make your audience feel the same admiration, wonder, awe, fear, pleasure, enjoyment, or whatever it is that you feel in respect to your topic. Remember, this is *not a persuasive speech:* you are dealing with characteristics of your subject that people generally accept as true. Your object is to convey to them a deeper realization of the size, complexity, rapid growth, or other attribute. The importance of good physical condition; the beauty of Kreisler's art on the violin; the immensity of the Grand Canyon; the peacefulness of the Northern woods; the majesty of Niagara; the risks of space exploration; the immense cost of government; the dedication of the research scholar, etc.—such topics, upon which there is no dispute, but which are often not deeply realized, are the ones with which you are dealing.

Read carefully the part of Chapter 7 which distinguishes the informative–impressive from other informative, and from persuasive speeches. Make a full outline.

11. PERSUASIVE-BELIEF SPEECHES

Your point of reference for all persuasive speeches is Chapter 8. Follow its instructions.

Select a topic of current local, state, national or international interest that is now in controversy. Read current newspapers and magazines and listen to radio–television discussions for ideas. Do additional reading in the library.

Remember that logical proof, including both good reasoning and good evidence—not just generalities or hearsay—is needed in this type of speech. Choose the side of the controversy in which, after consideration, you believe. Then organize and outline your talk to win the agreement of the audience.

12. ADDITIONAL PERSUASIVE-BELIEF SPEECHES

Debates on questions of policy. Debate is in no essential respect different from other forms of persuasive speaking. The object is to get agreement or belief from the audience. The affirmative side upholds the proposal; the negative opposes it.

The ability to present a strong, persuasive argument in favor of your viewpoint, to defend it against the attacks of an opponent, and in turn to overthrow his arguments, is one that is demanded not only of lawyers, but of businessmen, professional men of all kinds, organization leaders, labor leaders, and in fact everyone who deals with people and seeks to persuade them. This persuasion must be carried on under fire from an opponent.

This assignment is one of the most important of the entire course. It calls for *teamwork* among those assigned, or who have chosen, to speak on the same side. Meet early; plan your outline cooperatively.

Suggestions for Preparation

1. Topics will be assigned that will deal with current local, state, or national subjects of controversy. With the aid of the instructor, they will be worded as definite propositions, for example:

> Resolved, that universal military conscription should be made a permanent policy of the United States.
> Resolved, that labor should be given a share in the management of industry.
> Resolved, that the United Nations should establish a federal world government.
> Resolved, that eighteen-year-old citizens should have the right to vote in all local, state, and national elections.
> Resolved, that courses in colleges and universities should be entirely elective.
> Resolved, that there should be no right to strike when public

utilities affecting the health and safety of the public are involved.

These are typical debate propositions. Read the newspapers, news magazines, and other sources for ideas. Submit propositions so worded that (1) the affirmative must advocate a change in the present policy; (2) that one specific policy is advocated; (3) that it is clear, and as brief as possible.

2. When your team lineup is announced meet the opposing team at once and choose or draw for sides.

3. Hold a team meeting, at which you determine the order of speaking and assign the various "issues" or important arguments to the different speakers. Work out a team outline, to be handed in at the opening of your discussion debate.

4. The order of speaking will be: First affirmative speaker, first negative, second affirmative, second negative, and so on.

5. With the exception of the first affirmative, leave open from 30 to 60 seconds at the beginning to answer and if possible refute the principal argument of the preceding speaker of the opposition.

6. Stress "reasons why" as your Principal Ideas, and examples, statistics, and testimony as your proof. Have an effective one-sentence conclusion summing up your point.

7. Each speaker on each side will then have a set time to make a speech of refutation. Order: negative, affirmative, negative, affirmative, etc.

Variations of Debate

The cross-examination plan. Rather than follow conventional procedure, this plan may be used. One speaker for each side presents the entire case. He is questioned for a limited period by one of the other side. Summing-up arguments are then presented.

The Forum. In this popular plan, rebuttal speeches are omitted. Instead, following the principal speeches, the members of the audience may ask questions of the speakers (1) to get information; or (2) to raise a doubt about the validity of the speaker's argument. The audience should be restricted to direct, brief questions, and usually "second-questioning" or dialogue between speaker and questioner is not permitted. This is an excellent audience-participation format.

Arguments on questions of fact. Debates usually take place on *questions of policy,* that is, whether a new line of action should be adopted by an organization, a public group, or a government.

An interesting variant of the usual type of debate is one on a *question of fact.* The dispute is *whether a given assertion is true.* This assertion may deal with *fact past,* for example, "Has the United Nations succeeded?" It may, and often does, deal with *fact future,* for example, "Will France regain her preeminence in Europe?" or "Will men be able to live on the moon?" or "Will the danger of communism in South America be averted?"

This, like the usual type of debate, is persuasive-belief speaking. The Specific Purpose is to convince the hearers that they should accept the arguments of the speaker on a controverted or uncertain topic. Principal Ideas, as in all other speeches of the type, must give logical reasons-why. Evidence is supplied mainly through examples, statistics, and testimony.

As a classroom assignment, questions of fact may be debated in the conventional manner, or with speeches followed by questions from the audience. An interesting arrangement, however, is to have one speaker present a prepared argument, and to be refuted, impromptu, by another.

13. PERSUASIVE-ACTION SPEECHES

This is to be a speech of the persuasive type which seeks direct action from the audience. In it you will demonstrate all the skills you have acquired in this course, both in planning speeches and in presenting them.

Early preparation and *rehearsal* are especially urged in carrying out this assignment.

Suggestions for Preparation

1. Select a topic in which you have complete conviction and a real desire to influence people. It should be a topic of sufficient importance to justify a real effort. Select one on which you have an abundance of knowledge, from actual experience or from reading. Remember, you will need plenty of examples, statistics, testimony, comparisons, and descriptive material to make your points logically convincing and action-getting.

2. Having chosen a topic, determine your Specific Purpose. *Write it down.* It must be stated so as to specify the exact action you want your hearers to take:

> To persuade my hearers to join the debate squad.
> To persuade the audience to adopt a definite schedule of exercise.
> To persuade my audience to buy a Blue Cross hospital insurance policy.

Note: Generally it will not be satisfactory to ask the audience merely to vote, or sign a petition, or "go out and talk in favor of this proposition."

3. Having determined your Specific Purpose, consider the choice of your Principal Ideas (the main points through which you hope to convince the audience that they should take the action requested).

> *a.* Consider *logic* in choosing them: they must answer WHY? in response to the question raised by your Specific Purpose.
> *b.* Consider motivation in choosing and wording them: each one should appeal to some want or desire of the hearers.
> *c.* Do not have more than two, or at the most three, for you must have time to develop them vividly and concretely.

4. Plan your Speech Details, to support each Principal Idea. All the details, especially examples, statistics, and testimony, are valuable, and for vividness use comparisons and descriptions. Paint a vivid picture somewhere in your speech. Use *activation.*

5. Plan your Introduction and Conclusion:

> *a.* Restrict your Introduction to a short statement, not more than two sentences, showing why the topic is of interest and value to the audience, that it affects their personal welfare.
> *b.* Make your Conclusion "echo," but not formally summarize, the Principal Ideas, and have it carry a strong appeal for action,

with emphasis upon use of the strongest motive possible. It should furnish a moving climax for your speech.

14. ADDITIONAL PERSUASIVE-ACTION SPEECHES

Persuasive speaking of the type seeking belief has been the subject of several assignments, such as the forum debate, the argument on a question of fact, etc. Likewise there may be additional assignments in persuasive talks seeking immediate action from the audience. They follow in general the over-all persuasive pattern:

Selection of a Specific Purpose calling for definite action to be taken by members of the group, or the group as a whole.

Choice of Principal Ideas that (1) give logical reasons why the action should be had and that (2) appeal to wants or desires.

Use of supporting material that constitutes evidence, i.e., examples, statistics, testimony; and in addition of comparisons that make the topic vivid and interesting.

Additionally, the speaker applies *activation:* he is actively enthusiastic himself, and he tries, by the means discussed in Chapter 8, to build reactions in the audience. He also tries to provide some means for immediate commitment to action on the part of the audience: having them sign a pledge, buy tickets, agree to attend a further meeting, or otherwise to involve themselves in an initial action that will commit them to the final action he desires them to take.

14a. THE SPEECH FOR A CAUSE

To urge support for a cause that is close to the speaker's heart is a good exercise in persuasion. It may be the cause of his country, upon which many foreign students have made fine talks. It may be a specific phase of the crusade against communism. It might be seeking support for an organization, such as the Boy Scouts, the Heart Foundation, the conservation of our natural resources, or one of a multitude of others.

The essential thing is that it must be a movement (cause) to which the speaker is personally dedicated—one to which he would be willing to devote a major part of his life.

14b. THE FUND-RAISING SPEECH

This may overlap with the speech for a cause, but is worthy of consideration as an assignment nevertheless. Campaigns for worthy organizations, for special civic or neighborhood projects, and for the support of institutions, furnish many excellent topics.

14c. THE POLITICAL CAMPAIGN SPEECH

Local, state and national political campaigns suggest the possibility of enthusiastic student speeches in support of candidates or issues, especially when election time is near.

14d. THE SALES PRESENTATION

Persuading the members of the audience, as individuals or as a group, to purchase some product or service, can furnish a fine exercise in action-getting speech. It is suggested that the product or service be one that is of substantial dollar value, so that time will not be wasted on the presentation of trivial articles. Such things as insurance, annuity contracts, automobiles, household devices of reasonable value, tailor-made suits, and the like are indicated. Purchase for parents or brothers and sisters might be urged rather than buying for one's self. In the sales presentation, exhibits and demonstrations should be encouraged.

14e. THE MORALE-BUILDING SPEECH

This is a "situation-speech," that is, one involving a special set of circumstances. The speaker, as the leader of a group, or as a person brought in to assume leadership temporarily, has as his purpose the creation or revival of enthusiasm on the part of the group for some project or enterprise in which it is engaged. For example, he might be the director of a United Fund campaign, addressing workers who are seeking pledges of funds to attain the campaign goal. He might be a plant executive or foreman, urging greater production efficiency upon the workers.

The Specific Purpose, then, is to get greater enthusiasm and effort from the speaker's followers or co-workers.

There are several steps by which he seeks to attain his objective, and these steps may serve as the Principal Ideas of the talk. They are:

1. To create or restore the confidence of the workers: that they are capable of doing the job, that conditions are favorable, that others are succeeding, etc.

2. To promise a reward (motivation). This reward may be monetary or otherwise a material one, or it may be the satisfaction of achievement and the realization that the workers are helping a worthy cause.

3. To suggest how the desired result may be achieved: a brief resumé of things to do according to instructions already given. To emphasize the necessity of following whatever plan has been adopted.

4. To predict that success will come, and to stress once more the social or other importance of the project upon which the workers are engaged.

This being a "situation" speech, it is necessary to set up a fictitious audience, rather than depend as is usually done on the class *per se* as the audience. For instance, the members of the class could be assumed to be workers in a church drive for funds, and the speaker the campaign director. If this creation of a "situation" were not done, about the only topic for speakers would be to persuade the members of the class to work harder on their speaking.

Conclusion on direct-action persuasive assignments. In this section we have tried to indicate various forms in which the Persuasive-Action speech may be practiced. All demand the same kind of planning and composition: all rest upon the speaker's own enthusiasm, plus good use of logic, motivation, and activation. Many other special types of direct persuasion may be used to advantage.

15. THE SPEECH OF FORMAL OCCASION

As discussed in Chapter 9, this involves speaking of the impressive-informative kind. The object is to stress admitted and acknowledged *qualities* or *characteristics* of the subject.

Included in this classification are speeches of formal occasion, such as those of dedication, commemoration, or tribute.

In general, the directions for the impressive-informative speech should be followed. In dedicating a building, a bridge, a scholarship, a stadium, a new housing project or airport, the speaker should consider the *significance* of the thing dedicated. It is not a matter of giving the history of the structure or institution; it is rather one of finding the *meaning* that it symbolizes. In dedicating a college library, one is not interested so much in how it came to be built (though tribute may be paid to those who planned it and those whose contributions made it possible), but rather its significance for learning, scholarship, education. Similarly with the dedication of other structures.

In commemorating a national or other holiday, one again doesn't review how it came into existence, but rather, emphasizes the meaning, the significance, of the occasion. A Fourth of July situation, for example, calls for discussion of the principles of democracy and their preservation in freedom, rather than an historical review.

In meetings designed to pay tribute to men living or dead, or to groups or movements of the past or present, again, the meaning or significance is the guide to speech design.

The speaker may conclude by appealing to his hearers to act, in general, in such a way as to live up to the ideals or ideas which he has discussed as existing in the institution dedicated, holiday or historical event commemorated, or the man who has been the subject of tribute. This use of the "application," as it has been called, is legitimate and sometimes moving. "Let us, then, emulate the patriotism and courage of Nathan Hale; let us defend our freedoms and offer our lives to protect our beloved land."

16. THE ENTERTAINING SPEECH

Reference to Chapter 10 will assist the student as he tackles this rather difficult assignment.

One point worthy of mention is that this sort of talk resembles the informative-impressive type, in that it selects certain aspects, qualities, or characteristics of the subject for emphasis. The entertaining talk selects those qualities that may provide amusement.

Propriety must be observed. The speaker who uses questionable stories or remarks may get laughter, but he also downgrades himself in the mind of the audience.

"Apply the elements of interest" a great teacher once advised the writer on the planning of an entertaining speech. With the subject and occasion decided, study what is vital, unusual, familiar, striking, etc., about the subject, especially in relation to the specific audience. Out of such analysis ideas for something entertaining, novel, humorous will undoubtedly come.

As stated in the chapter on this sort of talk, the *subject* is not the inherently entertaining part: it is how the subject is treated by the speaker.

17. IMPROMPTU SPEAKING

The ability to speak in an organized, coherent way without previous specific preparation is a most valuable one. Many occasions in personal and public life call for an instantaneous reply or comment. One either replies or comments adequately, on the spur of the moment, or the opportunity is lost, perhaps forever.

In Chapter 6, toward such end, methods of "preparing" impromptu talks are set forth. "Off-the-cuff" comment may be called for in class, either about the composition and delivery of speeches, or about their subject-matter. In debates, and other forms of persuasive speaking, refutation may be employed. Another form of impromptu speaking is to ask and answer questions during forum discussions. Thus in a lively class, much impromptu talking may occur.

However, there may be a few meetings in which impromptu speaking, with topics "drawn from a hat" are used. In such situations, it is perhaps better to have the topics to be used published in advance, or the areas of subject-matter to be used made known. In real life, most impromptu speaking is done on some phase of a topic under general discussion, for example, at the meeting of an organization called to debate the question of erecting a new building, or increasing dues.

In order to assist in full-hour programs of impromptu speaking, we make the following suggestions. Remember to refer to Chapter 6 for some techniques of "impromptu-izing."

1. At the beginning of the class hour, the first speaker will come forward, and draw his topic from a hat. He will have *two minutes* to prepare his talk, while the instructor explains some detail of the contest.

2. Before the first speaker begins, the *second* speaker will draw his topic, and will prepare it during the two minutes the first speaker is talking, and so on through the contest.

3. The timekeeper will give a warning by tapping with his pencil at one minute thirty seconds, and a second tap at two minutes, at which the speaker will stop.

4. The class will vote (no speaker voting on his own name) on each speech, by using the ballot form at the end of this section:

   a. Each speaker's name shall be written down.
   b. Opposite his name a grade shall be put down, between 75 and 100, inclusive. *Give no identical grades.*
   c. This grade shall represent your judgment of the value of the speech, regarding 75 as poor, 85 as good, 90 to 95 as excellent.
   d. Opposite your own name mark a big X—no grade.

5. A committee of the class will take up the ballots immedi-

ately at the end of the contest and will report the three speakers who, by vote of the class, were the topnotchers.

6. Simply voting for "best speaker" is an alternative method.

BALLOT FOR
CONTEST IN IMPROMPTU SPEAKING

How to use this ballot: (1) Write down the name of each speaker as it is announced, in the space provided. (2) At the end of each speech (not before or after) assign the speaker a grade not lower than 75 nor higher than 100, on the following basis:

> 75—a poor speech, but he tried!
> 76 to 85—from rather poor to fair to good.
> 86 to 90—better than average.
> 91 to 95—a splendid talk.
> 96 to 100—a most unusually good talk, well organized, developed, and delivered.

At end of contest, use the final column to rank speakers, 1, 2, 3, etc.

NAME OF SPEAKER	TOPIC	GRADE	RANK
1.			
2.			
3.			
4.			
5.			
6.			
7.			
8.			
9.			
10.			
11.			
12.			
13.			
14.			
15.			
16.			
17.			
18.			
19.			
20.			
21.			
22.			
23.			
24.			
25.			

18. CONVERSATIONAL SPEAKING

The scope of the chapters in this book has not included the forms of conversational speaking: the interview, the roundtable discussion, the conference, etc. We have pointed out in Part One, however, fundamental principles of oral communication that should be applied in conversation of a serious nature. In Part Two we have discussed speech-planning for the various general purposes: to inform, to persuade, to entertain.

It is, if the instructor sees fit, perfectly feasible to make assignments of a conversational nature. Each of the kinds of *speech* we have discussed has its counterpart in interview or discussion situations. Thus assignments could be made for informative interviews, impressive-informative conversations, persuasive-belief and persuasive-action interviews or conferences.

To do this with complete success, additional reading in books devoted to the discussion or conversation should be assigned. The present authors have set forth some of the principles and specific requirements of conversational speech in their *Effective Business Speech* (McGraw-Hill, 1960), especially in Part Three of that work. And there are many good texts in discussion that are readily available for additional reading.

Index